Praise For *Second Wives*

Susan Shapiro Barash combines her professional and personal insights to help women create solid bonds with their husbands and avoid feeling second-rate as Wife No. 2.

— *Publishers Weekly*

I've never been a second wife, but if I planned on it, I would first read—and heed—Susan Shapiro Barash's significant book, Second Wives. *With engaging vulnerability, Barash arranges for us to creep into (and learn from) the lives of real second wives.*

— Sherry Suib Cohen, journalist, contributing editor of *McCall's Magazine* and best-selling author of seventeen books including *Secrets of a Very Good Marriage, Looking for the Other Side* and *Big City Look*

Barash brings her experience as an academic and, more importantly, a second wife to this useful book on how to navigate the sometimes murky waters of remarriage. [Second Wives *is*] *instructional for women who want to know what issues can arise from becoming a second wife.*

— *ForeWord Magazine*

Susan Shapiro Barash has discovered a mammoth area of interest which has largely been overlooked. Second Wives *compellingly addresses a complex topic with uncanny skill and insight. Once you've taken the plunge, it's difficult to put this book down. She is to be congratulated.*

— Carl S. Burak, M.D., psychiatrist and author of *The Cradle Will Fall*

Second wives, though a large portion of contemporary society, have received little systematic attention. Susan Shapiro Barash's book corrects this gap by offering insightful answers to the complex questions that inevitably arise. This timely work deserves wide readership.

> — Nechama Tec, Professor of Sociology, University of Connecticut and author of *Defiance: The Bielski Partisans, When Light Pierced the Darkness* and *Dry Tears: The Story of a Lost Childhood*

The book is for women thinking about becoming a second wife and those who have already taken the plunge.

> — *Tulsa World*

According to Susan Shapiro Barash, even though the divorce rate is over fifty percent, the idea of a second chance at happiness still prevails. Her research indicates that second wives, despite trials and tribulations, can be winners in every way. At last a unique book that provides hope and insight into the fast growing world of the second wife.

> — Lauren Lawrence, columnist and author of *Dream Keys for Love: Unlocking the Secret of Your Own Heart*

Susan Shapiro Barash's book is great. Women discover that there really can be another chance.

> — Lewis Burke Frumkes, humorist, radio show host, author of *The Logophile's Orgy: Favorite Words of Famous People* and *Manhattan Cocktail and Other Irreverent Observations on Life* and co-author of *The Mensa Think Smart Book*

SECOND WIVES

SECOND WIVES

THE PITFALLS AND REWARDS OF MARRYING WIDOWERS AND DIVORCED MEN

by

Susan Shapiro Barash

New Horizon Press
Far Hills, NJ

Susan Shapiro Barash
    Second Wives: The Pitfalls and Rewards of Marrying Widowers and Divorced Men

Cover Design: Robert Aulicino
Interior Design: Susan M. Sanderson
Author Photograph: Alonzo Boldin

Library of Congress Catalog Card Number: 99-75939

ISBN: 0-88282-182-2
New Horizon Press

Manufactured in the U.S.A.

2004   2003   2002   2001   2000   /   5   4   3   2

This book is dedicated
with profound love to
my husband, Gary

digamy: a second marriage after the termination of the first
Merriam-Webster's Collegiate Dictionary

"I think you are happy in this second match,
for it excels your first."
William Shakespeare
Romeo and Juliet

"Well let there be sunlight, let there be rain
Let the brokenhearted love again"
Bruce Springsteen
"Sherry Darling"

TABLE OF CONTENTS

AUTHOR'S NOTE

This book is based on extensive personal interviews of second wives and experts in the fields of matrimonial law, finances, psychology, family therapy, counseling, and private investigation. Fictitious identities and names have been given to all characters in this book except the contributing experts in order to protect individual privacy. Some characters are composites.

ACKNOWLEDGEMENTS

I extend my gratitude to many people. Above all, I thank my children, Jennie, Michael, and Elizabeth Ripps, for their patience and love. I am indebted to others: my mother, Selma Shapiro, for her unending support; my father, Herbert Shapiro, for his wisdom and impressive research; my brother, Mark Shapiro; my aunts, Bea Sandler and Ruth Brok, each for listening; my father-in-law, Theodore Barash, for his counsel; and my closest friends and extended family for their interest and energy.

The professionals who contributed their thoughts to this book deserve a special acknowledgement. Brondi Borer, a New York City divorce attorney, specializes in mediation and nontraditional family law. Dr. Ronnie Burak is a clinical psychologist with a full time private practice in Jacksonville, Florida, where she also teaches at the University of North Florida. Dr. Donald Cohen is a certified marriage and family therapist practicing in Weston, Connecticut and co-author of *My Father, My Son*. Cynthia Coulter George is a Fellow of the American Academy of Matrimonial Lawyers and Co-Chair of the Academy's Gender Bias Committee. She practices divorce law in Greenwich, Connecticut. Dr. Michele Kasson, a licensed psychologist practicing in New York City, is a staff member of the Lifeline Center for Child Development. Antoinette Michaels, ACSW, is an ordained Interfaith Minister and founder and president of the Hope Counseling Center in Sayville, New York. Amy Reisen is a matrimonial lawyer practicing in Millburn, New Jersey and an advocate for non-contentious divorce. Christopher Rush is an international investigative consultant and licensed private investigator. Mr Rush works in White Plains and Mahopac, New York, specializing in managing investigations into complex, high profile criminal, civil, and matrimonial matters. George S. Stern, President of the American Academy of Matrimonial Lawyers, has had a divorce practice in Atlanta, Georgia for thirty years. The excellent team at New Horizon Press, especially Joan Dunphy and Joseph Marron, understood the potential of this project and are responsible for its birth.

    There are those in the world of books and academia who warrant acknowledgement: Cynthia Vartan, Arthur Salzfass, Lori Stuart, Edward B. Shils, Suzanne Murphy, Lewis Burke Frumkes, and Carol Camper. My typist, Karen Wilder, and my student researcher, Ryan Lonnergan, deserve credit.

    I extend a heartfelt thank you to the many women who have come forward to share their deepest thoughts and emotions with me. Their stories are the life force of this book.

PREFACE

by

Dr. Donald Cohen

In my practice I have observed a variety of second wife scenarios. It is my belief that many second marriages, which are without a doubt on the rise, are much stronger than the first. This is because so many people go into a first marriage for the wrong reasons or are too young to really understand their needs, whereas later in life one often better understands her/himself. In a first marriage we tend to look to the partner to live out our other half, the undeveloped part of ourselves. In a healthy second marriage, same attracts the same, in contrast to opposites who attract. As we mature, we need to be with someone who sees the world in the same way that we do and who lives in the same zone. No longer do we want to be with someone different from ourselves, but a soul mate whose values and goals we realize as similar to our own.

One should marry from one's heart, not for reasons that seem right, not because we feel we ought to. Ours is a generation that has been misguided in terms of this. As a result, some couples have grown together, while others have grown apart. A marriage can only survive— whether it is a first, second, or third—if the partners exhibit self-aware-ness and practice open communication, not a monologue, but a dialogue. In addition, the ingredients which make for a successful marriage are: a mutual respect, a best friendship, a shared honesty, and an integrity in the relationship.

It makes sense that a man would look for what was lacking in his first marriage and then set out to fill the void, to do things right in his second. However, a husband may not always reach this level of introspection. If a man has been willing to examine his role in his failed first marriage and to recognize what was missing there, he is more evolved and mature. Thus, the more mature and developed man has clarity when he finds his second wife and, as a result, his commitment is full fledged and healthy.

A serious relationship after a divorce or widowhood often leads to a second marriage, despite what we hear about so many people living together rather than marrying or remarrying. Second marriages occur because people want the comfort; men and women alike seek out the security and permanence of a marriage, even in the face of a previous failure. While the second wife may not be haunted by the first wife, what really determines how the triangle plays out between the ex-wife, husband, and second wife is the message which the husband gives to his second wife. If he makes her feel loved and connected so that their life together is teamwork, then the second wife is not as threatened by the past history of the first marriage. What counts is the creation of a new life together.

Issues that continually cropped up in interviews Susan Shapiro Barash conducted with second wives need to be addressed. The most serious are: when the second wife is the cause of the first divorce, when there has been a tragedy in the first marriage which spills over to the second, and when there are children from the first marriage and stepparenting is a part of the package. Other serious issues include money and lifestyle choices and the second wife's place in terms of her new husband's priorities.

The Lover as Second Wife

Sometimes a marriage breaks up over an affair. If the husband takes his lover as his second wife, there is a question of morality. If a married man proudly chooses to marry his lover and tackles the dissolution of the first marriage, then his guilt is lessened. There is more guilt if he is not honest about how he met his second wife. If he denies that this affair was the catalyst that led to his divorce, and instead harps on the negatives of the first marriage, there is also more guilt. The deciding factor in how a husband feels about leaving his first wife for his second is what kind of marriage he had. If he tried to improve his first marriage through therapy and feels that he did all that he could to make the marriage work and still failed, then it is easier for him to leave without guilt. Without therapy and an examination of what was missing in the marriage, there is a more difficult transition—difficult for him to understand where things went wrong and difficult for him to explain to others why he is choosing to end the marriage.

The Biological Bond and Loss

Another scenario that can cause concern for the second wife is when there is some kind of tragedy that affects her husband and his ex-wife, such as the loss of a child. When the first family is brought together by such a sad event, it reinforces the biological connection or shared past. The second wife is not a part of this picture. She feels unanchored. This may be very frightening for her, and she may even feel unwelcome to share in the grief. For her, it is not only the tragedy that is sad and threatening, but her husband's involvement with his ex-wife, and possibly their efforts to comfort and console each other, that cause the second wife pain and anguish.

Coparenting and Stepparenting

When there are children from the first marriage, it is important that the second wife and her husband's biological children are open to each other. Both the second wife and the children, through the husband, need to work on their relationship. If there is a "we-ness," a sense of inclusion and connection, the second wife can transcend a myriad of problems.

A second wife who also has children from a first marriage is, in a manner of speaking, on equal footing with her husband. When she has children of her own, her instincts may compel her to be generous and to make as much of an effort toward bonding with her stepchildren as she does her own children. A second wife might also find herself with a stepchild who connects with her. In the case of a young child who lives with his father and not with his mother due to a custody arrangement, the second wife has more of a chance to become close to him. Nevertheless, the first wife determines how some of this plays out. If she wants or accepts the child being with his father, but she is in competition with the stepmother, then she will often interfere with the new wife and the child building a rewarding relationship. If the ex-wife encourages the child to be close to his stepmother and to her as well, then a healthy relationship can occur. The second wife who advises the children to appreciate their mother and to look for her positive qualities is conveying the right values to the children. The stepmother needs to be clear, both externally and within herself, that she is not the mother. It is irresponsible for her to try to exert power, which may hurt the child in the process.

Decisions That Involve Money

A significant issue for married couples concerns finances. This is especially true for second wives. A shared bank account, where his money is
hers and her money is his, is the optimal way for husbands and wives to
handle their money so that they can totally share their lives together.
However, it is not always possible in second marriages for this type of
arrangement to work due to things like bad credit, lawsuits, child support, and alimony payments. A second wife who pools all her assets
with her husband may find herself responsible for such debts. Each
partner may be better off placing a stipulated amount in their joint
account and utilizing personal accounts for marital responsibilities such
as alimony and child support payments. Financial counseling is often
beneficial for an equitable arrangement that suits the new marriage. If
the underlying issue that the second wife is up against is about money,
she and her husband have to create their own set of standards. A major
issue becomes how the second wife's lifestyle is affected by her new
husband's obligation to his first family. This is sometimes a bitter and
ongoing battle. The husband's responsibility to the first wife may be pre-
emptive. As in most cases, the extent to which the husband makes his
second wife confident about their life together determines in large part
how she interacts with his first family and subsequent responsibilities. It
is very important for the second wife to feel that her opinion is valued
and that new financial decisions are made together.

The Second Wife as Number One

The capacity the husband has for giving his second wife a sense of being
loved as the new "we" and not comparing her to his ex-wife will influence in great part their present and future happiness. If he has children
from the first marriage, his integration of the children and second wife
has a tremendous influence on everyone's future. A husband who makes
his second wife aware that she is the main event in his life will have a
great chance of success in his new marriage. If he polarizes the two pivotal parts of his life—his second wife's role and his children's role—he
is keeping his life from being in balance. This tone is set by how he
treats his second wife. She and the children will respond to each other
accordingly, following his cue card. Comparisons and preconceived
notions cause friction and unhappiness.

The solution is to share a wonderful, emotionally rich life together. A major component of that newly established couple relationship is a romantic life independent of the children. There must not be a competition between the children and the second wife. When the second wife is with her husband, he needs to make her feel that she has his love and attention. His children need to feel the same, as do hers; the children need to feel special when in the company of their parent. When the children seem to demand a major part of the parent's time and energy, then it is critical that the partner makes the spouse feel valued.

In the case of second wives who enter into a marriage where both partners have been married before or where she has been a second wife several times, it is helpful to share each other's entire story. It is helpful to communicate what kinds of families the husband and wife come from and their histories. How one's parents' marriage worked, as well as how one related to his or her parents is telltale. People tend to do to others what was done to them. It is practical to learn about all of this before one becomes a second wife.

There may be unresolved issues involving the first wife if the husband felt unloved in the marriage and did not face these problems. The pain he brings to the marriage with the second wife often occurs because he was not honest in the first relationship. If the emotional separation from the first wife has not been established by the time of a new marriage, the second wife suffers. The new marriage may have dangerous problems if the husband still is playing out past issues with his second wife.

If the new husband, wife, and stepchildren feel comfortable with their places in the family, there is not usually a problem with the second wife's position. However, if the first wife hasn't developed new interests and relationships, she may be jealous and resentful of the second wife. Healthy boundaries need to be established. Ideally, these are implicitly set by the husband so that the second wife feels appreciated and secure. The first wife's unhappiness is not the husband's problem any longer. Both he and his second wife should take a stand, letting all know that they are entitled to be happy.

INTRODUCTION

It is believed by many that Lilith was Adam's first wife, but the two argued and the relationship did not last. According to the story, Adam felt that Lilith's place was to lie beneath him, but when she refused, she was banished from Eden. Then Eve was created from Adam's rib, and for a while they were happy together. Lilith, meanwhile, was trying to re-enter the Garden of Eden. Adam explained to Eve that Lilith was a demon who threatened women in childbirth. But when Eve saw Lilith one day, she was curious and doubted Adam's word. That Lilith was another woman intrigued Eve, and they became friendly. Adam was the common link, having been a husband to both women.

Millions of women are second wives or will become second wives. With a divorce rate of over fifty percent in this country, the concept of a second marriage, taboo only several decades ago, or relegated to movie stars, has become standard. Today second wives can be found anywhere at any age and have many different versions of their role as such. It is not only a woman in mid-life who sets out to begin again or a young woman who meets a man ten years her senior. There are second wives who have been so for twenty years and those who have just embarked upon this journey. One may become a second wife at any juncture or a second wife several times, depending upon the circumstances.

I well understand the world of the second wife, having been one for sixteen years in my first marriage and for two years in my second marriage. During and after my divorce, I realized that the odds of remarriage to someone without an ex-wife were slim. Yet there is a remarkable difference in becoming a second wife in one's early twenties and becoming a second wife in one's early forties. It is with a certain maturity that I face the slim shadow of my present husband's first wife in our marriage. In my second role as second wife, I am more secure, but aware of her existence. Yet I remember vividly the specter of the first wife in my first marriage; it loomed large before me. Although there were no children from my husband's and her marriage, her mere existence was intimidating enough. That she was ten years older than I and had moved onto another life of her own was little consolation. My point of view was that I could not share anything for the first time with my husband. He had done it all with someone else, from choosing china to taking vows. On the other hand, I held fast to the belief that this man was excellent marriage material by virtue of having failed once. That is, he wouldn't dare fail again; he'd learned from his mistakes. I convinced myself that I represented the present, while she was his past.

Long ago I was assured that the one woman on earth a second wife should never have to worry about is the first wife. Then why was it that it took me so long to get over this other woman? And why did we go out to celebrate the day she announced her next marriage, when she proclaimed herself as someone else's second wife? Why was it that people made remarks to my husband such as, "Oh, I didn't know you were remarried," or worse yet, called me by his ex-wife's name? And could I ever predict that years later I would divorce this man, all the while wondering if what had transpired between us, what had gone awry, was a repeat performance of his first failed marriage. I could not help asking myself, would the next woman to stand up to the plate be threatened by me because I know who that man is and who he isn't? She will have to learn. She will have to believe that he has finally achieved a self-knowledge that will make the third time the charm. It is not my concern, however. I exist as the current ex-wife, who was identified as a second wife for the entirety of the marriage.

The second wife is common in our society. One can perk up her ears and hear a woman explained as such anywhere and everywhere, be it the auditorium before an elementary school play or a subway stop. Nevertheless, for some people the connotation remains, *second wife, second hand.* Unless someone is or has been a second wife, it is difficult to understand how far-reaching the implications are. Yet, whatever the evolution that brings it about, second wives will multiply. Many provide second lives for their husbands, a new family, and another shot at happiness. Some reap the rewards the first wife never had, such as the success and stability that often come with a man's maturity. If there are children from the first marriage, the issue is more complex, and the relationship between the ex-wife and husband is ongoing.

The interaction between the husband and his ex-wife needs to be fixed in such a way that boundaries are firm and well defined. A second wife may feel threatened by an ex-wife without any children in the mix as well as one with them. There is the knowledge, always nagging, that she was not the first, that in passionate moments she may be compared to her predecessor. Is the husband thinking about his first wife during an amorous afternoon with his second? Is the second measuring up to the first? She might feel inferior not only about sex, but about any ritual of marriage. A second wife who believes that she stands in the first wife's shoes is very insecure. According to many therapists, the second wife often yearns to be number one, knowing it is an impossibility.

In some cases, the first wife is envious of the second. When she sees that the second wife influences her husband in different ways than she, it often evokes hostility. She may hear that her ex-husband is going sky diving even though he always told her he was afraid of heights, or she hears that he has built himself a mansion when he claimed total poverty during their divorce only eighteen months before. And the second wife may grasp at these changes, these differences in their marriage, to help set it apart from the first.

When each of my three children were born, I could not help thinking, *Well, now I've topped her. I've bore him children and she never shared that with him. I have taken him to a place he's never been before with anyone.* Still, obviously, it wasn't the glue; the marriage did not last. Second marriages carry more responsibilities, fears, and risks, children included. There is more risk, because having failed once, no one wants to make another mistake.

Eventually I was too immersed in daily life with our children to think about his first wife anymore. The finish line grew murky and I stopped wondering if I were the winner. For the millions of second wives who prevail, I hold this shift in focus up to them. There comes a point, hopefully, when the second wife becomes more confident and no longer looks back.

Though I had wondered about his first wife many times, it was only when I decided to leave the marriage, ending my tenure as second wife to this particular man, that I began to speculate as to what had plagued his first marriage. I realized too late that hearing his first wife's story—her version of what kind of husband he was—might have enlightened me. Second wives rarely seek out this opportunity, nor is this sort of communication often readily available to them. Instead we wonder in silence if the mistakes were the same, if the pitfalls are a repeat of the past. Second wives are often too strong minded and intent on success to consider the possibility of meeting the first wife and gleaning wisdom from her side of the story. We are too loyal to this man, too sympathetic to his ordeal for an ex-wife's saga to hold water. While a perverse curiosity exists, with each woman speculating about the other, a second wife adheres to a stubborn stance that this time it will be better. She defies odds she doesn't know exist. When there is no chance for solidarity between the first and second wife because of biases from the start, the second wife loses the chance to gain information that may be vital to making her marriage a success.

Despite the proliferation of second wives, little comfort or expertise has been offered to this singular and large slice of the population. Yet, conducting my interviews, it became apparent to me how challenging it has been for second wives. Many of them are dealing with the same problems and the same frustrating situations. Even with a heightened awareness, coping with the problems of a second marriage isn't any easier today than it has been in the past. It is for this and, of course, for my personal reasons that the topic so intrigued me. My hope is that this book will shed light on the matter and provide guidance, so that second wives no longer feel alone and isolated in their roles.

Everywhere that one turns, it seems, one finds a second wife with a tale of her own. There are few support groups to assuage the fears and concerns that second wives endure. Throughout history and literature, second wives like Anne Boleyn, Henry VIII's second wife, the second Mrs. de Winter from the novel *Rebecca*, and Edith Galt Wilson, second wife of President Woodrow Wilson, have been portrayed as indecent women, while the first wife assumes the role of martyr, having sacrificed her youth for a man, only to be dumped for someone new. The implication often is that the "someone new" is a conniving home-wrecker who doesn't deserve happiness or a successful marriage. There are many famous and visible second wives. Among them are Marla Maples, who was Donald Trump's second wife, Rachel Hunter who was married to Rod Stewart, Pattie Scioffa, who remains Bruce Springsteen's second wife, and Nicole Kidman, married to Tom Cruise. In the past, there was Elizabeth Taylor, Richard Burton's second wife, two times, in fact, and Mia Farrow, who was both Andre Previn's and Frank Sinatra's second wife. Psychologists and sociologists have confirmed that second wives, whether they know it or not, are in pain to varying degrees. It is a difficult role and the negative label of second wife is not easy to evade. Despite the time period or their station in life, for many women the awareness of being a second wife never dims totally. For this reason, there is a bond which exists between second wives, a sisterhood of sorts, even if left unexpressed.

For this book, I have interviewed hundreds of women who are second wives across the United States and in some European countries, from disparate walks of life and of all ages. The outcome of these interviews is the twelve categories of second wives I have devised. While each group has its own concentration, there are many commonalties that overlap. For instance, a several times married second wife may also fit into the chapter on dealing with stepchildren, or a second wife dealing with a vengeful first wife may also fit in the competitive category.

Second wives' tales are diverse, yet with a similar echo. Many women confess to feelings of resentment and distrust, coupled with the sensation that they are always number two. Sometimes the second wife is accused by the first wife or others of having been the lover who destroyed the first marriage. Whether or not the second wife was having an affair with her husband while he was still married, the label of home-wrecker seems very unfair. After all, she may reason, if his first marriage was happy, why was he seeking out another woman? Can a relationship be broken if it's not already in disrepair, the second wife asks herself, especially in the case where a husband has been unfaithful? Meanwhile, the first wife whose husband has been unfaithful feels betrayed and is bitter; her self-esteem has been destroyed, her world has tumbled. At the outset, the second wife of such a man may be too eager to marry him and make the marriage work to question her husband's history of duplicity. Once settled into the marriage, however, she may begin to worry that his adulterous past is an indication of his future behavior. How the husband behaves—not only in the case where the end of the first marriage resulted from him engaging in an affair, but in any situation with his second wife—sets the tone for their marriage.

Undoubtedly, second wives' concerns extend to ex-wives and children as well. For many second wives, there is the fear that the ex-wife is still in the picture. This is especially true when children are involved. In some cases, the children may be used as pawns, particularly if the ex-wife is without a love interest and an occupation or activity. In addition, the financial obligation of a man to his ex-wife and family is very real and something that the second wife cannot wish away. While all of these issues may be discussed by the couple ahead of time, the realities set in once the wedding has taken place.

For many second wives, it is the emotional impact of their positions that plague them. Being a second wife is to never have been the man's first wife. She may be on edge, uncertain of the future. She may ask herself, *Will he make the same mistakes in our marriage that caused his first marriage to fail?* Questions about their future as a couple crop up. *He divorced one wife, he might divorce me*, the second wife begins to worry. As her stepchildren vie for their father's attention, the second wife may find them intrusive and become jealous. The friends whom her husband brings to the marriage may reject her out of loyalty to the first wife; the friends whom she brings may not be as welcome as she anticipated. Because of one or many of these reasons, the second wife may feel excluded. And she will always be second.

In my experience, being a second wife keeps one at a distance from others who have not had the experience. Once, I took my middle child, a toddler at the time, to a nursery school interview and ran into two women with whom I had gone to college. They were there with their first born children of their first marriages. They couldn't believe that I had a child older than my toddler. Then I overheard one whisper to the other, "Of course she has two already; she's his second wife." I felt hurt, set apart, rejected, and pigeonholed.

In many sitations over the years I have seen assumptions like the one I experienced persist. Because of this I began to realize how many second wives struggle with the preconceived notions of others when they take on this role. I felt compelled to research second wives, speak to them, and learn through each woman's individual voice. My research led to a better understanding of my own feelings about being a second wife. How I wished there had been books available to me from the start, books that would have provided information and guidance, and would have made me feel less alone. So many second wives have voiced the same thought to me, that knowledge of other second wives and their feelings is both consoling and strengthening.

Regardless of how the first wife feels about the second and vice versa, a perverse curiosity exists. The second wife may gossip about the first wife, or the first wife will pump mutual friends and her children for information on her ex-husband's new wife. Each woman is interested in the other, some in every detail. And the tales told in this book are those stories: confessions of regret, competition, fear of a ghostly presence, and reconciliation. It takes a very long time to shed this particular ghost, as these confessions will confirm. Tales of shared emotions and shared paths abound. How and whether time heals and settles the triangle created by the second wife, her husband, and his ex-wife, is something individual to each narrative. The new marriage, dancing to its own beat, collides with the past and hopefully moves forward in a rhythm of passion and love.

PART ONE

SECONDARY DILEMMAS

CHAPTER ONE

IDENTIFYING WITH NUMBER ONE

Terri never expected to be positioned in the same way that her husband's first wife was during their marriage. "My husband, Andrew, got divorced to marry me. He was very kind and attentive when we were dating. We did not have an affair, but he was contemplating returning to his marriage when we met. Andrew was legally separated but not sure about getting divorced. Then we began to date, and he filed for divorce within six months time. It was a whirlwind courtship; he showered me with gifts and took me to exotic places. Andrew was always charming and handsome. He had a regal quality, and I fell for it completely.

"In retrospect, I think I should have paid closer attention to what Andrew was like when we were alone together and not out in public. He was moody and nasty and unpredictable. He would depress me, his moods were so low and he was angry about every little thing. I knew that his first wife had left him and that he had dated like crazy once she was gone. He traveled with women and had two at a time. Andrew was not a good candidate for marriage, I knew that in my heart. But he made promises to me and made me feel so special. I fell for it. He missed being married, that was the irony. He once confided he had cheated on his first wife and had a mistress in another city.

That was a red flag I missed. After we'd been married for four years, I began to understand what his first wife had felt. I knew that she had a temper, and when he provoked her, she would be as belligerent as he is. I could not be like that. I was intimidated by him.

"Finally, I left for the same reason that Andrew's first wife had left. I packed two small suitcases and was out of there. I did not care for one material possession, although he was obsessed with material goods. I remembered what Andrew had told me about how his first wife had left him. She took nothing but some books and one suitcase full of clothing. She went to the local YWCA and took a room. He made her want that kind of escape and he made me want it too. Three years later, I know that Andrew still womanizes and hurts people. I hear it through mutual friends."

In the throes of passion, it seems unthinkable that there will ever be difficulties in a marriage to a man self-described as a long-suffering ex-husband. The second wife views herself as a savior, a woman who has made all the difference in her new husband's life and has given him a second chance. Neither the horror stories that some husbands have shared about their first wives, nor the secreted, guarded bits of information that others have made available can in any way guide the second wife. What she learns about her husband she must learn through trials and tribulations. How he handles his second marriage may be very unlike how he handled his first. Or it may be exactly the same. He may view all wives as interchangeable. For men who see their spouses this way, only the faces change, while he remains the same.

It is often stated that a man's place in the world is not affected by his divorce. If he remarries, he may require a similar domestic environment. Second wives may find themselves in the same position as the first in terms of expectations. For this reason, the second wife could possibly feel that she is simply simulating what the first wife offered. The husband's particularities—about how to run a household, about socializing, about sports—can make her wonder about his first marriage. How did his ex-wife cope with him when he was idiosyncratic and demanding? What was it about him that irritated the first wife she wants to know, now that she, the second wife, is suddenly feeling less than euphoric with his style?

"I always say to women who are marrying men who were married before, to go sit down and interview their first wives," remarks psychologist Dr. Ronnie Burak. "The information that she has is very valuable. If the husband tells the second wife that the failed marriage was all his first wife's fault, beware, because he takes no responsibility for himself. If he has felt this way once, he may feel this way again. Generally, we tend to repeat our patterns."

The National Center for Health Statistics reports the average duration of a first marriage is eleven years, and of the second marriage, seven. The strain on the second marriage is often attributed to a vocal ex-wife, children, and finances. The lasting effect of the first divorce may take its toll on the new marriage. For the second wife who believes that her husband has become enlightened since his first marriage, there may be tremendous disappointment. His relapse to a behavior he promised to have shed or never to have had can prove too much. The new marriage is burdened with problems from the past. For those who remarry after divorce, the hurdles to overcome are evidenced in the statistics. While seventy-five percent of women and eighty-five percent of men who divorce remarry, the rate of divorce amongst second marriages is sixty percent.

According to the Academy of Matrimonial Lawyers, the five most common reasons why marriages fail are: financial difficulties, infidelity, lack of commitment/preoccupation with other activities, poor communication, and a midlife crisis/change in priorities. It becomes obvious that no one is invincible, no marriage is guaranteed. When the news broke that the so-called idyllic union of Donald Trump and Marla Maples had broken up, it was apparent that second wives were as vulnerable as first wives. None of us is totally protected; there is always the risk that a marriage will not work out as the woman (or man) had hoped. While many second wives speak of their roles as the bearers of the second chance, that chance is fraught with risks often generated by leftover problems from a first union. Loss is the by-product of divorce; loss of hope and loss of a dream. And unfortunately, loss begets loss.

Lauren has been a second wife for thirteen years and has always viewed her relationship with her husband, Ross, as special, but

nevertheless acknowledges problems: "This marriage is more to his liking, yet day to day, after all these years, I forget he feels this way. I've
begun to see how his first wife felt about his strict focus on business,
how aggravating it is even to me. There are times when I know that I
react to Ross negatively, that I understand why he was divorced. Ross
can be very tough. He has put in a great effort to change for me, but I
still feel trapped at times. It is his nature to make someone feel that way.
Ross acted one way before we were married and another after. The bottom line is that I understand the anger and the hurt."

For Irene, one of the women I interviewed, the same disappointment that existed in the first marriage has occurred in hers. "I married a man who appeared to be wonderful at first. Henry had a wife who
had a child from her previous marriage. He treated this child as his, and
I was very uncomfortable with the entire situation. But he didn't give the
child much time. He and his ex-wife, Ellen, had terrific fights over
money. She depended on him for financial support. It's too complex to
say Henry simply wasn't any good. He kept them attached to him out
of her need. He seemed to stick around deliberately without any real
feelings for the child. Being an insecure, new bride, I was happy that
Henry didn't pay them proper attention. I was relieved that it didn't take
anything away from us. As I got older and wiser, I should have wanted
him to care about them, it should have rung alarms in my head that he
didn't care enough. After a while, he let go of some of his anger toward
Ellen and began to be combative with me.

"He used to tell me how lucky I was that he put her out of the
picture. He called her a hysteric. Meanwhile, he kept telling me when he
compared us, I looked much better than her. He told me I was a star
compared to Ellen. I didn't realize what poison this talk was. Then he
began to treat me as he treated her—poorly, cruelly. He would yell at
me constantly. I began to think of her more and more. I knew what she
had endured. Both of us had misjudged him completely. Both of us had
been duped. All the promises he had made were lies. Henry told me I
was chosen because I was second. It wasn't true. I knew that I was just
like Ellen when it came to him—I had to get out. And I left. Today, I
am a second wife to a calm, kind man. I do not question this man's character because I know it."

In many cases, the second wife views the first as a thorn in her
side. Everything that the second wife has witnessed until now (through

her husband) makes it obvious that the first wife is a nasty, vindictive woman who has single-handedly ruined her husband's life. The second wife takes her husband's word verbatim, initially. It is only with time that she begins to see what the first wife tolerated.

Such husbands reveal themselves to their second wives after the courtship and honeymoon are over. Their patterns reemerge and each second wife finds herself in the same position the first wife was in. She begins to recognize her plight, seeing that this man is not evolved and that he has continued the same role from his first marriage. The second wife suspects the first wife's complaints might have some validity.

TRUE COLORS
It is when the husband shows his real self that the second wife has empathy for the first wife. At that point, deep down the second wife may have a gnawing sensation that there was some truth to the first wife's version of the story.

The painful lesson of True Colors is demonstrated by Olivia's situation. Olivia related to her husband Jim's first wife and Jim's subsequent live-in girlfriend from the start. "All of us in this story are from the same background and religion, and still, there has been a divorce and a failed relationship. It takes a tremendous amount of energy and luck for these things to work out. Jim has a child with each of them, and I really understand what happened in both cases. I watch how carefully they care for their children compared to his cavalier form of fathering. I feel more responsible for his children than he does. It seems that it is the women in his life who do the parenting. I sometimes imagine that we'll have a baby. Then I'll be the third woman to mother his offspring, alone raising his child. I won't admit this to my husband or to either woman, but I know what it must have been like for them. Jim can be very contrary and controlling.

"My stance is supposed to be that an ex-wife is negative by definition, especially if the husband has been burned. I also know that romance and expectations are not like the reality of marriage and that is why so many first wives leave. In my husband's situation, both women left him. Day to day living is not the same as courting. It is strange to admit, but sometimes when the ex-wife or the ex-girlfriend brings over the child, I feel like I have a friend in the world—someone who knows what I'm going through. I have actually sought out the ex-wife's advice on my career because she knows how my husband would react to it. I depend on her wisdom. I suppose I trust her on some level, whether I should or not. I know she doesn't want Jim back, and she knows exactly what I'm going through."

Therefore, in certain circumstances, the second wife can experience the same frustrations with her husband that his first wife did. "When it comes to parenting the children with his first wife, the father is often cast in the role of sugar daddy because there is not the day to day interaction. The second wife sees this and can resent her husband's laissez faire attitude toward his children, her stepchildren," says Dr. Ronnie Burak. "If she has her own children and they do not get along with his, it is a problem. This is compounded if he does not do any disciplining. He may be afraid to rock the boat. He may harbor too much guilt for leaving or for breaking up the family. This man cannot instill discipline because he is afraid he will lose his children. The second wife then feels defeated. She will have the same dissatisfaction as his ex-wife, because he is not enough of a disciplinarian. The first wife needs her ex-husband to discipline their children to maintain continuity when they are not under her supervision. The second wife wants her husband to discipline his children so she doesn't have to, thus making it easier for her and the children to get along. Hence, the second wife wants the children to be disciplined, and so does the first wife. In this case, the women are bonded. Both the first and the second identify with each other because they are stuck with the discipline."

Renee became a second wife to Gary, who had three young children. "I wish that someone had warned me that marriage is work every single day. One has to have a tremendous maturity to have a successful marriage. It took me many years to figure this out. Now I'm more realistic and more settled down. I look less toward Gary to make me whole. Gary's ex-wife, Elaine, was clingy and demanding, and my husband hated it. Then I became his wife and realized why she was clingy and demanding. She could not get his attention otherwise, and now I was experiencing the same dilemma. I became close to Gary's children. They were not the minus in the marriage. I began to agree with Elaine that they needed more than what they got from their father. Even his children suffered.

"The minus in this marriage is my husband. When we were first married, Gary was so troubled. I saw that he had preconceived notions of how wives could behave and be treated. I began to see that he put me in the same place as his first wife. I knew that whatever I put up with, Elaine had put up with the same. He was not able to talk about anything that mattered, and it was frustrating. I know that she had the same issues. Gary wanted things the way he always got them, the way he was used to. It was as if my needs mattered less. It had happened before. He was repeating his mistakes. I realized what torture it was to be with someone who could not allow you to be yourself.

"I was ready to leave the marriage before Gary agreed to go into therapy. It took several years, but we have learned to work on our difficulties. I know that he has been more open to his children and spending time with them because of me. Every time I do something with them, I think of Elaine. In a strange way, we share the same goals for them—that they are secure, satisfied, challenged, and strong. My husband is not as tuned in to their needs but is working on it. I believe that both their mother and I deserve the children's respect. After all, it is she and I who protect them, who see it all."

HUSBANDS WITH WALLS
As Renee learned, if the husband cannot communicate with his second wife, chances are that he was unable to communicate with his first. If his fathering faltered during the first marriage, it will suffer during the new marriage as well.

Communication is a key element in a successful marriage and cannot be fostered through the walls put up by a husband who has trouble expressing his emotions. If a husband admits to his second wife that he and his first wife rarely discussed their feelings, she should pay attention. When it happens to her and she cannot express herself nor get a reaction from him, there will be great frustration. When this lack of communication extends to the husband's way of dealing with his children, the second wife can expect little difference in the relationship now that they are married. However, if she listened when he told her he had trouble communicating with his first wife, she would have little trouble recognizing his behavior as repetition. She would also be better equipped to both deal with her own frustration and to look for ways to help her husband.

It is wise to seek counseling before becoming a second wife to a man who has children from his first marriage. Despite rosy illusions in the throes of romance, his attitude toward his children and former wife influences the new marriage. The second wife, regardless of how in love she is with her husband, ought to understand the dynamics of the first family. If she does, her presence and positive energy may bring harmony to everyone involved.

In order for the new wife to be a positive force however, she must use her own powers of perception and objectivity to evaluate the situation.

IMPROVEMENT REQUIRED
How one's husband deals with his first wife and children will have great impact on the second marriage.
• Watch how he handles his first wife and children
• Know why the first marriage failed
• Do not ignore telltale signs of irresponsibility
• Discuss all concerns ahead of time
• When problems arise in the new marriage, clear the air
• Go into therapy together
• Go into individual therapy
• Help him to achieve the balance he needs between the old and
  the new

There are other aspects which bear careful scrutiny. The financial area is a major trouble spot in many second marriages. Strangely enough, finances often cause the second wife to easily identify with the first wife's plight. Suddenly she realizes what she is up against. Her husband's attitude about money is what the first wife had to abide. It is further complicated if the first wife's maintenance interferes with the finances of the second marriage. The second wife may now understand that her husband has never been easy about sharing the wealth, even if there is plenty to go around. Or she may realize that her husband has always had extravagant tastes and that his treatment of her in terms of gifts and material possessions is not unique.

HOW HE COUNTS HIS MONEY

Until a woman becomes the second wife, she cannot really know how her husband feels about money. Once she understands it, she begins to see how finances affected the first marriage and may empathize with his first wife.

On occasion, second wives find finances to be such a critical issue that they will divorce their husbands over it. Cynthia George, a divorce attorney, has witnessed this. "There are problems in a remarriage with a second wife who has no money. If the first wife had no money and the divorce was expensive for the husband in terms of payments or the settlement, he is very guarded. The husband may insist on a prenuptial agreement or he will be very controlling of his money after what he went through in his divorce. In a prenuptial agreement, I try to move money from the man to the woman each year of the marriage. She'll get a certain amount of money if she's insecure. There are cases where the guy will write a check for $500,000 on the day of the wedding so that he does not have his new wife coming to him and asking for money. This eliminates one of the causes of divorce in a second marriage. It gives the second wife her financial freedom, something the first wife might not have had."

Another issue that wreaks havoc on the second wife is if her husband perpetuates the problems of his first marriage in his new relationship. Yet it is possible that he will learn from his past mistakes and do things differently in future relationships. A second wife can learn about her husband if she is aware of the kind of relationship he had with his first wife. She can then identify patterns that have carried over into their marriage. For example, if in the past the husband walked all over his wife, he may try to do the same thing in his new marriage. If the first wife did not feel like a true partner, but less equal than her husband, the husband may approach his relationship with his new wife in the same way. However, his second wife is a different person than his first wife, and she will likely have different responses to her husband's actions and behaviors. "When the new marriage is different from the first marriage, this man will not get away with the same things," comments Dr. Kasson. "Perhaps the second wife will not tolerate this kind of behavior. Or, maybe this time the husband is looking for an emotional equal, whereas the first time he was not. He might find a second wife who stands up to him. And he might like it. Or he may fight it, feeling that the first way worked better than the second. It really depends upon the man." If a second wife keeps her eyes open and is confident of who she is and what she wants in the marriage, she is well on her way to making things work. She will not have much success if her husband is not aware of her needs and feelings or of his own past and desire for the future. Past mistakes can help a self-aware man know what he wants or doesn't want in his next relationship. This, in turn, will benefit his second wife.

THE PAST VERSUS THE NEW LIFE
The relationship held by the husband and his first wife will not necessarily be mirrored in his second marriage. In an equal partnership, the dynamic is specific to the two individuals.

Unfortunately for Rory, problems from her husband's past did encroach on the happiness of their marriage. To compound the problem, Rory also was lacking self-confidence. She could not confront her husband about his actions and her husband did not recognize that he was bringing his past into his present marriage. "Generally speaking, our marriage works. But, I do think of Billy's first wife. I think of her most often when we go on vacation. I know that my husband will not give up his favorite haunts, so we go to the same places every summer that he went in his first marriage. I have wondered if we are actually in the same room, in the very same bed. It makes me unhappy.

"I do wish that Billy had opened up about her. If he had told me more at the start, then I'd have felt better all along. I hate wondering and trying to imagine how it was. Sometimes, when he kisses me at night, I think that maybe she is on his mind. It chips away at my confidence. I try to imagine how they were together. It makes me unable to have sex with him. I can only imagine that he was once in love with her too, and they were intimately involved. I just shut down. I know friends who have become second wives and have moved into the first wife's house. I do not know how they do it."

Rory is an example of the second wife who I found to be most disturbed by her husband's previous marriage: one who has self-esteem problems and does not feel she is unique. Such a woman's insecurity is often underscored by her husband's inability to create a new life with her. She cannot put the first wife behind her because he perpetuates his former life with his new wife. Instead of exploring unfamiliar personal terrain and creating a sex life that does not rival the first but surpasses it, the second wife finds herself walking in the first wife's shoes.

One of the repetitive patterns I unearthed occurs when a second wife asks for a divorce. Such a break-up can be devastating to her husband. He now has two failed marriages and perhaps two families. In his mind, despite all of his efforts, he could not succeed. His ego is shattered and his self-esteem is at an all time low. While this man may become introspective and ask himself what it is that he repeatedly does wrong, he might also deny that it is his fault in any way. He instead may view the situation as having chosen poorly twice or that his luck is not good. It is only if this man is able to look inward that there is an opportunity for him to change his methods.

OPPORTUNITIES ABOUND
If the husband can view his failed marriages as an opportunity for self-improvement and not blame his wives, it is a plus. Learning from one's mistakes is key to successful relationships.

Many a second wife enters marriage believing she is safe because her husband has been through it all already. She assumes that his knowledge and experience make him capable of a greater level of commitment. When she finds herself in an unhappy position, she begins to wonder about the first wife. Was he the same with her? Was he unreasonable, narcissistic, unyielding? When it becomes apparent to him that the second marriage is failing, the less mature man will regret his mistake in marrying this woman but will not have remorse beyond this. If he left his first marriage for his second, and it does not succeed, he may not be sorry that he broke up his family, but that his life did not work out as anticipated.

"Sometimes the second wife has a fantasy that she can correct what was wrong in the first marriage. The second wife does not want to think of herself as being in an ongoing negative pattern. She has to believe that this time it is new and separate from his past," comments Dr. Ronnie Burak. "It is a huge disappointment for the husband when he assumes that he is in a whole different world with the second wife and it fails. He believes that the first marriage failed because of his poor choice. Now he has chosen again and may come to believe it is not that he has chosen poorly twice but that he is deficient."

Many times, the marriage fails when the second wife cannot get her husband to realize what is lacking in their relationship. After repeated attempts at communication, the second wife might give up hope. For the second wife, the concept of failure is discouraging, as she greatly desires success. Only if her husband recognizes his deficiencies and how his past mistakes are being replayed can he use his hard-earned wisdom to improve the new marriage.

LACKING INSIGHT
If it is the husband who is not fueling the marriage, and if he does not recognize his shortcomings or limitations, the marriage will suffer.

One second wife who has become aware that her husband seems to lack insight states, "My husband, Jay, looked to me for a new life, and I wanted to give it to him. He gave me this big speech about how in his first marriage they were out for dinner constantly and never at home. He said he wanted me to fill the cupboards and make our house into a home," laments Carly. "I don't think he ever meant it, but I wanted it. I wanted a home life. We had discussed our supposedly shared values, and Jay had been adamant that he wanted just what I wanted: a quiet life, children."

"I know that his first wife wanted a family life, too. I know that she stayed for years, thinking it would happen. Then Jay wanted a divorce, and she was crushed. She gave him the best years of her life, sacrificed her desire to have a child, and still he divorced her. Then I came along, and it seemed he wanted what she wanted, but with me. Instead, he is exactly the same. I'm beginning to think that Jay cannot change. We are still together, and I am not ready to leave, but I am very disappointed. I do not believe that he will divorce me, but I also do not think that I'll get what I want out of the marriage. I can see that this is Jay's problem, not mine and not his first wife's. I know that he is good at getting divorced and being divorced because he paid close attention to the whole ordeal with his first wife. He protected himself, and he would do it again, except there would be more money at stake since he's been doing so well lately. It doesn't frighten me nor does it make me worried about my future. I have come to see similarities between me and his first wife. No matter how he treats me, I seem to want to be here. My focus is on keeping the marriage going. I guess he really gets his partners hooked."

"When the second marriage dissolves," says Cynthia George, divorce attorney, "the husband finds the process easier than it was the first time around. He knows what to expect and how it will happen. If the first divorce took place after fifteen years and he is now forty, there might not be a great deal of money to deal with. However, if the second divorce takes place ten or twelve years later, when this man has made more money and has become a success, money is now an issue. He considers himself someone who made it through a divorce and survived, and he is genuinely surprised divorce is more demanding this time. In particular, if the second wife and her husband have no children, the husband cannot figure out what the problem is. Why would she want so much of his money? Why is she behaving this way? He is genuinely baffled and at a loss. After the second divorce, he has been through quite a bit."

If the issues from the first marriage remain unresolved, the husband may bring them to the new marriage. A second wife is not always prepared for this, and as problems carried over from his first marriage begin to surface, she may become confused. Then, if the problems are insurmountable and the second marriage fails, the husband will likely be crushed. He did not see the break-up coming, just as he did not realize the unresolved problems of his first marriage had seeped into and destroyed his second. He has great difficulty facing this new failure and loss, shocked as he is that another marriage has ended.

TWO TIME LOSER
- The husband has high hopes for the second marriage
- He sees it as a second chance but has not yet resolved past relationship issues
- His second wife gets frustrated with his past problems
- Finally, she gives up and leaves him
- He is shattered now over two lost marriages

In some cases when a second wife must live with a husband who had relationship problems never addressed in his first marriage, she finds herself dealing with those same issues unsuccessfully. When Edie met her husband, he told her of his wife's infidelity and the terrific pain he endured throughout the divorce proceedings. "His wife, Marlena, did not want custody of the children, and he ended up with two young children, ill prepared for parenting. My husband, Harold, is a surgeon with a rigorous schedule. He was virtually clueless as to how to take care of these two little girls. He definitely wanted a second wife who would pitch in, who welcomed the idea that he had kids and was the custodial parent. It was almost like marrying a widower, Harold's commitments were that time consuming. The girls had not seen their mother in months and yearned for a mother figure. They really needed someone. But I don't believe that his having been married before has served me well. I don't believe that he and his first wife dealt with their emotional issues, and that created problems for us.

"After some time, I actually understood why Marlena left him and why she had a lover. He is quite egocentric and unavailable, emotionally and physically. The hospital seems to be his world, and he needs little more to keep him going. Even on Saturdays he will go in to the office and work. I know that Harold wanted to improve upon his first marriage when he entered the second, but he was unable to do so. He did not want to make the same mistake again. Yet there have been so many similar difficulties. It's as if the years have not brought him maturity. He believes that he is now more patient and a better listener and, on some level, he is. However, there are other aspects to Harold's personality that have not changed, and cannot be changed. I think he probably acts the same way in our marriage and does the same wrong things that ended his first marriage. As our life together went on, I began to understand his first wife's plight. Yet, I also believed that Marlena did not fulfill his needs and that I was better suited to him. All of this had kept me there longer, but recently, I filed for divorce. Despite the children and the life that we have built together, I cannot be with him. I think of his first wife constantly, what she felt, how she had to go. If I did not file for divorce, I would have become like her. I, too, would have taken a lover."

Unlike Edie, a second wife who is determined to move beyond the first wife's issues has a chance to grow with her husband. There is a respect for the individuality of both partners and an acceptance of their differences. No matter how strong and accepting she is, however, he must be able to recognize his role in their problems (whether it is leftover from his previous marriage or new issues) and be willing to make changes.

WHEN THE SECOND WIFE SHOULD STAY
• When he agrees to therapy
• When he admits his errors and asks her to guide him
• When the intimacy is real

On the other hand, if the second wife and her husband cannot work out their problems, if he remains intractable and aloof, the second wife may find her marriage of short duration. For even the most loving, patient second wife cannot solve her husband's problems for him.

WHEN THE SECOND WIFE SHOULD GO
• There are irreconcilable differences
• He has not gained insight or flexibility
• There is no support system, no attachment

Each of the women in this chapter identified strongly with the first wife and, especially after some time had passed, sympathized with her. In fact, once many of them were second wives for a time, they discovered why the first marriage broke up. Some were able to adapt to their new life and overcome problems from the past; others found themselves mired in frustration over dealing with issues from his first marriage or their husbands' continuation of past behaviors and beliefs. The women who did the best entered their marriages with their eyes and ears wide open. They were able to talk openly with their husbands about the problems of his first marriage, and thus avoided some of the same pitfalls. Yet even they did not take the opportunity to speak to their husbands' first wives early on. Upon reflection, many wish they had done so to better understand the other side of the story. For some, such open dialogue could have saved them heartbreak and misery, for if they knew before they married what they eventually learned, they say they would never have walked down the aisle. It is obvious then, that open communication before the wedding is just as important as after. Without it, the second wife enters her marriage blindly, unaware that she may be setting herself up to repeat her husband's doomed first marriage. With it, a second wife is armed with information that will help her avoid replaying past mistakes. Once married, the lines of communication must continue to stay open between a second wife and her husband. If they both openly discuss and acknowledge their past relationship struggles, they can work together to eradicate residual problems in their new relationship.

Many of the women interviewed came to realize that because communication between them and their husbands was stilted or nonexistent, past problems could not be brought out into the open where they could be dealt with. When a second wife is alone in seeing problems in her marriage and is unable to get her husband to acknowledge or talk about them, she may find herself fighting a losing battle. Eventually, as in Edie's case, if the problem continues, ending the marriage may seem to be the only solution. It is difficult for some second wives to take this step, especially after they tell themselves that they are a man's second chance at happiness and they will do for him what his first wife could not. For a second wife who believes this, a divorce will make her feel a failure. Yet there is only so much a partner can do on her own to save a marriage. Every marriage is different; divorce may be the only solution for some while counseling or therapy may help others get back on track. In the end, about half of the interviewees in this chapter chose to divorce their husbands while the other half remained in the marriage, committed to working it out. For the second wife whose marriage does prevail, according to a nationwide survey, eighty-eight percent of husbands feel happier and are more committed to the new marriage than they were to the first. As author Thomas Moore describes it in his book, *Soul Mates*, the "soul centered image" of marriage is one where "the individual has room to play out his eccentric possibilities. We may honor a marriage's soul by discovering what it wants."

CHAPTER TWO

COMPETING WITH
THE FIRST WIFE

"During the first five years of my marriage," Susanna explains, "I was always trying to outdo Grant's first wife, Kirstin. If her hair was long and highlighted, so was mine. If she cut hers short, so did I. And my husband fed right into it. Grant would tell me how she had looked during their marriage, how striking she was—tall and thin and dreamy. I was told more than I ever needed to know: how she wore hats and mini skirts and came to parties late, looking so beautiful she would take everyone's breath away. I was totally threatened by this, and while I had little confidence that I could compete, I would run out and buy exotic dresses and primp before a family event anyway. Eventually his cousin asked me why I was doing this, why I was trying to look like Kirstin. My answer was unhealthy: I did it because I thought he still wanted her.

"Kirstin was remarried the day after the divorce was final and had clearly made another choice, but my husband would speak of her as though she was still there. And they did keep in touch. She sent him postcards and called him at work, which made me crazy. That was what made me think we were in competition. I remember once, Princess Diana was interviewed about her marriage to Prince Charles. She made a comment about how crowded it was for the three of them, Charles,

Camilla Parker Bowles, and herself. I really identified with what she said. It felt crowded to me, too. But one day I stopped caring—I simply lost interest. My husband and I had spent enough time together as a married couple for his first wife to recede. Or I grew up and lost interest in her. Or I became more interesting myself. And when Grant compared us, I yawned. Eventually, he just stopped talking about her."

There are various aspects of competition between first and second wives. This occurs particularly if there have been children in the first marriage, because they can become powerful weapons in divorce. However, the competition between the first wife and the second exists in its own sphere and may have a life of its own, regardless of children. Competition and comparisons between the first wife and the second are ongoing as the stages of the new marriage unfold. The first wife watches, perhaps jealously, wondering if the second is having another kind of experience: in sharing a baby with her ex-husband, in lifestyle, travel, in the entirety of the marriage. At the same time, the second wife wonders if her experiences with her husband are similar to those of the first wife, or if she is doing better. Is she better equipped to handle their lifestyle, their children, their home? Although the years march forward and hopefully both the first and second wife establish themselves in their own lives, the comparisons do not always stop.

AREAS OF COMPETITION
- Appearances
- Athletic ability/physical fitness
- Domestic style
- Parenting
- Romance
- Sex
- Career/financial success
- Values
- Goals

Neither first nor second wives like to admit a competition with the other. While it may not always be articulated, it often exists. For many second wives, this competitive drive plays on their insecurities.

They are aware that nothing they share with their husbands is original; he has already done it with someone else. An insecure second wife is continually measuring how well she does, how much better she is at it than his first wife was. How dire the competition is depends upon the circumstance of the break-up of the first marriage. If the husband has cheated and left the first marriage for the second, there is a different dynamic than if it was the first wife who left.

Dr. Michele Kasson views the competition between the first wife and the second as specific to the situation. "If the second wife was the husband's lover, then the first wife lost out way before the marriage ended. She has to work very hard at regaining her self-esteem. The second is then in a place of superiority if the first is bereft and did not want to lose her husband." This kind of persistent competition makes the second wife think of herself as the winner. She views herself as having won the husband over: emotionally, physically, and financially.

If the first wife has chosen to leave the marriage, she may be perceived to be in a position of superiority. Because of this, the second wife often feels less than secure and is frequently compared to and reminded of the first. The husband may not realize what the problems were in his first marriage and the second wife may have her own unreconciled past. In such cases, the second wife keeps sensing the shadow of the first wife and feels she cannot measure up. Thus, a version of the Rebecca syndrome surfaces; in this case it is generated by competition, not by marrying a widower. If the first wife has literally flown the coop, then the second wife senses her ghost. She feels that the outside world compares and contrasts how she conducts the new marriage as opposed to the first wife. There is little relief coming from her husband; it seems to her that he, too, is scrutinizing her.

THE REBECCA SYNDROME
This occurs when the first wife is deceased or absent and the second feels she is a replacement. She feels she is competing with an invisible enemy. She worries that she is being constantly scrutinized by her husband and others and cannot measure up to the ghost of her predecessor, as did the second wife in the book, *Rebecca* by Daphne Du Maurier.

An instance of the Rebecca Syndrome is shown in the relationship of Erin and Bruce. Erin's husband, Bruce, was abandoned by his first wife on a business trip to California. In shock and totally baffled by her departure, Bruce pulled his life together slowly. "When he met me," Erin said, "he was ready to be involved with a woman, but could not shake the 'training' of his first wife. Bruce was heavily influenced by his first wife's methods, so he couldn't understand me or my style. I fell in love with him, but there were certain behavioral patterns that I did not like, a certain authoritative attitude that I couldn't live with. He kept imagining that I was just like her and assumed that I'd put up with that kind of relationship. When Bruce finally looked at me and saw me for who I was, another kind of person altogether, he stopped treating me that way. I think that despite the fact that he was left behind by his wife, which really hurt his ego, she had been pretty difficult to get along with.

"I felt that I had to fight to be recognized and not compared to her. I showed him that I was more solid and more dependable. She and I were night and day. She was blonde, thin, and high strung. I am an average build with dark hair and more patient, sort of quiet. I suspect that Bruce wanted someone else right away. He is incomplete without a partner. But he chose a different type of woman this time, and I wanted him to come to terms with that. He had to let go of his past habits and stop thinking about how I was like her or not like her. Bruce had even asked me to cut my hair short because he'd asked his ex-wife to do that. I refused to do it, explaining that this was who I was and I didn't want to be like her. I'd say I've fought long and hard for him to let go of who she was versus who I am. It's all worked out, but it took a full year and tremendous perseverance on my part. Each of us has to fight for our own place."

Because Bruce was attached to his ex-wife's ways does not mean his first marriage was a happy one. Author Daniel J. Levinson, in his book, *The Seasons of a Woman's Life*, reminds us that "The divorce rate underestimates the degree and depth of actual severity of marital problems... it shouldn't be assumed that just because a marriage has endured that it was necessarily a good, happy marriage."

The truth of Levinson's theory could not be more significant for Joyce. "I had a very difficult first year with my husband because I married him right after his wife, who had been very ill, died. We met at the hospital and were very careful not to get involved throughout her illness. It was a horrible ordeal and he had a small child who was left without a mother. I know that the first wife and I are like comparing apples and oranges. She and I were from different cultures. I kept thinking that if I did something one way, she'd have done it another way. I began to get depressed, assuming this woman was a better wife and mother than I was turning out to be. My husband and I finally spoke about her. He made it clear that he had been committed to their marriage but was not happy. It took me a while, but I see now that he is both committed and happy. And I am happy now, too."

In a situation where the first wife is alive, happiness may be more difficult to attain that it was for Joyce. In fact, the relationship between a second wife's happiness and a first wife's happiness cannot be underestimated. This is true for Dana. Divorced with two children, Dana became a second wife to Mark eighteen months ago. Although Mark's first wife immediately remarried, she remained in the picture because of their three children. "I think that in me, my husband chose an improved, upgraded model of his first wife. He is attracted to certain qualities, an aggression, an inner strength. I think she realized that too, and it makes her angry. She didn't care what Mark did when she left him for someone else, but now that I'm in the picture, she has an opinion. I do not like that he is in touch with her so frequently, and if he has any exposure to her without it being about the kids, I object loudly. I also have pointed out that I do not speak with my ex-husband for any reason. I have two children who are teenagers, and they make all their arrangements with their father and call him on their own. I set this as an example. But Mark defends her. He tells me that she cannot draw the line with him the way that I have with my ex-husband. I say to him that there is only one wife in our house. I wish we could get along or at least be civil, but she makes it clear that she hates my guts and resents my place. She is miserable about our relationship, so I'm not happy either. But I'm independent and strong, so I'm moving away from those angry emotions. I suspect, as time goes on, she'll learn to pull away too, to release some of her anger."

As can be seen in Dana's case, there is a direct correlation between the first wife's happiness and the second wife's happiness. Once the first wife has let go of anger or resentment towards her ex-husband or his second wife, she can go on with her life. This may mean remarriage of her own, moving away, or making peace with her ex-husband and his new family. The second wife will subsequently feel the burden of conflict released and will find herself happier and more secure in her marriage. Most important, a man who has trouble letting go of his past and who entertains lingering feelings and memories of his first marriage will gain the freedom to break with the past. He is then able to concentrate on the future with his second wife.

TRANSITIONS
The competition ceases once the first wife is happier or the second wife is more secure. The key lies with the husband, who must separate the past from the present.

Unfortunately, there are some husbands who cannot separate the past from the present. They may purposely choose a second wife who is very similar to the first in looks or style. When this happens, comparisons are easily drawn by outsiders and the two women may feel interchangeable. And no matter how happy or secure each wife feels in her new life, it is not pleasant for either one to be told that she looks like the other. Often the second wife is told that she is a younger version of the first, and the first is told that her ex-husband has married someone just like her. It is not that men are necessarily blindly making the same mistakes as they did in the past or that they intend to hurt their first or second wives when seeking a mate. As noted psychologist Dr. Ronnie Burak explains, "We all unconsciously look for a certain kind of person. Whatever need was there that drove us to choose the first person is still there in some way. What the husband hopes for is that he will find a similar person, but without the flaws of the first. For example, a tall, slender redhead who is kind instead of a tall, slender redhead who is heartless."

Many men and women have been choosing the same type of person with whom to become involved from the time they were teenagers. It is only as we mature that we can decipher the qualities that work and do not work in a potential partner. While the positive characteristics of a previous partner can be sought in the next partner, it is unhealthy for a husband to repeat his pattern to the point of another failure.

OVER AND OVER
- We search for someone to complete us
- The second wife has similar traits to the first
- The first wife resents being replaced
- The second resents being a replacement

This repetitive pattern may be seen in Angie and Ted's relationship. When Angie met Ted's first wife, Rachel, she was astonished at how alike they were to each other. "My husband has always told me that he likes a certain kind of woman, someone who is tall and thin with dark hair. He loves that I'm a singer and a great deal of our time is spent on music. I had never met his first wife, and since they had no children together, she seemed to be in the past. But we do live two towns away from each other and it was my hairdresser who introduced us. I was quite shaken by how similar we looked. Even our style of clothes was the same. I had heard about her because Ted's sister and Rachel are still very friendly. She kept telling me that we would like each other. My husband kept telling me that I am a better cook and am prettier than his first wife. I've always felt that his family has been drawing comparisons and watching me very closely. They have never said anything, but he's come out and told me how much happier he is with me. Then he tells me that she wanted him because he is so macho. He believes that I am attracted to the same things about him. It seems unfair, the way that he dumps me in the same category and presumes so much. I bet he did that with her too. When we were married three years ago, he told me that I reminded him of his first wife, which I did not like. I had refused to meet her when his sister offered, and then I ended up meeting her anyway. What I wish is that we did not look the same. I feel as if he simply traded one wife in for the other."

In Angie's case, not only was she hurt because she felt like a replica of Ted's first wife, she was inundated with commentary and unsolicited opinions. The similarities she shared with this other woman were discussed by his family, his sister, and even a hairdresser. Although it may be difficult, it is best for the second wife to ignore outsiders' opinions and pay attention to what is significant: her marriage, her husband, herself. The information provided by others is not always honest or helpful. By virtue of time, the first marriage and comparisons to the first wife will lessen.

IGNORE OUTSIDERS' OPINIONS
If family members and friends remark that you and the first wife are alike or unalike, do not pay them any heed. Do not question their loyalties or intentions, but simply press on with your own life and your own identity.

Caitlin is another second wife who experienced the negativity generated by comparisons. "I feel that Cliff's ex-wife and I are very similar in many ways," admits Caitlin. "I am a bit heavier, but we are both small with dark hair and dark eyes. Oddly enough, we even have the same interests. We both love animals. I am a devoted mother to both my kids and stepkids, and I've been told that until the divorce, Anita was an excellent mother. But we're not the same people. I am more career-oriented than she is, and she is more combative. I do not like to fight. So what my husband got was someone who is very much like his first wife but not willing to make waves, in fact, determined to keep peace.

"I thought at first that I could learn something from her. I thought that since we interact through the kids, it might be wise to glean some wisdom from her. But I didn't have a chance. She really resents me, not me personally, but that I am married to her ex-husband. Anita seems to forget that she has a boyfriend and that she was the one who wanted out. And Cliff has never mixed me up with her in any way. I know that I make him much happier than she did and I know why he is attracted to what I offer. I think that now, since we have hit forty, we are more aware of what works in a marriage and what takes away from the possibility of survival. I am no longer threatened by comparisons to her; I know who am, what I want, and what I bring to this marriage."

Even if a second wife attains confidence and security in her own position and her own marriage, she can be undermined by a first wife who is seemingly waiting for this new marriage to fail. For these first wives, there is a fantasy that this second wife is not actually who her ex-husband wants or needs. She holds on to the hope that he will see through his second wife, will leave, and then return to her. To this end, for the first wife who is still in touch with her ex-husband, most likely because of children, she will put herself in direct competition with the second wife. To the dismay of the second wife, especially an insecure second wife, the first wife may imitate the new wife. For instance, if the new wife is blonde, she may become a blonde. Or if her ex-husband has chosen someone very intellectual, she may go back to school.

FIRST WIFE'S MODUS OPERANDI
- Dismisses the new marriage
- Flaunts her abilities: mothering, career, looks
- Imitates the new wife
- Undermines the second wife

Meanwhile, the second wife finds herself living under the shadow of the first. She realizes what the first wife's strengths were and she strives to do as well. This may manifest in her career, parenting, socializing, and caring for or romancing her husband. To protect herself from fear of losing her husband, she may harbor a fantasy that she is the only woman ever for him. When she feels herself in competition with the first wife, she needs to believe that this is the only marriage that has ever really existed for her husband.

SECOND WIFE'S MODUS OPERANDI
• Attempts to outdo first wife
• Embellishes the romance
• Dismisses the first marriage

"Even if a first wife wants her husband back, she may have a need to show him and his new wife how terrific her life is without him," says Dr. Ronnie Burak. "Her manner of competing is now relegated to showing off. She will show off her boyfriend, her latest achievements, her new look, as much and as often as possible. The second wife is most likely quite relieved that this first wife has new diversions in her life, especially a new love interest. But she does not appreciate the first wife's attempts to be in the picture, in any way."

Lannie has been a second wife for fifteen years and has two older stepchildren; together she and her husband, Bob, have one child. "Bob's first wife, Elsa, has been divorced once and widowed twice since. I think Elsa mates and kills like a black widow. She is a power monger, even with her children. She tries to control her son who was recently married. She is the same age as my husband and has always resented that I am so much younger. We are not one bit alike. We are opposites in looks and personality. Compared to her, I'm a relaxed person. She is not nurturing or warm and friendly, which I am.

"Bob was unhappy with her, but he is the type to stick things out. Elsa was the one who wanted out. Then she contested the divorce, because by then we were living together. We lived together for five years before the divorce came through. I was pregnant when I married him, because I could not wait. I was getting older and she was holding up my life, which made me very angry. But because Bob was head over heels in love with me, I was never threatened by her. I saw the two of us as very different. I think Bob realized what did not work for him and decided how to suit his needs in the second marriage."

The husband who is clear on why his first marriage failed will often seek in a second wife a relationship that is seasoned and improved. He takes the knowledge of what failed in his first marriage and uses it as a cautionary tale. The second wife benefits from his sensibility.

KNOWLEDGEABLE HUSBANDS
• He has learned from the mistakes of his first marriage
• He communicates his needs to his second wife
• The second marriage incorporates his life lessons

Isabelle realized that her husband, Seth, postponed their wedding because he was afraid of marriage after his divorce. "To this day, I hate his ex-wife, Debbie, for what she did to my husband and the effect her behavior has had on people's perceptions and expectations of me. Because of her, he and his family questioned if I was in it for the money. Seth's mother made it difficult for me, saying that I even had the same looks as the first wife. I blame her suspicions of me on how Debbie conducted herself. Everyone was criticizing me, saying that I had the same intentions as his first wife. They insisted that I sign a prenuptial agreement, although I could not have cared less what Seth had in the bank. If his ex-wife was in it for the money, that was her thing, not mine. I wanted to be Seth's wife for years before we finally got married.

"To this day, when I think of Debbie, I see her as a ship that always comes in to port. She is always there, even at a distance. Their child is an anchor, the guarantee that she'll dock. She will sail in and out of my life, this ex-wife, for the rest of my days. Even my stepson compares us. He will say to me, 'My mom does it this way, can't you do it like she does?' Meanwhile, Seth is very neurotic about money and it is because of his alimony and child support. To me, all of these bad feelings come from being compared to her and not judged for who I am."

The unfair comparisons to Debbie hurt and undermined Isabelle in her role as Seth's second wife. Yet as hard as it is for a second wife to be scrutinized by her mother-in-law or other friends and relatives, it is doubly as upsetting to feel the same glare from her new husband. Yet for Seth, such trepidation over remarriage and his inability to trust Isabelle was inevitable. He had suffered through his ex-wife's painful hold on his finances, both during and after their marriage. At the same time, Isabelle was insulted at the suggestion that she sign a prenuptial agreement. After all, she loved and trusted Seth and thought it absurd that she would be marrying him for his money. With this in mind, still, in a second marriage, it is a good idea to take care of the finances before they can become a point of contention.

According to Cynthia George, divorce attorney, problems in a remarriage can be avoided. "Sometimes second wives get so insecure about money because their husbands' behavior can be unpredictable and confusing. Both women, first wife and second wife, are nervous about money. It becomes a question of what the first wife had had in the marriage and what she has attained though her divorce. In the new marriage, the second wife finds herself competing with the first wife's history. Eventually, when the second wife realizes her husband is taking care of her financially, she is relieved. She may be in a better place financially than the first wife and the husband is ahead this time. Hopefully, the past mistakes over finances will not color the future."

Competition between first and second wives is not only over finances. The results of my research show that when a baby is born into a second marriage and there are stepchildren, the energy shifts. A stepmother who may have been involved, even dedicated to her stepchildren, now has her own child. The competition between the first wife and the second may escalate regarding the children. Ninety percent of second wives I interviewed feel that having their own baby changes the dynamic. While the second wife may welcome her stepchildren into a relationship with her baby, she makes the relationship with her own child primary. If she and the stepchildren did not have a strong and well-established relationship before the birth of the baby, the interviewees state that the gulf widens. Most second wives feel the first wife is keenly competitive about her children coming ahead of the second wife's child. Ideally, with her own child, the second wife now feels complete. Her new marriage is no longer focused on the children of the first wife and the feelings of competition that go along. Instead, it is well rounded with an emphasis on her relationships with her husband, their child, and her stepchildren.

BABIES AS ARMOR
- The new marriage profits from the baby's arrival
- The second wife and the first are on an equal playing field
- The second wife feels vindicated

On occasion, having a child in a new marriage brings acceptance on the part of the ex-wife and the present couple. Nellie is a young mother and stepmother to a six-year old child. "My husband, Tom, is in the Navy and travels for work, so I am in constant touch with his first wife, Peggy, because of their child. I was jealous of Peggy until we had our own baby. Not only had Tom slept with her, but she was the mother of his child. I tried not to compete over their daughter but to simply be as good to her as I could be. And his ex-wife did remarry and built a new life for herself. I had to waitress for a while when we moved here, and she did too, to make ends meet. We sort of understand each other. There are many similarities between us. But when I look at how close my husband and I are in this marriage and I know how distant they were in their marriage, I know that what we have is only about us. I have calmed down and have decided there is enough room for all of us: him, me, her, their daughter, and our baby."

In certain cases, having one's own child brings no improvement in the relationship between the parties. "His ex-wife is always there because of the children," complains Allie. "I thought that it would change once we had children of our own, but it hasn't. There was a constant competition because he was better to our sons than to his daughters from the previous marriage. It's not that he doesn't love his daughters; he had just always wanted boys. I try to be understanding of his ex-wife, but she thinks it is some kind of show down and that her children are competing with me and mine. She tried to turn her kids against me in order to stir things up. She is very neurotic. She has nothing in her life to think about but how to get back at me. I think this is often the pattern with ex-wives who are bitter over the divorce or who haven't moved on with their lives. For years before we had our own children, I was miserable at family get-togethers with my stepkids because their mother would be there. Only now am I feeling stronger and less affected by her vindictive behavior."

Other times, when there are children from the first marriage, the second wife may think she is in competition with the first wife for the children's affections. This competition may work both ways. The first wife/mother sometimes feels as if the other woman who now has her husband may soon also win over her children's love. She may lose everything to this woman. So, while the first competes to keep her children's love and loyalty, the second competes by being sugar mommy, taking them to the zoo, being lenient, buying them toys.

CHILDREN AS WINNERS
When the second wife is genuinely interested in her stepchildren and the first wife encourages a healthy, loving relationship between her children and the second wife, everyone benefits.

CHILDREN AS LOSERS
When the first wife feels threatened by her children's relationship with the second wife and/or the second wife tries to win the affection of her stepchildren by spoiling them, the children become confused and worry about betraying one woman by having a relationship with the other.

Regardless of the potential pitfalls of dealing with stepchildren, some women are not worried about the negatives. After her divorce, Nanette purposely chose to date men who had been married before and had children. She eventually married such a man. "His first wife resented me in the beginning and felt that we were competing over her kids' attention, but she's relaxed since then. She sees that I'm supportive of her children and my husband and I offer them a very nice lifestyle. Frankly, she is unable to do this for them. As far as he goes, maybe I'm projecting my own divorce, but I do not believe she really wants him back. I know that I see my own ex as yesterday's news. It is fine that he is remarried. It works out all around. So, the only problem here with the first wife is that she vies for her kids' attention. I am not trying to make her kids mine. But I accept that they are part of the package and I do include them. That's the part she has trouble with."

Often, competition over a child is not so much about the child, but about jealousy for the new couple and their relationship. "Unfortunately, my husband didn't get it," regrets Audra. "One time Brian was telling me that he and his ex-wife have a great friendship. I told him that I thought she was jealous, insecure, and inflexible. I knew that she was trying to seduce him whenever she had the chance. Brian's ex-wife acts as if I took her husband away, which is not the case. I know that it has extended to how she keeps her daughter from us. It bothers her if I have anything to do with her. I have always been good to their daughter, who is a difficult adolescent. But Brian's ex-wife can only regret things, like the fact that she doesn't have him anymore or a family that is in one piece. No matter what Brian does, she thinks it's not good enough for her or their daughter.

"My husband has been unable to get away from his former life, even when he thinks he is committed to this one. I am always feeling he's watching me to see if I can do as well as his first wife in the same situation. There are too many crossovers and I need him to start fresh."

"Control through the children is common," says Antoinette Michaels, relationship counselor. "If a first wife has a hard time of things in the new marriage, it is a reflection of how her ex-husband reacts. There is a great deal of anger directed toward the second wife if the husband left the marriage for her. If it was a mutual coming apart, the second wife has less hostility directed at her, but still feels that comparisons are being made continually. The question becomes, how fair is the husband to both women?"

The forming of a triangle between the first wife/husband/second wife depends upon several factors. If the first wife hasn't moved on with her life, she will likely try to maintain contact with her ex-husband. How he responds to her demands and how he handles his perceived obligation to his first wife is important. If the husband firmly adheres to his new life and does not relent to his ex-wife's wishes, then the second wife is in the right place and so is the first.

FOREVER A TRIANGLE
- The first wife misses her former life and holds on however she can
- The second wife wishes her husband had no baggage
- The husband struggles to be free and unencumbered

Even if the first wife is not trying to stay in her ex-husband's life, a second wife may create other problems with a first wife. Some second wives are jealous of the one who came before and obsess over what they have missed out on by not being first. Yet as Marina demonstrates, this is the second wife's problem, not the first's, and it is thus up to her to find peace and happiness in the role of second wife. Marina appreciates her role as second wife and does not mind that she is not the first in many instances. Nor is she the least bit concerned about the first wife. "I understand my husband is not at all interested in having children because he is too impatient. This is acceptable to me. I believe his ex-wife had a problem with this. Also, they were the same age and I am younger. I come from a different era than my husband and his contemporaries. I enjoy being with his friends, especially the friends who his ex-wife did not like. I feel young and fresh. I realize that my husband thinks I'm special. I like being looked at as the younger wife while around my husband's contemporaries. It's a chance to remain young, a shot at longevity."

"What we often see," remarks psychologist Dr. Donald Cohen, "is a situation where the unreconciled differences in the first marriage become a part of the competition in the second. This competition can be played out in a number of ways. Either the first wife will not relent with her ex-husband, or the husband cannot completely let go of her, even as he remarries and begins a new life. For the second wife, there is a need to compete however she can. She may even compete by flirting with the ex-wife's boyfriend at a family gathering."

Unlike Marina, who is secure in her role as a second wife, Sheryl still feels the need to compete with her husband Edward's first wife. "I know that I have won by becoming a second wife, and yet I can't resist competing when the opportunity arises." Sheryl admits. "Because my marriage to my husband is a result of an affair which broke up two marriages, there is great animosity from both our exes toward me and Edward. I will not say I am proud of what happened, but I can say it was worth it to me. The first wife really hates me, and I feed right into it. My husband wanted to break free of her during their marriage. Even if he had not met me, he would have eventually left her. He has told me repeatedly that he purposely chose me because I am so different in looks and in every way of dealing with life than his first wife.

"At a party where we had to be together, she cried to me. She told me that she doesn't want to share him. But I have no intention of sharing him, because he is mine. She will only see me as the person who took her husband away. She's in denial over the fact that their marriage was in trouble for years before it actually ended. I was so into competing with her that I had my hair done and bought a new outfit for this party.

"Her way of mothering their children is another story altogether. I have children from my first marriage and so does Edward. It isn't a simple story, and I know I ought to be more gracious, but I can't. And she can't be either. We are competitive because of him. She knows how aware I am that she still wants him. She forgets that when she was married to him, he never came home. He was avoiding her, and then he was with me. I've won this battle, but we both still compete. Even when I know it's sick, I am vicious when I talk about her."

Many of the second wives I interviewed did not have as

vindictive or angry a relationship with their husbands' first wives as Sheryl did. Yet it is a good example of how a husband's, a first wife's, and a second wife's perceptions of themselves and each other can differ. As Dr. Donald Cohen notes, "The comparison between the first wife and the second is often striking. A husband imagines that he is embarking on a new life, while the second wife imagines that she is the victor, the one who wakes him up. This is in direct opposition to the first wife, who, in the second wife's eyes, put him to sleep. Oftentimes a first wife and her ex-husband are the same age while the second wife is considerably younger. But this does not always succeed. The projections can outgrow themselves. Once the second wife is no longer in need of a father or the husband is no longer in need of a daughter, the relationship is doomed. Only if the projections are kept in equilibrium can it survive. If the husband marries a younger woman to preserve his vanity, it is a tricky business. A more positive relationship results when a husband chooses a second wife who is his contemporary, as they will likely share a common frame of reference. This second wife has the same maturity level and a similar life experience to that of her husband."

Yet, as Marina's case demonstrated, being contemporaries is not mandatory for a successful second marriage. Beverly and her husband, Michael, share a similar story. Their lives are quite unlike that of Michael's first marriage. "We live in the city, while they lived in the suburb. They had separate lives and weren't together much of the time. Their separate lives extended to the nighttime. Michael and I are in a marriage where we do everything together. With his first wife, he was constantly looking for an escape. She was as determined to pursue her career as he was, and there was no time for each other. Although I am fifteen years younger, I do not need to be immersed in my career. I can go to work without it becoming a major event. I can be available in the way that she was missing for him.

"For all of my awareness of the first wife, I have never had the feeling that she came between us. I am aware of her existence and what kind of relationship they had. But I know that if he still wanted that, he'd be there."

In Beverly's case, Michael sought qualities in her that were contrary to his first wife's personality. This is common for many men, particularly if they were the unhappier of the two in the first marriage. For example, when a first marriage was traditional, with a husband as breadwinner, who worked hard to promote his career while the wife put her career on hold or abandoned it to raise the children, the second marriage often does not focus on the same traditional values. The pivotal aspect of the second marriage may instead be a nurturing relationship between the husband and wife. There is less of a focus on their careers, combined with dual parenting. However, if a husband chooses a second wife who desires to be a homemaker and mother, it is likely that his first wife was very career-oriented. If a husband recognizes what he liked and didn't like about his first marriage, in a second marriage, he will seek out a woman who complements his needs.

HIS NEEDS FIRST
- When the first marriage ended because the husband did not feel appreciated, he will wisely choose a second wife who puts him first.
- When the first marriage ended because the wife chose to have a career ahead of the marriage, the husband will now search for someone who has different goals.
- When the first marriage ended because the husband wanted some one with interests of her own, he will look for her the second time.

In Alanna's situation, her husband Victor's first wife was simply not prepared to be anything but a housewife. Victor wanted a more exciting partner, someone of equal worth in the workplace. "Victor and his ex-wife, Marla, are exactly the same age, while I'm a bit younger. I know that he is happy to be with someone whose career is in the making. It is extremely important to me that I will practice medicine and I am now finishing my residency. I know that Marla had no such ambition. She was absorbed with her children and the PTA. It is not how he wanted to live the rest of his life. The bottom line is, he found her very boring. I am much more outgoing and I have more social skills. I'm extroverted and she was introverted. She read books all day while the kids were in school. Marla preferred staying at home, choosing the status quo over anything new.

"What concerns me is Victor's attitude toward marriage after his divorce," Alanna confessed. "Victor became wise to things during their divorce, and he refused to ever put himself at risk again. He never wants to be criticized, and he never wants another divorce. He thought long and hard before he married me."

What troubles many second wives are husbands who compare everything that their first wives did to how they conducts themselves. If the husband mentions the first wife very often, even if the first marriage is clearly over, it is not easy for the second wife. "Whether the marriage was good at times, bad most of the time, or somewhere in between, there was an attachment and a history which the first couple shared," says Dr. Ronnie Burak. "The second wife has to be strong and understanding. If her husband left the marriage, it is always easier for the second wife. But if the first wife left him, the second wife feels more insecure and constantly compared."

Even the most secure of second wives feel threatened by comparisons, especially when the marriage is young. A second wife who hears that she looks like the first wife, but is not as pretty or plays tennis almost as well as the first wife, often becomes disheartened. If she is told or perceives the interaction with her husband is not as romantic or sexual as it was with the first wife, the second wife will be put on the defensive, and her self-esteem will suffer. An attentive, sensitive husband makes his second wife feel secure and cherished.

LIFE BEFORE / LIFE AFTER
- The past cannot be wiped out
- It is difficult not to make comparisons
- The longer the marriage, the longer the history
- The husband must be sensitive to these concerns

When a husband is unable to show a caring attitude, his second marriage usually falters. It took Sacha a long time to realize that her husband, Evan, could not make an emotional commitment to her because of his historical love for his first wife. "I have always known that Evan loves me. Yet when his ex-wife had a baby with her new husband, he visited her in the hospital and brought her a gift. I was devastated. I have always wondered what it is between them. He has always had a thing for her and speaks of her in glowing terms. So what was it about the marriage that didn't work? Here I am, the present wife, feeling less than the first wife. I have my husband, but I do not really have him. It's as if she has some kind of hold over him, some kind of magic that I can't compete with. I feel it even when we are intimate. I feel it when we go to parties, I feel it when we play tennis together, whatever we do.

"One time, we were at a restaurant and ran into people Evan

went to college with, and he introduced me using his ex-wife's name. I was absolutely horrified and so hurt. He said it was just a slip, but it made me see how long he'd been with her and how he wasn't really finished with that relationship on some level. My only hope was that our life together would become more important and that the past would somehow disappear. What I have learned is that the past does not disappear and that it has enormous influence over the present. For my husband, who has no kids but had a wife he loved, there are ways he treats me that I know he did with his first wife. He has a whole attitude in terms of being a husband that was cultivated and nurtured during the first marriage. On one level I suppose, I benefit from it. On another level, I'm never first, never the only one. Evan's first wife plays him like a fiddle, calling him at work whenever she wants. I wish she would disappear, for my sake and the sake of my marriage. On the other hand, there have been times when we have been together when I'm able to forget his past, when I do feel important enough. And he has told me that our sex life is better. When I feel secure in our relationship, I say to myself, this is where I want to be."

Although it is tempting, it is illogical and impractical for the second wife to negate the first wife. Rather, it would behoove her to take advantage of her husband's experience. What happened in his failed marriage will hopefully be a lesson to him that he takes into his second marriage. The second wife may like to hear from her husband that his first marriage failed because it didn't meet many of his needs and desires. Still, no matter what he says, it is often very difficult for her to reconcile that her husband had a sustained intimacy with another woman for years. This time cannot be erased, but the insecurity caused by it can be eased if a husband avoids making comparisons between his first and second wives and focuses on his current marriage instead of the past. For example, when a husband appreciates his sex life with his second wife, she deserves to know about it but doesn't have to know how it compares to the one he had with his first wife.

THE QUESTIONING SECOND WIFE
While the second wife would like to believe the first wife never existed, these thoughts are unrealistic. She should acknowledge the first marriage's existence, while recognizing that it is in the past. She should focus her energy on her marriage, which is the present and the future, and avoid making comparisons.

While comparisons and competition can be damaging to the second wife's confidence, they are not always negative. It is when she feels she isn't measuring up to the first wife that these comparison are dangerous to the second wife. If she focuses on the positive—the things she offers her husband that the first wife couldn't or wouldn't—she will become more secure in herself and her marriage. For some, like Cathy, this is not as difficult as it may seem.

When Cathy met her husband Bart, he was unhappily married to a woman since college. "I was taken by a date to their home for dinner. I kind of liked his wife, Barbara, when we first met. It seemed they weren't getting along from the beginning. I watched them send darts across the table to one another. So I came away from their home knowing that they were not happy. Several years later, Bart and I ran into each other in the city. He was not yet divorced, but was separated. He and Barbara were planning to be divorced and their child was five years old. We began to date and once we were an item, Barbara resisted the divorce. I was very polite to her because of their child, and while she hated me underneath, she also behaved decently to me on the surface.

"My husband gave her everything in the divorce and I have always resented his huge child support payments. His child is now in college and we have three children of our own. Barbara has behaved badly throughout. I hoped that our children would make a difference, but I think underneath, I always knew it would be this way. She competes with me through their son about money. Will he give more money to his first family than to his second? This woman is a miserable and angry person, but she was the one to instigate the divorce. She has never worked a day of her life, while I've been working my entire adulthood. I know that my husband found in me a different kind of person than his ex-wife is."

Even though Cathy does not question the solidity of her marriage and sees how much more positive it is than Bart's first marriage, Barbara, an angry and bitter woman, still manages to intrude upon the peace and happiness of Bart and Cathy's marriage. Most often, the second wife is antagonized by the first wife's hold over her husband through their children. If Cathy did not have a family with Bart, she may not have been so secure in her marriage and may have felt threatened by—or even jealous of—Barbara and Bart's parental connection. First wives who keep the children as an ongoing link are particularly upsetting to second wives.

WHAT UPSETS THE SECOND WIFE
• The idea that her husband has children with his first
• The realization that she may never share children with him
• If the first manipulates the children as pawns

When a second wife has insecurities caused by the first wife's parental connection with her husband, his lack of sensitivity can worsen matters. Antoinette Michaels, relationship counselor, believes that it is up to the husband to correct the situation with the second wife when it comes to dealing with the children. "If the husband does not include his second wife in his first family's events, this is not a good sign. The first wife sees this as her power and may play it for all it is worth. The real question here is one of priorities. If the second wife feels left out, especially if she has done her share of caring for her stepchildren, she will be hurt and disappointed. The husband is responsible to balance his children and his second wife without competition."

Even with good intentions, competition between a first and second wife is almost inevitable. Whether the competition surrounds the stepchildren, physical beauty, or finances, it clearly has a harmful effect on all parties. Yet it is most damaging to the second wife who is trying to build and maintain a stable and fruitful marriage, amidst the conflict and negativity created by competition. A second wife who steps back and does not become a part of the competition has the ability to enjoy her husband and her marriage. Her acceptance is integral to the happiness of the new relationship.

HOW TO STOP THE COMPETITION
• Distance yourself from feuding and competition
• Accept that you came second, knowing that you are now first in his life
• Do not get caught up in the drama
• Carve a life that is present and future

Of the women who discussed being measured against their husbands' first wives, the prevailing comparisons are for physical appearances, and the outstanding competition is over finances and children. If the second wife is younger, she may feel triumphant physically. If the first wife was a great beauty, then the second wife may feel too plain. Competition over finances works both ways: the second wife has a financially secure life while the first wife does not, or due to alimony and child support, the second wife's quality of life is diminished. The topic of children also works both ways: if one woman has children and the other does not, the mother will forever be connected to the husband through the children in a way the other woman cannot.

Fifty percent of second wives interviewed on competition with the first wife believe that they are being compared on a daily basis to the first wife not only by their husbands, but by family and friends. The other fifty percent recognize the competition between themselves and the first wives, but are very comfortable with their own strengths and relationships. They keep their own marriages private and sacred, distancing themselves from the intrusions of the first wives and children. Although these women view their roles as improvements over first wives', they do not dismiss the first marriage nor do they linger on the past or comparisons. Instead, they focus on the present and their own marriages, confident that the future they are building with their husbands is promising.

CHAPTER THREE

REVENGE OF
THE FIRST WIFE

"I was very aware that nothing about me was similar to Graham's first wife. Yet when we were engaged, I decided our wedding had to be unlike his first, since I knew all about it. He had told me everything in detail," confides Mary. "There was this constant sense that we were being compared. I had a perverse curiosity about her. I knew he had been in lust with her and that it was not a connection based on friendship or mutual support.

"From what my husband said about their separation and previous relationship, I was very suspicious that he was still sleeping with her. I could not trust him, even when I confronted him and he denied it vehemently. I think that he was not over her, but there was no way that they could live together. After several months of being married, I followed him one day and he was meeting his ex-wife at a hotel. I wish he had never told me how sexy she was to him because then I would not have been uncertain. My uncertainty was the demise of the marriage. I think that Graham's first wife kept seeing him to ruin our chances of success. It was a power play. After their marriage ended and Graham and I got together, I had all the power. Then, when she and Graham had their affair, she had all the power. I did not stay even one year in the marriage."

A First Wife's Sexual Revenge

Despite the efforts of the second wife, the presence of a vengeful first wife may undo the second marriage. This is especially true when the first marriage relied heavily on a sexual connection. In such cases, the second wife may feel threatened and insecure, and for good reason. A first wife who has had a sexual hold on her husband may attempt to maintain control over him and thereby his new marriage. If the second marriage is a result of an affair, it is even more likely that the first wife will exercise such power by, for example, seducing her ex-husband for revenge. Then the two wives' roles are reversed; the husband is now cheating on his second wife by having an affair with his first wife.

COMPARATIVE SEX
If the first wife was left for the second, she can get back at the second wife through revenge sex and may take pleasure in becoming the other woman

According to Antoinette Michaels, relationship counselor, the husband who continues a sexual relationship with his ex-wife is relatively common. "I have frequently seen clients where the first wife sleeps with her husband when he comes over to get the kids. The sexual relationship still exists although they are both divorced and may both be remarried. The cause for this ongoing relationship is a lack of boundaries coming from both sides. And the first wife likes getting even. There is a feeling of possessiveness and entitlement that the ex-husband and ex-wife have for each other."

One second wife who experienced the trauma of dealing with revenge sex is Joanna. Joanna became a second wife eight years ago, at the age of twenty-six. "From the start, I was suspicious that my husband, Tate, still had a relationship with his first wife. There were no children between them and no real reason for my husband to keep in touch with his first wife. But he did. And I never trusted him, because while we were dating, he would see her. When we became engaged, he took her to dinner to tell her. And I thought that they had sex that night. That was the feeling I had. I asked him, but he laughed at me and said, 'Of course not. You never have to worry about her.' I worried about her because we had had an affair, and she knew it. One time he went away on a ski trip. I knew she was an excellent skier and had this suspicion that she was also skiing that week. I didn't have the courage to ask."

Joanna explains her own feelings. "I think it is an ego trip for Tate, but for his ex-wife, it is about revenge. I actually have evidence that this is going on. I know she is getting back at me for breaking up the marriage. She is taking pleasure in this business of having sex with my husband. I am at a total loss."

In instances where there has been divorce and ex-spouses have ongoing sex, the first wife often feels victorious. It is a way of holding on to and controlling her ex-husband while wounding his new wife. The second wife suffers because her husband has betrayed her and her self-confidence is slipping away.

REVENGE SEX
- The first wife does not want to let go
- Sex becomes power
- Finally she can get back at the second wife
- He is never truly in the new marriage if he sleeps with his first wife

Ongoing physical relationships between ex-spouses are heavy blows for second wives to bear. Tabitha was twenty-five when she married a man ten years her senior who had been married to his first wife for six years. "When I met my husband, Gregory, he was separated from his first wife, but undecided about a divorce. I believe that meeting me made the decision for him. After we met, Greg suddenly wanted to be divorced. He had been living alone for six months at the time. Although his first wife, Lucy, really pushed for the separation, when he came to her for a divorce, she changed her mind and wanted to work things out. He told her it was too late, he had met someone else. That was a big mistake. Lucy didn't like that one bit. Greg would still see her for meals and drinks when we were first dating. And he would give her things. He actually gave her his car. He also gave her the television set from the living room of his apartment. I thought that was strange. And Lucy would call him all the time to discuss her work. There were no children between them, so I found it hard to understand. As I look back on it, six years later, I see that I should have said more, since it bothered me terribly.

"I remember that a few months after our wedding, Greg received a call at midnight from Lucy, who was hysterical. She said that she had to see him, that it could not wait until morning. I was appalled and crushed when he put on his clothes and went to see her. Not only that, but he did not come home until seven the next morning. I knew that he had had sex with her. I absolutely knew it—I would put my life on it. That is how positive I am. I confronted him and he denied it. I told him that if she ever called again and asked to see him, I would leave him. Either she calls at the office, or he really respects my wishes because it has never happened since. But I do not trust my husband when it comes to his ex-wife. It is not easy for me. I do not feel confident about her. I know that she wants him on some level, maybe not as her husband again, but kind of as her plaything. I know that she wants him so I can be cheated. She is angry that he asked her for a divorce and then married me."

The Vengeful First Wife

A sexual connection is not the only threat to the second wife. For many, there are ghosts which cannot be vanquished because of continual encounters in which the first wife makes her presence known. If the first marriage was long standing, there are certain styles and patterns that were established that the second wife wants desperately to change. If her husband is resistant, she senses the influence of the first wife and feels unnerved. Other times the second wife is discouraged by the aggressive or territorial nature of the first wife. She questions why her husband claims to want a new life while he allows his first wife to have a hold over him.

There are many tales of first wives who simply cannot put the past to rest. In such cases, the first wife is vengeful if she has not established her own life and is extremely resentful that her ex-husband has found someone else. This manifests itself in trying to influence the children/stepchildren against the second wife and in terms of money. If the first wife is negative, difficult, and visible, there is no question that this causes problems for the second wife. "With time, in most cases, everyone calms down," says Dr. Ronnie Burak. "But there is always the wife from hell who persists. For example, the first wife's resentment of the second wife may be fueled by what she sees and hears. As a result, the second wife's displeasure increases when the first wife does not fade into the background."

George S. Stern, President of the American Academy of Matrimonial Lawyers, views the relationship of a husband to his former spouse as one of the main points of contention in second marriages. "After stepchildren, pity and obligation to the first wife is the biggest problem in second marriages. The first wife is always upset if her ex-husband is doing well financially and emotionally and she stays in touch as best she can. She knows it makes the new wife miserable."

One of the most famous second wives of all time, Anne Boleyn, who married Henry VIII of England in 1533, faced the revenge of the King's first wife. In order to marry Anne, the king had to separate the Church of England from the Roman Catholic Church. He was so determined to divorce Catherine of Aragon, his brother's widow, that he dismissed the Cardinal who could not obtain an annulment. Because Henry had so many mistresses, Catherine tolerated Anne at the start. Both women lived in the same palace. Anne's role was maid of honor at the court. Often the two women played cards together, an event Catherine particularly enjoyed because it displayed her adversary's deformity: her sixth finger. Ultimately, Anne was unable to provide the king with a son. It was this flaw that resulted in her beheading in the Tower of London. Henry's first wife was more fortunate—her life was spared.

In modern-day life, the stakes between first and second wives are not as high as they were for Catherine and Anne. Nonetheless, there are many unhappy, angry first wives who feel they have gotten a raw deal. Sometimes the anger can escalate to frightening levels. This kind of hostility is something that a second wife is not always prepared for.

For Melanie, the anger incurred by her husband Kyle's first wife was frightening. "My husband's original divorce decree was for reasonable visitation rights, but Kyle's ex-wife, Georgia, was controlling about it. In the beginning Kyle had to fight for more because it was so limited. To add to that, it was so traumatic whenever his daughter did come to visit because Georgia portrayed Kyle as an evil, awful man to their daughter. Georgia created such drama around the visits that staying with us was perceived as this horrible punishment. My husband is not a patient man and did not handle this well at all. His ex-wife was behind all of it, scheming and being unfair. Georgia even had parties when her daughter returned home from her stays with me and Kyle, as if it were worthy of celebration."

Eventually Georgia remarried, but no improvement between Kyle and his daughter ensued. "At first I was hopeful, then I realized that nothing had changed in terms of his ex-wife's controlling their daughter's attitude toward my husband," Melanie sighed. "Georgia's angry sentiments toward him prevailed, and because my husband can be so stubborn, her influence ended up destroying the relationship. Georgia put her child up to saying she never wanted to see her father again. This is a situation that has been ongoing; there has not been any reconciliation."

Like Melanie, Chelsea has had to deal with a vengeful first wife. Chelsea's introduction to her husband's angry first wife came about long before she was even married. "The divorce was in the works when I first met Alicia. I was miserable. Her presence hung over me and I couldn't stand it. I think that Alicia was strange from the start. I met my husband through a personal ad and Dale must have told Alicia this. She did many nasty things, such as make disparaging remarks, insinuating that I was a desperate woman because of how I had met Dale. She would repeatedly ask my husband if he really wanted me, if this is what he would settle for.

"Although I am younger than Alicia, which really bothers her, comments like this destroyed my self-esteem. I believe her own self-esteem must be very low. Right after my husband and I got together, she went off with a young surfer from a completely different socio-economic class. It was her rebellion and her show of anger. Alicia also said terrible things about Dale to me. If I even answered the phone when she was calling him for something, which I didn't like, she made a negative statement about me. Alicia really couldn't resist saying bad things, and this even continued after she'd moved on and began new relationships. However, finally she seems to be less important and I feel that I come first. Dale and I are married and Alicia no longer has the same control."

The best change possible for a second wife who hopes the first will vanish is that the ex-wife remarries happily. Her contentious attitude may dissipate once she has found a rewarding relationship of her own. If the ex-wife has children with her new husband, this usually improves the situation further. Another change—that of relocation—works because the contact is reduced to long distance telephone calls, and with time, the calls usually diminish. The troublesome first wife who moves on with her own life successfully will relent and no longer try to exert influence over her remarried ex-husband.

FIRST WIVES AND CHANGE
Certain positive occurrences make a difference in a vengeful first wife:
• When she finds someone or remarries
• When she has a baby with her new partner
• When she moves out of town
• When she recognizes her waning power

From Lover to Wife

"How the marriage was broken up affects the first wife's behavior toward the second," says Dr. Burak. "If the husband left and the first wife did not want out, there are feelings of betrayal and a subsequent need for revenge. If the first wife still has feelings for her ex-husband, she may be jealous of the second wife. On top of this, the settlement might be less than she would have liked."

If the first wife is spurned, she will be angry. If there was an affair, the anger may escalate. Once it is apparent to the first wife that her ex-husband and his lover are going to become husband and wife, she feels even more rejected and becomes livid. Her anger may be so far reaching that she will continue to interfere in the new marriage whenever the opportunity arises. The second wife needs to be polite but distant from her husband's first wife. However, this may not easily be implemented—some women cannot tolerate the presence of the first wife at all or may have trouble keeping their distance, especially if the first wife is overbearing or omnipresent or if an affair with her husband led to their marriage and she is afraid she may get the same treatment as the first wife.

Trust became an issue for Nicole once she became a second wife. "When we were lovers, I did not consider if I trusted or believed in him. It was simply a matter of getting together as much as we could, whenever and wherever. Then I became his wife. He actually left his marriage for me. I became frightened. If he could do it for me, he could leave me for someone else. The first wife's anger became all too understandable to me. She was vicious. She called me a whore and said I had ruined her perfect world. He told me to ignore her, that she was prone to mood swings and was an unhappy woman. She went to small and great lengths to hurt me. She told the dry cleaner and butcher not to do business with me. At the health club, I was ostracized because of things she had said. She told my husband's friends terrible things about me. I was freaked out. But I also understood. I kept asking my husband if he understood how vengeful she was. He said to ignore it. He said she would calm down. She has never remarried, but eventually we moved away and had two children. All of these changes helped. However, when my husband calls in late sometimes, I feel myself remembering how he lied about our affair. I have trouble trusting him."

While the affair that resulted in marriage has caused Nicole's trust in her husband to remain shaky, because of all that they went through over their affair, Victoria trusts her husband unconditionally. It was hard for both Victoria and her husband, Tony; they never meant to break up a family. "Tony and I never meant to fall in love. We met in the workplace when we were sent to another city to set up stores for our company. It just happened. I never meant to destroy a marriage. The anger I encountered when his wife learned about me was incredible. She actually flew down here and stormed into the store. She began screaming at me in front of hundreds of people. She told me I was dirt beneath her feet and that she would never touch Tony again as long as she lived. She said I had contaminated him for life. She screamed at him at the same time, saying that he'd see his children again over her dead body. Then she stormed out. People were staring at us. It was mortifying and Tony was broken up. I could see that. It was the beginning of hell for him. I could never have fathomed that someone would go to the depths that she has. She even orchestrated his losing his job. She called up his boss and told him about us. He had to get an attorney in order to see his children.

"What is so amazing is that we have stuck it out—that we are still together. There are some days when everything is fine and some days when my husband's loss overwhelms him. He misses his children so much that it is palpable. She has been punitive through the children. Whatever we did by having an affair, she has done worse."

Trust is both an essential component of the marriage and a troubling point for second wives whose husbands had affairs with them while married. The magical affair that she and her husband engaged in can be a destructive repercussion in the second marriage. The second wife now asks herself if she can trust a man who has cheated on his first wife. Lovers and spouses are like apples and oranges, and goals and values alter with the nature of the relationship. Second wives with these pasts are often concerned their husbands could do the same thing to them that they did to their first wives.

TRUST AND THE SECOND WIFE

If an affair leads to the second marriage, the second wife may suddenly be stricken with the realization that she too could suffer what the first wife suffered. Now the first wife's anger is more understandable if not tolerable. As a lover becomes a second wife, expectations and values change. She may worry she is next to be cheated upon.

Nevertheless, affairs are often the aftermath, not the reason for, marital discord. "Failures in a first marriage may have had to do with a lack of communication and a lack of clarification. So the husband has an affair, leaves the marriage, and ends up in a new marriage with his lover. The second wife begins to be anxious. She needs to have confidence that this is not a pattern but a reflection of an unhappy first marriage. Meanwhile the ex-wife can be very bitter," says Dr. Michele Kasson.

If the second wife can view the first with sympathy, she may be better able to deal with her. Adrian views her husband Marcus's ex-wife, Nora, as someone with problems. "I look at this woman as needy and dependent. Nora calls our house to speak with my husband, babbling on and on. She wants to sue him for more money, because she has nothing else to do. She has plenty of money, so it can't really be about money. The children are grown up and his commitments are finished. He and I are totally connected. He is the love of my life.

"Nora was so positive that my husband would come back to her. She played strange games, which I suspect were her way of getting back at us. She called us in the middle of the night. I know this because we traced the calls. She sent letters that looked like ransom notes to my office, saying Marcus would want her back one day. She called his sisters and told them I was dangerous and after my husband for his looks and lifestyle. We did not even have a lifestyle, we simply share a life where we love one another. She got married and cooled off for a while, but when she got divorced, she called Marcus up and asked him if we were still married. Our paths have not crossed in five years, but I sometimes shudder when I remember what Nora did for the first two years of my marriage."

My research shows that many second wives feel discontented with obstreperous first wives. Many try to be encouraging when their husbands complain, yet the status quo disturbs them. When the first wife's anger toward the new marriage is blatant, whatever the reasons for the divorce, it causes problems in the second marriage.

RESENTMENT FLIES
The second wife wants to support her husband's settlement with his first wife, but resents the energy it requires. The first wife cannot stand that her ex-husband is happy with another woman, regardless of the circumstances which precipitated a divorce.

Children as Pawns

Kaki and her stepchildren are very close. "We have a joint custody arrangement, so the stepchildren spend time with us every weekend. I think that the children love their mother because she is their mother. The attachment to me is out of choice. They genuinely look forward to our time together. This drives my husband Mike's first wife to distraction. Anna goes crazy and tries in every way to sabotage our plans. The irony is, Anna doesn't want the children to be with her any more than they are, she just wants them to dislike the time spent with their father and me. She is angry with me and angry at herself. Anna cannot focus on the positive. The cost of living has escalated, and she is dissatisfied with her settlement from Mike. She is constantly calling Mike at work and complaining about this. What transpired was her poisoning the kids against us. This was terrible, particularly for my husband. We have reacted to her behavior with honesty and it has paid off. At first we chose to ignore it, but there was so much tension, the kids couldn't hold it in. We sat down and discussed what kind of relationship we hope to have with them and how their mother cannot affect our relationship. This way of dealing with Anna's manipulation has paid off."

Like Kaki, Betsy does not take issue with her stepchildren, but struggles with her husband's ex-wife's presence in the picture. "I wish that my husband, Brent, would figure out a way to make plans that do not need to be changed all of the time. I wish that the schedule for his children was written in stone. Then there would not be conversations with his ex-wife, Liza, about every little thing. I observed Brent with his children before I allowed myself to take on the responsibility of having a new husband and four stepchildren. The children are not the problem. The problem in my marriage is Brent's ex-wife. I am even connected to her through the children. I do not wish to be connected to her in any way for any reason. Liza insisted on living in the basement of our house for a period of time after we were married. I could not stand it. And Brent let her do it. Finally, I asked that he put an end to our living arrangement. It was too strange and uncomfortable.

"There have been times," admits Betsy, "when I've tried to imagine their sex life. I cannot imagine it. Actually, I think of how they have these children together, and I cannot imagine the joy it would have brought to them. To me, it seems that they were never a couple, an item. And when Liza shows up to get the kids or there is some incident where we run into each other, I hate it. Liza did bad things to Brent during the marriage and she's been very rude to me. She will march right into my house and walk right by me to get the kids. She will leave, slamming the door without even saying good-bye. And why is she in our house to begin with? What right has she to be there? After I see her, it's as if I don't want my husband to touch me. I guess I'm very turned off that he ever saw something in her."

Nothing is more critical to the first wife than her relationship with her children being colored by the new couple: her ex-husband and his second wife. The intentions of the first wife vary, depending on her own situation. Some have new husbands or lovers and are pleased to hand over the children to their exes and the new wives so they can spend time alone with their mates. Others are deeply angered and worried that the second wife will exert influence over the children. Most first wives do not relish sharing their children with other women.

TWO MOTHER FIGURES
Many first wives worry that if their children love their stepmother, they will lose them. If they are young children, she feels uncomfortable about entrusting to someone whom she has not chosen.

The fears of both second and first wives about the first wives' children compound an already difficult relationship. Lela was warned by her father-in-law against her husband's first wife's retaliation. "Although I was not responsible for the divorce, Myra, my husband's first wife, was angry that the marriage had failed and blamed me. Her attitude is that she is allowing my husband and me to live in this town, as if it is within her control. My husband, Tim, and I fight about her nonstop, which is exactly how Myra wants it. Her way of showing me her feelings was to tell her kids evil tales about me and to try to seduce my husband. I do not believe for one second that Tim fell for it, but it makes me unhappy to know she tried and continues to try. When Tim has to see her, even for a few minutes, I'm anxious. Myra once called me when I was engaged and told me that it was a fight to the finish. I know in many second marriages the wives wish that their husbands had never had children. In my case, I wish he'd never been married. And yet, I love his children. She's the one who makes me so miserable. I can feel her anger, even in the weeks when I do not hear from her, when there is no interaction whatsoever."

POWER AND VENGEANCE
Children, finances, and sex can all be seen as weapons of the first wife.
If the husband feels obliged to the first wife, then her command is
extensive. The second wife cannot get out from under.

Some first wives attempt to undermine second wives through
the children, money, and by seducing their ex-husbands. When the husband has not broken free of a relationship pattern with this woman, it
will cause problems in his new marriage, and his second wife may feel
despair. In this situation, the second wife needs to express her unhappiness to her husband and fight for a separate and complete life with him
without any interference from his ex-wife. Often counseling from a therapist is imperative in order to get the couple on the right footing.

"There is always the first wife who cannot resist playing with
her ex-husband's life," says Antoinette Michaels, relationship counselor.
"But there is also the second wife who was the catalyst for the marriage
to dissolve. The first wife reacts to her, either through the children,
finances, or whatever emotional hold she might still have over her ex-
husband. The triangle persists, despite the divorce and the supposed
newly formed lives."

SOLUTIONS FOR THE SECOND WIFE
• Communicate your dissatisfaction
• Establish boundaries
• Change the patterns
• Seek couples counseling

Having been married for twenty-two years, Deirdre regrets the
first ten years when her husband, Sam, insisted they live near his ex-wife,
Paula. "Because of the children, Paula was always there. There have been
aftershocks throughout. Then the children grew up. Recently, my husband has been denied access to visit with one of his grandchildren. That
is the form of the punishment dealt to him by his ex-wife. I think this
has happened because Paula has never recovered from the divorce. My
attitude for many years has been that what is over is over. I used to be
surprised that Paula didn't get it. I'd say to myself, can't she let it go
already? I didn't need this ex-wife around, hanging all over him. Paula
was trying hard to lure him back and thought it was kept secret from
me. Ages ago, when we were first married, she actually invited him on a

date. It was embarrassing for everyone. My husband was naive enough to tell her that it upset me and Paula took great pleasure in learning this.

"My husband's past has echoed throughout our marriage, negatively and positively. Sam was always a good father to our child because he had raised two already. His commitment level to our marriage was remarkable—a direct result of having been in a poor first marriage. Sam was always civil and decent toward her, even when Paula was making a blatant play for him. I simply could not worry about what I could not change. In a sense, I pitied Paula for thinking she still had a chance with him. I have always known what our marriage means to my husband."

Though his ex-wife made it difficult for him, Sam, with Deirdre's support, tried to be a good father to his children from both marriages. Yet many times this is not the case. If a father is not there for his children, it affects not only them, but his first and second wives as well. "The question becomes, does the husband hold up his part of his parenting responsibilities, or does he abdicate them to his first wife? If the first wife is left with angry, depressed, hurt children who miss their father, there is a problem," comments Dr. Ronnie Burak. "The first wife has to explain for him and cannot. In many cases, the father is a sugar daddy while the mother tends to the nitty gritty." At the same time, the children may focus their anger not only on their father, but his new wife, who seems to them to be responsible for taking their father away in the first place.

It is only with determination that the second wife is able to effectuate the life she desires with her husband. If she views herself as unlike the first wife and as the one who offers her husband a second chance, she is motivated to make it happen. An acceptance and understanding of her husband's circumstances provides the new couple greater stability and a stronger foundation. And, with this, they will be able to handle the problems that arise when parenting his children and their own children.

DAY TO DAY
The first wife often takes care of the daily grind with the children. The husband and second wife many times provide the treats: movies, outings, the fun of life.

Endless Encounters
"I know that I am not a confident second wife," reports Thea. "Hank's first wife has caused several scenes and I've felt very uneasy. This is my second marriage and one that I desperately wanted. I am totally in love

with my husband and I thank God that we are together. However, for some reason, I am obsessed with his ex-wife. I know very little about Hank's past, but I do know that his ex-wife, Carla, still writes to him and that they had a tempestuous relationship and violent scenes. I know that she still calls him at the office and has tried to meet him for lunch or dinner. This really hurts me and I sometimes wish that Carla didn't exist at all. One night Carla had a flat tire and was downtown by herself. She called up, and when I answered, she told me to put Hank on the phone right away, that it was an emergency. I was astonished at how fast he responded to her. Carla wanted him to come downtown and help her, but I told him to call the police for her. I thought that was sufficient. She is not his responsibility anymore. But I know that she did it on purpose; it was a way of trying to bait him.

"Carla travels for work and so does my husband. Once, Hank had dinner with her when they were both in the same city. He told me about it, but I found it inappropriate anyway. Hank said Carla had been the one to instigate the meeting. What mattered to me was not only that she instigated it, but that he went. I said that I did not want him to do it again and he agreed. He has given me his word. I know it's just Carla's way of trying to hang on."

"First wives can be very angry," says Cynthia George, a divorce attorney. "When they repeatedly see the kind of life they've given up through divorce, they resent that the next wife is living it. Sometimes it is much better than they had it, because of the years of success these men have accrued. The first wife's inclination is to open up the case again, to see if they can get more money. Usually it is an ironclad agreement and there is little wiggle room. But the concept of renegotiating the signed contract is almost irresistible to an unhappy first wife who feels that she was cheated out of something. And in many instances, she was. It is the nature of divorce; there is loss in every way."

THE CALM SECOND WIFE
- Protects her turf
- Considers herself the opposite of the first
- Will not allow anyone to come between her and her husband
- Accepts her husband's baggage

Despite the second wife's attempt to keep her marriage stable, an ex-wife can cause friction in many arenas. After Claire became

Monty's second wife, his first wife, Tammy, tried to get her ex-husband back. "When Tammy didn't succeed with her plan, she asked for more money than what was agreed upon in the divorce decree. Tammy wanted him back—that was the bottom line. What she did was to put us through three years of hell while Tammy toyed with him. She would do anything to be with him, hoping he'd miss her and that they could reconcile. Then the money issue became Tammy's form of revenge. That was the worst. We ended up in court.

"Monty and I are both photographers and do not make a lot of money. Tammy is an attorney and actually makes a good deal of money, so I cannot imagine why she has made money an issue. That makes it all the more obvious to me that using the finances is simply a form of getting back at him. In the settlement, Tammy ended up with their home and most of the marital assets. The whole thing is so twisted, and yet, it won't go away. I have heard that she divorced her second husband recently and has two young children. Maybe Tammy will now focus on her latest ex-husband and leave my husband alone."

What happened to Tammy, and what often happens to other women and men, is that they repeat the same patterns and mistakes in their second marriages. These behaviors can cause the demise of the second marriage. "I see many second divorces," George S. Stern, President of the American Academy of Matrimonial Lawyers, comments, "because these second marriages have the same issues that the first marriages had. People do not really change and they tend to marry the same person the second time. When this happens, the old traits arise in the new marriage. The ex-wife will weave in and out of her ex-spouse's life, depending upon her own situation. If she has two ex-husbands, she may hang on to both, depending upon the circumstances."

REPEAT OFFENDERS

The ex-wife who remarries and divorces again may wax and wane in terms of how she enters the second wife's life. When she is content, there is no word from her. When she is miserable, she reappears. There may be a clearly discernable pattern when multiple marriages occur.

This type of repeating marital patterns is illustrated by Aimee's husband's ex-wife. Aimee was surprised when her husband, Guy, told her that his ex-wife, Carol, was divorcing again. "Carol's affair had caused the break-up of her first marriage to Guy. Within days of their divorce, Carol was remarried. I doubt that she would have left the marriage if not for the man with whom she'd had the affair. She was deeply in love with him and it caused my husband tremendous grief. While Guy admits that they did not have a happy marriage, he also felt compelled to remain because of their young daughter. By the time I met him, he was almost over his ex-wife, but wounded underneath, I think.

"Carol was not angry, nor was she vindictive. She simply got on with her life and left their daughter to us. It wasn't easy on the child, but Carol was immersed in her new love. Then they began to have problems. That was when Carol seemed to resent the happiness that I brought to her ex-husband. Now that she is divorcing her one-time lover, she not only leans on my husband, but seems angry at me. Maybe Guy was supposed to be waiting on the back burner for her all the while. My husband is strong and protective of us, so I am not worried. But I certainly never expected this kind of behavior from his first wife."

Another second wife who is experiencing problems with her husband's ex-wife is Fern. Fern's husband's ex-wife has contacted him whenever she has been in a crisis mode. "My husband's first wife remarried about two months after we were married. At first, all was quiet. She finally stopped calling my husband to see if she could win him back. She had a baby and moved an hour away. Then her husband began to travel for work and she would call my husband when he was out of town. I resented this and told him so. I thought it was a way of upsetting our equilibrium, of stirring the pot. I think she wanted to shake me up. She'd always hated me and hated that he had remarried within a year of their divorce.

"About five years ago, I heard that she and her husband were breaking up. They were fighting for custody of their child. Her husband already had a girlfriend and I think she was devastated. She asked my husband to help her find a good lawyer for a custody battle, and then she asked him to loan her money. That was when I said that I was very sorry that she had a problem and that she was getting divorced, but that his obligation, financial and emotional, was to me and to the child I was carrying. I think he heard me, but he somehow felt her tugging at him anyway. It was her way of holding on, feeling safe and punishing me. The latest news is that she is remarried, for a third time, to a successful surgeon. I doubt we will hear from her for a while."

It seems to the second wife there is no escape when the first wife behaves as though she is entitled access to her ex-husband, for whatever reason. If the husband makes himself available to her, the second wife begins to feel as though she doesn't count. After a while, these manipulations take their toll on the new marriage.

ENDLESS ENCOUNTERS
Some first wives feel comfortable contacting their ex-husbands in a crisis, big or small. He represents a safety net of sorts for her, a person from the past who was once there for her. The manner in which she will seek out her ex-husband's advice is varied. For the second wife, such encounters are difficult and unfair.

"In many cases, the kids are used as a weapon by the first wife whenever the opportunity arises. This happens between ex-spouses particularly if there were unresolved issues in the first marriage," Dr. Donald Cohen explains. "For the first wife, it is both a way of hanging on and a form of retaliation against the second wife. What works best for the second wife is if she steers her husband clear of the situation. At the same time, it is wise for her to encourage her husband to spend time with his children from the first marriage."

"I believed that Chuck's first wife and I had an amicable relationship. Harriet was remarried and many years had passed," said Margot. "When our daughter/stepdaughter became engaged, we agreed to co-host an engagement party. A week before the party, we went to the restaurant to try out the food and had a perfectly lovely evening. Harriet told her daughter that under any other circumstances, she and I could have been best friends. But Chuck had warned me about Harriet's sneaky side, and said she didn't really mean it. I never anticipated that the gesture of co-hosting a party would backfire. To me, I had the best interests of my stepdaughter in mind. The night before the party, I called Harriet and asked what she would be wearing. She said she wanted to be very low key and to let her daughter be the star. I agreed and wore a very simple outfit. When I arrived at the party, Harriet was dressed to the nines, as were her friends. I was really hurt by such a ploy. I found it unfriendly and downright cruel. I never trusted her again, not even when it concerned the children."

Without a mature attitude on the part of the second wife, such incidents can have repercussions, and even with a good attitude, handling a manipulative first wife causes problems. "What I came to realize is that

Harriet is very needy and won't give up. Unfortunately, her anger has fil-
tered into our household. I have often wondered if it is best to fight her
or to let it slide. Her dictum at first was that her children could not love
her and still love me as their stepmother. But I love the girls and am like
a Mother Bear to them. Eventually she came to accept this. Yet this was
only one of several hurdles for me."

Margot explained, "In the beginning, she would make Chuck
feel guilty if he didn't want to go to some leftover family event. There
were so many things that came through both his family and hers that
they seemed to still be included in. And because of the two girls, it was
continual. What bothers me the most however, is that Harriet has kept
my husband's name, even when she remarried. It is a way of hanging on
and I resent it. I did not take his name because she kept it. It was her
way of getting back at him, at us. And of course, that brings us to the
question of money. He is overwhelmed by financial commitments
because of his obligations to keep two households going. She demands
more each month, an extra expense here and there. Chuck is so tense he
can barely breathe. The wedding was another added expense. The two of
them were supposed to share the cost, but in the end, we paid for ninety
percent of it and she paid for the flowers. Her control over us is exces-
sive. My secret wish has always been that she would move far away."

Since it is impossible to deny the existence of the first wife, the
second wife concentrates on time as the great equalizer, and she waits it
out. The hope is that, as the years pass, the first wife will marry or move
away, and that as the children inevitably become adults, the child support and alimony cease to be a financial drain. Yet this is a tricky business; even if the first wife does move away or remarry, she may move
back or divorce. In short, such changes may help alleviate strain but they
do not always guarantee things will improve. Still, time does help heal
and along with these changes, the passage of time will often diminish
anger or bitterness, thereby improving the situation for everyone.

BITTERNESS AND IMPROVEMENT
The second wife does better when several events occur:
• The ex-wife moves out of town
• The stepchildren grow up
• The husband stops paying alimony/child support
• Time elapses—not months—but years

Although almost half of the interviewees claimed that the revenge of the second wife was quite prevalent, the majority of second wives were able to overcome the situation. Issues involving stepchildren, according to *American Demographics*, are among the most contentious in second marriages. This is exacerbated when the first wife places them strategically in an ongoing battle with her husband. Those second wives interviewed who have stepchildren were equally divided in their feelings toward those stepchildren: half of the women described a productive and comfortable rapport despite the first wife's wrath, and half expressed their dissatisfaction with the relationship they share with their stepchildren. Money matters and children are major challenges for the second wife and play substantial roles in the first wife's efforts at revenge. However, it is the sexual seduction of the first wife that is most dangerous and menacing to the solidity of the new marriage.

What matters most to get a second wife through such difficult ordeals is her own strength and self-confidence. Her husband must also display strength enough to resist his ex-wife's ploys to stay in his life, set boundaries for his ex-wife, and be considerate of and responsive to his new wife's fears and concerns. His weakness in dealing with his ex-wife will magnify any damage caused by her, which in turn may strengthen the first wife's resolve to destroy the new marriage. If the three adults cannot sit down together and work through their problems in a civil manner, therapy would probably greatly benefit the newly married couple so they can better handle the problems until the first wife's vengeful efforts wane.

CHAPTER FOUR

GUILT EQUALS MONEY

Dora was not prepared for her husband Matthew's level of commitment to his first family when she became a second wife. "I knew he had responsibilities, but I didn't realize how much guilt he had on top of it. Matt paid for the kids and for everything for his ex-wife, Amanda. After a while, I really resented it. There was a time when he had lived in his car during the first year of the divorce to make ends meet for them. Then things changed, and by the time we were married, it seemed that everyone was set. But that wasn't the case. There were unanticipated financial needs and he was the one to pay.

"What bothered me so much was not merely the financial aspect, but that Amanda was so bitter—and wrung him out as a result. She turned the kids against him, calling him a deadbeat. She would tell them the most personal, negative things about him. She succeeded in influencing them, initially. For five years, Amanda badmouthed Matt while he gave her all of our money. Adding to this was the fact that we had to mend the relationship with his two children. There was a huge argument that Matt and I had over money. He was paying the bulk of his salary to Amanda and his kids and was religious about doing it. My feeling was that the money should go to the kids, but not to her. And throughout, the kids were leery of us because of her negative comments."

"In a traditional marriage that ends in divorce, the most common outcome is that of a husband whose lifestyle improves and an ex-wife whose lifestyle diminishes," Amy Reisen, divorce attorney, explains. "The husband, if he is the breadwinner, is in control of his career and has more opportunities in his life. A woman who has not worked and now finds herself divorced has to reinvent herself. For her, there is a loss of status."

Childless second wives entering their first marriage quickly learn the definitions of *alimony* and *child support*. Alimony, known as spousal support, is based on income. There are different kinds of alimony, but traditional alimony, in which the man as the breadwinner provides an income stream to the wife, is the most frequent type found in divorce. Traditional alimony, also known as permanent alimony, lasts until death, remarriage, or cohabitation in some states. Rehabilitative alimony is short term, to put the ex-wife back on her feet or to pay for her to further her education, but is not an income flow that matches the amount if the marriage had endured. Alimony is tax deductible for the husband but taxable for the wife. In the case of child support, taxes are paid by the husband and the support is due until the child is emancipated. This emancipation is defined as either eighteen years of age, when the child graduates from a four year college, enters military service, until death, or until the child marries. Child support in most jurisdictions is based on income as set by child support guidelines of the federal government.

Alimony is a contentious issue for many second wives. They may question why the first wife should be granted this money or why their husband feels compelled to give as much as he does. While few second wives question the need for their husband's children to be well taken care of, child support may still cause a problem. For example, a second wife may feel cheated if her husband gives more to his children from his first marriage than to their children. Also, many ex-husbands and their second wives may fear that the first wives are using the child support payments for their own purposes, instead of using it for the care and well-being of the children.

Whether the second wife is initially schooled in the definition of alimony or not, she is often displeased that it impairs her husband's finances. At the outset, she might have been more open to it because she was so intent upon becoming the second wife. Yet once this has been achieved, her view of alimony may be altered. Every time that money is paid to the first wife, the second wife feels irrationally cheated on several levels: financially, emotionally, and physically. She feels cheated of being first, of having her husband all to herself, of having an easier time with money in the marriage.

ALIMONY AND THE SECOND WIFE
- She begrudges the first wife the money
- She rarely accepts the deal completely
- Her husband's obligation is a constant reminder of his past

In many cases, after the wedding has taken place and the new life is about to begin, the second wife naively believes that the long haul is behind her. Although she's reticent to admit it to anyone, there were times when it didn't seem promising that they'd ever really be married. At the same time, her husband may be wracked with guilt. If he has children from his first marriage, his guilt centers on them. If his first wife is miserable and not adjusting to single life, whether she wanted it or not, he worries about her.

If the dissolution of the marriage came about because of an affair, there is even more guilt for the husband to deal with. His first marriage is over, having ended in divorce. Now, as he remarries, he sees all that his actions have done to those around him. He worries that he has ruined his children's lives. He fears that he greatly reduced the quality of his first wife's life by asking for the divorce. There is little to say that will convince him otherwise. It is very frustrating for the second wife who witnesses her husband's guilt and is unable to change the past. In these types of situations, the husband usually tries to compensate with money. He tries to buy his way to freedom—freedom from guilt, freedom from his perceived debt.

According to Antoinette Michaels, relationship counselor, men vary in their approach when it comes to guilt and money. "Some men do not feel guilty at all and others are extremely guilty. If a man does not feel the guilt, it is because he has blocked it out and makes his own kids less significant in order to cope. In other situations, I have seen husbands who make their children more important than the second marriage because of their guilt. Obviously the middle ground would be the way to go, where the man will strike a balance between his new life and the old."

For Claudette, whose husband felt enormous guilt over his children from his first marriage, her role as second wife was difficult. "I thought I'd be secure and that he'd stop thinking about her and putting the kids ahead of me. I wanted the marriage to be about us. I wanted the solidity of being a second wife. Instead, I have to cope with his unending guilt, and he is blind to her controlling methods. I think that she resents that he married someone younger and more glamorous than she is. Her way of getting back is to constantly telephone with problems pertaining to their kids. I have never stopped feeling threatened by the first wife, mostly because of their children. When we were dating, he used to stay over some nights at her house. This I found really hard to take. It was a way of not giving up what he had, even though it was over. I waited it out and we did get married. Now he just has guilt, but no more overnight visits to her place to see the kids."

The husband who acts on the affair, divorcing his wife to marry his lover, is filled with hope and expectation. It might not be until the second marriage is official that his elation sags, and he becomes tortured by his decision. This is a menace to the second marriage, especially when the first wife becomes ubiquitous. Lifestyle, expenses, children, and a too visible first wife hover over the new couple.

GUILT OVER HIS ACTIONS
- He leaves his wife for you
- The future is rosy
- He marries you
- He cannot live with his decision

"Because of Howard's and his ex-wife's mutual children, there is still contact," says Polly. "I saw that my husband went through a terrible divorce and had fights over the children. He was such a mess about his divorce, he once gave a cab driver his old address. It killed me that he was still so locked in the past. I felt like I did not count. His guilt was consuming him. Howard's ex-wife then remarried and everything was better for a period of time. Then, when his first wife's second divorce came through, I became worried because Howard felt so responsible. And it took years for him to work out his conflict about not being a part of his children's everyday lives. In my opinion, one takes too much from one marriage to the next. It is an impossible battle with lots of scars everywhere. Mostly I think that these men can't get their first families out of their minds. And it is the second wife who pays for this."

"Regardless of how set a second wife feels, the idea of stepchildren always puts her on edge, particularly if she has no children from a previous marriage, or has never been married. If one partner does not have children, he or she may not understand the responsibilities," states relationship counselor, Antoinette Michaels. "The priorities are difficult for the non-parent to accept. If both partners can communicate, it can work."

THE OUTCOME OF HIS GUILT
- The new marriage feels in jeopardy
- The first wife seems to still be in the picture
- Money becomes a point of contention
- There is stress everywhere

If the husband feels guilty about his children and the affair he conducted which broke up the marriage, he may stay in touch with his first wife and write checks to assuage his negative feelings. Some husbands begin to relish the life they left behind. The second wife is quite angry that this is going on and the first wife cannot tolerate the existence of the second. The children are miserable because so much has been taken from them and there have been so many changes. The husband begins to feel weighted down, confused, and discontented.

SEVERING THE TIES
- Guilt over the children keeps the ties intact
- Guilt over what was an affair keeps him paying
- He misses the life he wanted to leave
- He is neither here nor there

In some cases, like Elysse's, a husband's guilt can be so extreme it destroys his second marriage. Elysse became a second wife to a man with a ten-year old son. "I did not anticipate Owen's remorse over the divorce. While his first wife, Kim, was trying to punish my husband through their son, Owen was overpaying her, hoping his money would appease her and ease his own guilt. He had wanted the divorce and she was very bitter and angry. Kim would play games using their son as a pawn: either she'd push his son on us or keep Owen from seeing him.

Because she had so much control over the situation, he kept paying her more and being nicer. He was no diplomat and he couldn't handle her manipulations or her conniving. He was really a prisoner and I became one, too. Then Owen lost his job, and I ended up giving him money that went to his son and ex-wife. I was extremely upset. I fed into his weakness by working so hard to bail him out. Finally I'd had it and I left. Our marriage was ruined because of his guilt."

Faith has been a second wife for ten years. Though she has thus far stayed with her husband, Faith, like Elysse, has been greatly disillusioned by her husband's behavior. "When we first got together, Ben had a business and boasted of being very successful. What I didn't know was that his business was declining and that he was emotionally attached to his first wife and child. By the time I realized this, I was in pretty deep. I've always had my own business, and slowly but surely, I began to enable him financially. By the time my stepdaughter was confirmed, I paid Ben's share of a big party that she wanted. My bitterness has grown, and while I've stayed in this marriage, I've been very lonely and let down. I maintain the hope that things will turn around, but watching my hard-earned paycheck go to Ben's daughter and ex-wife is brutal. I actually believe that it sickened me to the point that I contracted cancer. I ask myself what I get out of this marriage and lately the answer is not much. If he has guilt about using my money, it has not been expressed to me. I believe I'm different from most second wives—I know some who worry about the payments to the first wife but aren't footing the bill. In my next life, I'll be sure to find a self-sufficient man. Whether or not he was married with children is not even the issue."

The importance of finances cannot be underestimated when it comes to a husband's feelings of guilt. In a situation where the husband has enough money to take care of his first wife and children without relying on his second wife's help, the outcome for all is usually better. If his finances are in a poor state and he is wracked with guilt, his second wife may end up having to help support not only him, but his first family. The result—as was seen in Faith's situation—is unhappiness and resentment on the part of the second wife.

RESENTMENT BUILDS
- The second wife resents the triangle
- The first wife resents the second wife

- The children resent their lost life
- The husband resents his confusion

Watching one's husband hand his money over to his first family can be a hard pill to swallow for a second wife, but having to give up her own money will likely be unacceptable to most women. Thus it is important for any woman about to become a second wife to ask herself: *What are my husband's obligations to his first family? How will these obligations effect me? How much responsibility am I willing to take to help him meet those obligations?* By taking the time to consider these matters, one can enter into a marriage with realistic expectations and be better prepared to handle even the most stressful and seemingly unfair situations. A woman might even come to realize she is unwilling to sign on for or continue to help with such obligations. Then the question becomes: *What's more important, avoiding this stressful situation or going ahead with this marriage and making it work?*

Joy knew that she wanted an older man for a husband when she became a second wife. She wisely considered the burden of his first family ahead of time and prepared herself to accept it in order to obtain what she wanted: financial stability. However, even with preparation, she could not anticipate everything. "To me, the trade off was about economics. I knew that an older man would be established, but he'd also most likely have children and an ex-wife. I wanted a powerful, successful husband, and if I had to pay the price in terms of his guilt over his first family, so be it. What I never anticipated was the extent of the guilt. It had to be because he had left them. So the children are with us more than I expected, and again it comes out of guilt. That is the residual effect of the first marriage.

"But nothing was a surprise here. My husband, Todd, is especially supportive of me, partly because of the type of man he is. What made everything change, including his guilt, was when we had two children of our own. Todd had sworn off having any more children, but I ended up pregnant. Starting a new family for us to share has solidified our relationship."

Cynthia George, divorce attorney, has seen many marriages in which the younger second wife ends up having children. "I tell these men who marry women ten and twenty years younger to be prepared for a happy accident. Here they are, signing papers to protect their finances and ending up with more financial obligations than they ever anticipated."

For many second wives and their husbands, children of their own cement their union and help ease the husband's guilt. Even with the downside of an added financial obligation, the birth of a baby may help to bring both families together. Even if the man's guilt is great, if he is able to take care of his new family and his first family without it being too much of a financial strain, the chances of everyone being happier in the end increase.

For Janna's husband, children were not an issue. His first wife, Amy, however, was devastated by their divorce. "My husband Duncan's guilt began when his first wife couldn't pull herself together. Duncan sure felt guilty, but not guilty enough to stay. Instead Amy would pose in a childlike way and a check would go to her weekly, not monthly. There were no children. I couldn't believe it, no kids and he was still paying her all of the time. She was very much in love with him and very dependent upon him. When we were first married, she would call him in hysterics and he'd go over to calm her down. That really bothered me. She tried to hold onto him in any way that she could. Once we moved to another part of the country, it got better. Eventually our own life took over, and there was nothing about the past that could get in our way.

"The fact that there was money always helped. It meant that ultimately all he had to do was write the check. It meant that one day Amy would find someone else to take care of her. Once she realized he wasn't there emotionally, one would think the money was a poor substitute. But who knows. What she did do was make him very protective of his money. Duncan definitely had a thing about it, and I understood. After a few years, Amy did remarry, and he never even heard from her again. That is every second wife's fondest wish—that the first gets a new husband and family so that the second wife's husband stops thinking about his first wife completely."

FIRST WIVES EQUAL GUILT
• The guilt creates control
• The husband is burdened by his past
• He plays into his first wife's demands
• The children are used as pawns

Dr. Donald Cohen reminds us that the second wife who feels truly important cannot be daunted by the first wife. "If there is strong desire and passion and he continually puts the rest to the side for her, the second wife can rise to any occasion. But if it feels like an ongoing competition and his guilt is obvious, the second wife loses her confidence. On the other hand, the more accepting of the situation she is, the more it works in her favor."

Entering a marriage with a man who has substantial obligations from his previous life is a huge undertaking. It might not be for everyone and plenty of second wives seem surprised despite what their husbands have revealed to them. These responsibilities dissipate but do not disappear completely. The most successful second wife is one who enters her marriage armed with information and who deals with her husband's responsibilities with patience and acceptance.

TRUCKLOADS OF BAGGAGE
A second wife who enters the marriage with her eyes wide open will benefit. Whatever comes with her husband: kids, a first wife, a dog, financial obligations, she accepts. There is no pretense, but instead, full disclosure between them.

Though it may be difficult, another way that a second wife can ease the tension of dealing with her husband's responsibilities to his first family is to try to put herself in the first wife's shoes. She may learn, for example, that her financial strain is nothing compared to what the first wife is dealing with. Christopher Rush, private investigator, who is often hired by a first wife within two or three years of her divorce, gives some insight on the actions of a first wife who is in financial straits. "When the first wife discovers how her ex-husband is living with his younger second wife, she is distraught. The lifestyle the first wife hoped for and worked toward has been denied. Instead it is being lived by the second wife. The first wife, who has put sweat into the first marriage, has been left with an unfair financial situation. The courts in our country so often grant twentieth century settlements in a nineteenth century light. It is only if the second wife finds herself divorced from this man that she realizes how badly the system can treat women."

When a second wife can look at the situation from the first wife's point of view, she may feel differently about herself, her husband,

and his ex-wife. She may develop an understanding of the first wife and with that, feelings of empathy. She may even become somewhat accepting of the first wife's behavior and demands that may have previously been perceived as incredibly unfair. This open-mindedness will cause negativity and anger to abate or at least be put into perspective. In the end, this will not only benefit the second wife, but all who are involved: her husband, their children, her/his children, and even his ex-wife.

Albeit, there are some women who don't have to imagine what the first wife's ordeal was like, for they have experienced it firsthand. In the case of Amber, who was a younger second wife until one year ago, the rewards of filling this role were quite exciting at the outset. "My ex-husband had left his first marriage and married me quite quickly. I had no children when I married him, and while his children adjusted, what worried me most was the wrath of his first wife. I think that she envied me, but I also envied her. Maxwell had become extremely successful while he was married to her and she had lived the life that I inherited. She hated me for that and she accused me of breaking up the marriage. I can't decide if my ex-husband's success at the time we married made this woman envy me more, but it turned out that both of us, as his first ex-wife and second ex-wife, had to fight for our due.

"I'm now on the other side of the fence, and I see exactly what she went through. I used to think that she got a very good deal and that his children did as well. Since then, he and I had three children together, and through our divorce, fighting for child support and alimony, I could only think of her. What I had begrudged her and the feelings I had for her when she would fight for more money now seem ridiculous. I think that even as a younger second wife, money is never secure. What I resented about his first settlement was that it seemed to be driven by his guilt. Now I feel that his guilt is only about the children, not about what he owes to his wives."

When a second wife finds herself in the same position as the first, the reality of the situation is often a rude wake-up call. It forces her to acknowledge her own past feelings about the first wife and her misconceptions about the man she married. The men, however, who suffer with more guilt about their children than their exes, are not all as unfeeling as Amber's ex-husband.

Mia also struggled with her husband's guilt over his children. "My husband, Peter, has always felt guilty about the children. He compensated monetarily when they were younger, but it was a chronic problem. Now that they are older, it seems to matter less. And I believe that Peter had difficulty letting go of his ex-wife even though he was no longer in love with her. He felt badly about the divorce and I was very disappointed by this. It was only when we had our own child that things changed. Then he stopped feeling so terrible about his first family. Until then I felt vulnerable, emotionally and financially."

Dr. Donald Cohen reminds us that there is a component of guilt and highly emotional situations with money in any second marriage. "The practical side deals with money. It works as a barrier to the new marriage on many levels. But if the second wife feels that she is getting her due, then the life that she and her husband share is the one that counts. There is not an issue."

The husband's guilt is not the second wife's problem, although it feels as though it is. When the husband is lost in his difficulties, the second wife should take care that she does not lose herself as well. She needs to insist upon time together that is sacred to the new marriage. Any interference by the first wife and/or their children should be addressed early on in the relationship and contained as much as possible.

PROTECT YOURSELF
- Do not lose yourself to his guilt
- Fight fiercely for shared time
- Do not let the first wife infiltrate your marriage
- Do not allow stepchildren to be used to infiltrate your marriage

"I could not wait until Doug's first wife moved away and remarried," says Lara. "The second victory was when my stepchildren went off to college. I know that it was strictly for the kids that Doug had contact with his ex-wife, Jocelyn, but I couldn't stand it. When we first began dating, there was such residual guilt that he was still taking his kids with their mother out to dinner for birthdays and special occasions. That stopped pretty fast—that I would not tolerate. What Jocelyn did that irked me most was manage to remain in the family and, because of the children, get invited to certain events. At first I did not go to family functions because she honed in. I kept my distance. But she was making financial demands on my husband and members of his family, using the kids as an excuse. I finally sat down with Doug and explained to him what Jocelyn was doing and how it was affecting our marriage. Until I made a fuss, he was guilty enough to go along with her antics. It was infuriating, really. I saw Jocelyn as someone who was a control freak that used the children as pawns. I really struggled with all of this, but Doug and I got it all straightened out, most of it before we were married."

PRINCE CHARMING WITH BAGGAGE
- You understand his guilt but hate it
- You see obstacles everywhere
- He works hard to please everyone
- In the end, everyone feels cheated

Like Lara, Catherine's major troubles came from the baggage—emotional and financial—that her husband carried over from his first marriage. Catherine's husband, Arno, tried to leave his marriage many times before he succeeded. "My husband was so entrenched with his in-laws and their lifestyle that he could not readily give it up. Yet, he was miserable with her. His first wife, Blanca, was constantly trying to remedy the marriage, with her parents there, rooting for her all the way. When Arno finally left, he was in poor condition financially because he had worked for his father-in-law. It was a huge break-up, not only for the two of them; the fallout was everywhere.

"Then I came along and it didn't bother me one bit that Arno had no money. I was wildly, madly in love with him. Nothing else mattered. I wanted him above all else. He had a child and then we had a baby together, and that was wonderful. His child spent a lot of time with us the first few years because he was so young. That was simply part of the picture. Had the finances been easier on us, my husband would not have felt so responsible and so bogged down. Also, his ex-wife watched us very closely. She married a very different kind of guy when she remarried and her life was not what it had been with my husband. I think she resented what we had, which was a life full of love and connection. Meanwhile, Arno had this nagging sense that he owed his child a lot more than he did. I think it had to do with his having opted out of the marriage."

There are very few second wives who wouldn't wish that the first wife, her family, and the children never existed. Meanwhile, in many cases, the husband is not only feeling guilty, but tries to assuage his guilt by providing for everyone. In the best scenario, the second wife should laud him for his efforts, but might feel too alone or cheated to be his cheerleader. Whatever frustrations the second wife feels, it's best to focus on their marriage, not his previous one. The more supportive the second wife is, the more confident her husband will be. He will have the strength to do what he reasonably should do for his first family without spreading himself too thin.

THE SECOND WIFE STANDS ALONE
- He needs your support
- Slowly you can show him the way
- The more he includes you, the better you feel
- Do not be threatened by the children

Masters and Johnson tell us that women and men are happiest in equitable relationships, where the love is kept alive because both partners put in emotional and physical energy. This kind of constancy is extremely significant in a second marriage where there are stepchildren and an ongoing connection to the ex-wife or ex-husband. It is only when the new relationship feels truly equal that the spouses are unafraid and secure.

Emma and her husband Ryan developed an equitable partnership. Even when dealing with his ex-wife, they have worked together and made tough decisions jointly. "Money and my husband's ex-wife have always been at the core of our problems," Emma recounts. "Ryan asked his ex-wife if she would agree to his not paying support until he got on his feet with his job change. Sondra agreed, but my husband did not get it in writing. She then subpoenaed Ryan and sued him. At that time, I had cancer and was recovering. We had many medical expenses. My husband and family helped, but my mother had died of this disease and I was in a very bad state. Ryan and I hired a lawyer and that increased our payments. I was at the lowest point in my life, enduring six months of chemotherapy and the ugly behavior of the first wife. Sondra then racked up a phony financial statement and claimed that she would sue us for past bills. At that juncture, we got a restraining order that stated that unless the implications were dire, she could not contact us. And finally she remarried. It has worked and we no longer hear from her. It is behind us, at last."

Feelings of guilt are often inescapable for a man after a divorce. It is obvious why a husband feels guilty when it was his leaving that broke up the family. However, if the divorce was a mutual decision or the first wife requested it, there is still guilt because this man knows that his absence changes the family dynamic. According to Dr. Michele Kasson, "Husbands have this keen sense that their children deserve an intact family and should be raised with their father there. Because it isn't happening, the guilt feelings never quite disappear. Fathers are not there for the day to day, to do the fathering as consistently as they would want. And money becomes the compensation. Since these men cannot give their time, they give their money. This may enable the children to have a life that is similar to what it would be like if the husband were there. It is the best that he can do as a responsible father. Of course, this is not true with all fathers; some turn their backs and are gone."

Kate's husband, Sean, carries so much guilt that he takes all the abuse and punishment his ex-wife can dole out. And according to Kate, Sean's first wife's behavior is both astonishing and despicable. "It is beyond anything that I have ever witnessed. What irks me the most is that Sean doesn't get angry but remains passive when there are problems. I have two sons of my own who are eleven and thirteen. My husband has three children, who are seven to eleven. All five of them live with us. It is so bizarre the way their mother, Angela, treats her own children. She needs money and doesn't work full time, so she is suing for sole custody as a means of child support. On occasion, Angela will drive a cab to make some cash or will waitress, but nothing steady. She hates the man she is with, yet remains with him. Angela is pregnant with his child, and her children from her marriage to Sean are watching all of this. And my kids hear about it too. Her kids are afraid they will be tossed out having just witnessed Angela throw her own boyfriend out.

"My husband remains quiet and I become so angry that he reacts this way. I adore this man and I wish Sean felt that he deserved more. Then he could stand up and fight. Instead Sean pays Angela for the kids, who live with us and witness her daily histrionics. I suppose what does go smoothly is that our children get along. My kids do not adore his children, but everyone does well together. Anything with the kids I can handle. It's the business with his ex-wife that I didn't expect. When I entered the picture, Angela was invisible. Once we got married, she went nuts. She became a big problem then, through the kids and about money, which made my husband feel incredibly at fault. I cannot shake this attitude of his. We have a long road ahead, that I know."

According to George S. Stern, President of the American Academy of Matrimonial Lawyers, money causes tremendous conflict in second marriages. "The first wife is aggravated if her former husband is doing well financially and she does not feel compensated in a commensurate fashion. What the first wife needs to remember is that the finances are governed by law and in most states no one can reopen a property division and revisit it."

When a marriage is finished, the first wife demands large sums in alimony and child support. The second wife may feel that the first is out to destroy the new marriage financially. A second wife who laments the money paid to the first wife will find little consolation. How the husband resolves the issues with his first wife has a direct effect upon the second wife. Money is a substantive point. If the husband and his ex-wife fight over every penny and if the first wife can easily lay a guilt trip on him, then chances are he will pay more than is necessary. It would be best if the ex-spouses could be more realistic about their finances and act civil toward one another.

MONEY, MONEY, MONEY
When all else fails in a relationship, money often speaks louder than words. The first wife may seek all that she can. If there are children, the stakes are raised. The second wife may accept the conditions, but resents having to do without.

Though money problems cause difficulties in many second marriages, it is the cluster of issues which inflict multiple blows. Brenda is a second wife who is now able to work through the obstacles presented to her. "I recognized Gerald's first wife's prejudice toward me and how it affected my stepchildren. My alignment with my husband has given me confidence. I was very young when I married Gerry and there were plenty of hurdles: we had his kids, my kids, money issues, and his first wife's anger. I was so in love with him and I thought it helped that both of us had been married before and knew what to expect. Because he'd been married before, he was stronger and tougher. He could stick it out.

"My story is a bit unusual because my own children ended up being raised mostly by my parents. They did not see their father after the divorce and I did not see them except on a weekly basis. In a sense, my stepchildren took their place. I did not resent them but welcomed them. And they had a mother, so I was being very brave. I knew that she was raising them, but I also understood that I had input. What mattered to me most was my husband. I have always put Gerry first and been there for him. Whether there were concerns about money or his kids, I was always supportive and patient. It has paid off. We have been married for nine terrific years."

A SECOND WIFE'S SENSE OF PLACE
- Confidence is empowering
- A solid commitment to the stepchildren cements the bond
- Avoiding competition with the first eases tension
- Teamwork helps the couple overcome problems
- The key is her unconditional love, patience, and acceptance

Meg was patient and accepting when it came to marrying Ethan, and the final outcome was positive for them both. When Meg met Ethan he was still married. "It was love at first sight, but once he left his marriage to marry me, it became something else. I was already divorced and knew from day one that he was married. He didn't believe in having an affair, so while we did, he would stop it at certain junctures because he couldn't live with himself. He is a noble man who was hoping to make his marriage work. My mother said to me that I would not have loved him so much if he could leave his marriage so easily. We began on unequal footing and it has had its moments, indeed. I waited for years for him to be able to leave his marriage. By the time Ethan left, we'd lost a lot of time together and some of the best years of our lives. He had no money after the divorce, but I did not care.

"It soothed Ethan to be able to leave his ex-wife financially secure," Meg continues. "That way he could put it behind him. And it helped him to feel that he had taken care of his child above and beyond the call of duty. He needed to do those things. And I didn't care that he had no money. I was totally in love with him. Even though it wasn't my first choice, I didn't mind that he had a child. I realized that when a woman meets a man at a certain time in her life, chances are he will have children. From the day we met, I understood it all. And I accepted it. That is why it worked, despite his guilt, despite his troubled leave-taking."

Often the second wife's unconditional love is what her husband depends upon during the divorce and its aftermath. At a time when her husband is wracked with guilt, his second wife's support and patience may be the sustenance that gets him through the ordeal. His guilt will ease with time, but unconditional love, support, and acceptance from his second wife will aid in the healing process.

UNCONDITIONAL LOVE
The husband enters the second marriage with a guilty conscience and emotional baggage. He worries about his first wife and children. With time and his second wife's unconditional love, the difficult dilemma can be manageable.

Of the second wives interviewed who view their husbands' guilt as bottomless pits in their marriages, about half are convinced that the marriages have improved despite this. For the second wives who cannot abide their husbands' attitude and behavior, one-quarter are divorced, half have put the relationship in abeyance, and the remainder are seriously contemplating leaving.

It requires courage and self-esteem to put the first wife in the background and to concentrate completely on the commitment and needs of the marriage. If a second wife reassures her husband that the finances can be dealt with, this lightens his load and offers him hope. A second wife who knows her husband worries about his duty to his first wife and family will win by assuaging his doubts and fears. Confidence and security in herself and her marriage will help the second wife. If she and her husband are able to wade through their troubles, their union will be stronger. If the second wife focuses on financial problems, on what is missing because of the first wife's demands or presence, or on her husband's shortcomings in dealing with these issues, she will only serve to weaken her husband's resolve. Ultimately, this will harm his self-confidence and their marriage. The second marriage that focuses on the couple positively and separates the problems of the past from the relationship of the present and the future, will reinforce security, love, loyalty, and support.

CHAPTER FIVE

INHERIT THE CHILD

Annie has disliked mothering since she married Barry five years ago. "My reaction to mothering is severe. I am married to a man who is fourteen years older than I, and we have two of his three children living with us full time. The other has remained with the mother. It is absolutely hell to be a stepmother. Barry's ex-wife, Rose, lives about twenty minutes away and is now getting divorced for the second time. She had left my husband for her lover, and Barry was devastated. To this day he is very insecure about our relationship and about his kids. The problem is further complicated by the fact that his ex-wife never cared about mothering. Rose did not bond well with her children and she left them when they were four, five, and seven. My husband was responsible for everything. He raised these kids by himself for five years and had full custody. Money was never an issue; she simply wanted out. So the kids never had a schedule of when they would be with her. Instead they waited to see, from week to week, if her plans with them would work out or would be cancelled by her at the last minute.

"Although I complain, I am very attached to my stepchildren. Yet if they do rotten teenage things, I disown them in my mind. And then I remind myself of how accepting my husband is of me and of what I came into. These children needed me

desperately and I came through for them. There is no turning
back now. Besides, I am into character-building experiences.
This is one of them, being a stepmother and second wife to this
clan. What I have learned is that there are limits on how to save
the world. Being in love with Barry is what has kept me going
throughout. The kid scene is definitely the most difficult part
of being a second wife, because they are not really my own. So
I care, but it isn't really the same. I suppose deep down I'll
always be ambivalent about the children for this reason."

The most taxing aspect of remarriage involves stepchildren and
the meshing of two families. Marriages need both limitations and freedom to keep both partners separate and to blend with each other. This
applies to an intact family also, where the advent of children is an added
element of stress in the relationship. In a situation where there has been
a divorce and children are involved, there are undeniable repercussions
in the parent's remarriage. If the stepparent has children of her/his own,
it creates another scenario altogether. Then there are two sets of children, causing financial, physical, and logistical burdens on the marriage.
There needs to be a strong foundation to survive the everyday trials and
tribulations of these blended families.

In the year 2000, according to Child Trends, a nonprofit
research organization that tracks data and trends concerning children
and families, over twenty-five percent of children will live with a stepparent. *Psychology Today* observes the positive traits of the blended family,
describing it as more supportive and more complex than the traditional
family. If the blended family can survive the first five years, the outcome
is a population of well-adjusted, flexible stepchildren. The key is that
there is co-parenting on the part of both ex-spouses and that the stepparent knows her/his place.

Masters and Johnson report that five out of six men and three
out of four women remarry after their divorce. *The Janus Report* reveals
that while second marriages have a high success rate, remarriages with
children from the previous marriage(s) have a fifty percent higher chance
of failing than those second marriages without children. This addresses
the fact that there are undeniable conflicts to be confronted by the second wife and husband who bring children into their marriage. Unfortunately, the second wife may find herself having trouble coping with the

idea of being a stepmother—a label that conjures up evil and cruelty in the minds of many.

The image of the wicked stepmother is a very familiar one in fables and fairy tales. In *Snow White*, the wicked stepmother/queen competes with Snow White for her beauty, and in *Cinderella*, the horrid stepmother turns Cinderella into a virtual slave and tries to keep her from attending the ball. In today's world, while there is not always an instant love for one's stepmother, they are not usually as nasty as those stereotypically portrayed in stories. Often, it can be the children who are cruel and nasty toward their new stepmother. Confused and upset about their parents' divorce, to them, a new wife seals the unhappy deal: now their parents are definitely not getting back together. To add insult to injury, the children may be forced to live with or spend a good deal of time with this intruding woman, a person who takes up their father's time and affection.

When a second wife becomes a stepmother in a situation where her new husband was widowed or where her stepchildren are very young, her responsibility is quite significant. With small children, her role is threatening and frightening for both the children and for her, yet they need a mother and caretaker. If the children are adolescent, her presence as caretaker is less important. Instead, she should respect the maturity level of these older children who are often more concerned with whether or not she is good for their father than with needing a mother. What children of divorce and remarriage sense is the loss of their father to their father's new partner. Often when the children see that the marriage is working, they feel better not only about their father, but about themselves. A stepmother who opens her home and herself to her stepchildren is setting the right environment for them. Yet she cannot totally alleviate the hurt many children feel when their father remarries: they are upset when his priorities shift from them to his second wife. In such cases, the image of the wicked stepmother may manifest itself.

Cynthia George, divorce attorney, tells us that serious difficulties and subsequent second divorces often arise over stepchildren. "If a woman with children becomes a second wife and her husband cannot tolerate the way that she parents her own offspring, she feels that she must choose. Either it will be her husband who gets priority or it will be her children. She loses either way. What she hears from both her husband and her children is, 'Mom, you like him better than me' or 'You put your children first.' It feels like an insurmountable dilemma to the second wife."

The love and devotion shown to the second wife notwithstanding, the children who are in the mix keep the relationship triangulated. The first wife remains in the picture because of the children. The second wife is up against not only the ongoing communication between her husband and his ex-wife, but his children, who he likely sees on a visitation schedule or a joint custody schedule.

"It is wise," suggests Dr. Ronnie Burak, "that a couple about to embark on a marriage with kids from previous ones seek the help of a counselor. Preventive medicine before issues actually arise is always a good idea. There are inevitable problems because children have enough trouble getting by when their families are intact. Having to deal with a wicked stepmother—someone who seems to be moving in on the father—often brings about resentment or anger."

As Catrice sees it, becoming an instant mother was not easy. "When I became a second wife, my stepdaughter was only nine years old and the custody was joint. My husband, John, helped by taking most of the responsibility, because I made it clear that I could not replace her mother, Lydia. But I'm there for my stepdaughter. She once told me that I'm much more of a parent to her than Lydia's second husband. What concerns me is how Lydia treats her own child. The poor girl has borne the brunt of her mother's lousy life. Lydia was totally dependent on my husband when they were married. I'm not like that at all.

"This attitude really took its toll once Lydia and her husband were divorced. We ended up with my stepdaughter living with us. Then Lydia threatened to take us to court over her daughter's choice of where to live. Meanwhile, I tried to give my stepdaughter the time and attention she could not get from her mother. I took her shopping and to movies, plays, and the library. I wanted her to be very happy and feel safe with us. After several years, my stepdaughter returned to her mother's house, and things have since settled down. It was a lot of turmoil to live through and I believe that much of it could have been avoided had we been emotionally prepared. What I have sensed from the beginning is the accountability that my husband, John, has to his child. So while I do not feel the same emotional ties to her, I know how he is bound. That is why I make the effort. We are there for her if she needs us; that is our common stance."

What is most demanding for many second wives with children and stepchildren is the meshing of two families. Every person in the blended family needs attention and wants to count the most. The second wife, whether she has children of her own or not, wants to be the most important person in her husband's life. Her children want to be more important to her than her new husband is, and her husband wants to be number one for her, while he wrestles with his own children's demands. They too, want to be first with their father. The children worry that their father favors his new wife and that she comes first. Often they do not feel as comfortable in his and his wife's new home now that he has remarried. The second wife may dread the day when visitation will increase or the children will ask to live with their father. When there are two sets of stepchildren, the stress increases. Both sets adjust to a life where rooms and possessions are shared, as is time with their natural and stepparents.

SHARING HIM

The second wife lives in fear that her husband will put his children before her. The children live in fear that their father will put his second wife ahead of them. The second wife worries that her stepchildren will move in with them. The children worry that their father's home is no longer theirs.

SHARING LIVES

When there are two sets of stepchildren and neither has her/his parents on a regular basis, they become territorial. Sharing a life, sharing a room, sharing toys with stepsiblings is extremely stressful. For these children, there is a tremendous sense of loss.

Adding the equation of stepchildren to a new marriage often causes pressures which are sometimes unanticipated. Maura was not prepared for the problems she encountered with her stepchildren when she became a second wife. "There were such false expectations. My husband seemed so sure of himself so I thought that it would go smoothly. Instead it was extremely difficult. I had three small stepchildren, plus one of my own and then we had a baby together. It was a very trying time for us and our difficulties with our blended family lasted for years.

"I look back now and I remember how it felt. But we managed

to raise everyone, and it made them better kids. They were more willing to give and bend, and weren't as spoiled as if they'd been raised in a normal American family. There were sacrifices and there were times of joy."

"I was in my thirties and never before wed when I married my husband, Sheldon," says Gayle. "By then, the men I had dated had been married before, and most of them had children. I wanted no part of a man who would walk away from his children. If he wasn't responsible to his own blood, then what would he do to a wife in adversity? The responsibility to an ex-wife is not the same as the responsibility to one's children, which never ends. The fact that the man I married was a good father meant a lot to me. I saw it as a part of his character.

"Sheldon's caring for his sons was a positive force. I, in turn, have been very supportive of my husband's children and his ex-wife. She remarried, thankfully, and they have no children together, just as my husband and I do not. In a way, his children are a connection we all share. I know that his sons' dreams of their parents reuniting were shattered when I married their father. The finality of our getting married was a difficult event for my stepchildren.

"I realize that my open-mindedness toward my stepsons is very meaningful to my husband. Not only did I give him the opportunity for another life, but I was there for his children. Sheldon made it possible by welcoming me from the start. He was on my side when his sons gave me a tough time. He was there for me and put me first. Sheldon demanded that his sons respect me."

"It is a situation fraught with emotional risks when the couple is in the ecstasy stage of a relationship and the second wife finds the children intrusive. Everyone is fighting for the father's attention," says Dr. Ronnie Burak. "The children are in pain over their parents' break-up and the realization that they do not have their father all to themselves is so hurtful."

In Racquel's case, the blending of families went smoothly. "As a second wife, I am the mother of two young daughters and a step-mother to two teenage stepdaughters. Three weeks into dating my husband, Marshall, I met his two girls, who were quite small at the time. Within six weeks time we were married. His ex-wife had already remarried by the time I entered the picture.

"The children were the only common bond, his ex-wife, Rosalyn, and I shared, and she did not get in the way of the marriage.

In fact, we supported one another. I wanted the children to be close to both their father and their mother and to see me as special beyond that. Rosalyn agreed with my approach and we all benefitted. What lasted a long time, for years, was my acute awareness of my husband's first marriage. That is the one thing that stepchildren unintentionally do—they act as a constant reminder of his past. But I know this is the marriage that counts now and I have welcomed his girls from day one. For my own daughters, these older girls have been a blessing. My stepdaughters are mine on some level after all the years I've spent with them. When my eldest stepdaughter recently married, she asked me to plan the wedding. I could afford to be generous, because everyone in this story was genuinely happy. There was no antagonism, but plenty of mixing: our girls with his girls and his girls' stepsiblings on the other side. We are truly the new traditional family."

"When the husband is on the phone with his first wife about the children, the second wife has to be tolerant," says Dr. Ronnie Burak. "When the second wife is on the phone with her ex, talking about the kids, her husband has to accept it. Both sides must gain confidence. The more time that passes, the more secure it gets. A life is being built together."

For those children who have the benefit of two sets of caring parents, there is a sense of security and of being loved. When there are disparate points of view and the child is being pushed or coaxed in opposite directions, however, it becomes arduous. How the first wife and second wife get along and how the husband orchestrates events make all the difference. A second wife who feels worthy as a stepmother contributes more to the blended family.

MIXING IT UP
- There are more than two adult players at all times
- Integrating values and traditions is not easy
- The rapport between exes influences the kids' reaction to the stepparent
- Being valued by her husband is what counts for the second wife

When there are children from both husband and wife's previous marriages, the second wife must include both sets of children in the new family. For her stepchildren, she should not be a disciplinarian but someone who is maternal and protective. If the children are teenagers and rebellious, the husband and his second wife must endeavor to keep the marriage and the family together despite the efforts of teenage stepchildren to pull the new couple apart. A son might tell his father that he is going back to his mother's because he doesn't like how the new house is run since the father has remarried. In this way, he is playing one parent against the other. In many instances, the children will like their father's companion until the relationship becomes more serious or evolves into remarriage. Then the competition begins: *does he love me more than he loves her? Does he love her more than he loves me?* If the hurdles caused by these feelings can be surpassed, there is a great potential for growth.

ENHANCING STEPCHILDREN'S LIVES
For the second wife who attempts to become close to her stepchildren, there is the potential that she will touch their lives. The best stepparents do not push themselves on the children and do not attempt to discipline them.

Sometimes, especially after bitter divorces, the custodial parent plants seeds of resentment against the other parent in their children. Janine has witnessed the residual pain that her husband suffers because of his children. "I am really fortunate. My relationship with my own children has remained intact after my divorce and remarriage. I realize that my husband, Tyler, has been hurt because his children were taken away from him emotionally. I have felt the pain, and because I have my own children, I can only imagine how he must be saddened. I see his ex-wife as boorish, selfish, and cruel. There was no need to do this, to treat him this way. The children would come to our home for weekends and scout the house for new things and ask us how much our possessions cost. It was so obvious that they were doing it at the behest of their mother. She had manipulated them. They were not very friendly toward my children at first, but as a second wife with great determination, I changed their resentment into positive feelings. Tyler's ex-wife had instilled too much mothering and set too many rules for these children. I ran our home on a less formal, more open basis. My husband was very grateful because in the end, it all worked out. The household rhythms worked better and there was not as much contact with her. Age and time has helped. The kids began to get along and we became a family, another kind of family altogether."

Another second wife handled her stepchildren with different, but also successful, guidelines. Judy's husband had adopted his first two stepchildren, before his ex-wife gave birth to twins. "Today, the first set of children are in their twenties, the twins in their teens, and we have two small boys together. I knew what I was getting into despite the fact my friends and my mother all warned me that I was crazy. If money had been an issue, we could not have done it. But my husband takes good care of his ex-wife and he takes care of his second family, so we are all very fortunate. The oldest two children are close to my age because my husband is twenty years older than I am. By the time that we married, I did not have much to do with them. The twins were at our house every weekend, which was not easy, and then we had our own babies on top of it. After a while, custody was changed and the twins were not here every weekend. I was smart about the whole process. I've worked hard to see that our family is the priority and I've been quite conscious of the requirements of his other children as well.

"If this marriage had been about romance and sex, I'd be a very disappointed woman. Instead it's been about warmth, love, and raising a family. At times I can be a little frustrated because of what gets put to the side. Other times I feel that this is the best it can be. It takes constant energy and thought, that's for sure."

Often, the couple in a second marriage will not find much time for sex and romance unless they make it a priority. Going away for an occasional weekend or having a schedule where all of the children are out of the house on the same night on a weekly basis is helpful. Do not underestimate the importance of spending time alone together, for him, for you, and for your relationship. Intimacy fuels the marriage and promotes closeness and trust.

WHAT ABOUT SEX?
- Establish rules of privacy
- Make sure there's a lock on the door anyway
- Try to find time to get away alone
- Do not put sex on the back burner

In some cases, the second wife does not or cannot incorporate her new married life and the children of her husband's first marriage. Shannon saw her stepchildren as the demise of her marriage. "I was always aware of my role as a second wife, it never went away. I had a great deal of contact with my husband's children and that was the issue. My husband, Gordon, made a mistake in telling them that I had been his lover. I saw his explanation as only partially honest. He told them what he wanted to without giving them all the facts, such as how long we'd really been together. His children were then set against me. They would never be happy with a woman who had taken their father away from their mother. His oldest child resented me the most. I was closer to the younger two. What is interesting is that neither Gordon nor his ex-wife are close to their children. Yet the kids made up their minds that it was my fault that the marriage had dissolved and behaved accordingly. They were discouraged by their mother from being open to me."

In an environment where the children have been swayed by their mother, the second wife has little chance of redemption on her own. If her husband is not on her side and does not firmly stake out the boundaries for his children, the new wife is left alone and frequently feels scrutinized and criticized.

A NO WIN SITUATION
- The children are influenced by their mother
- Without her husband's support, the second wife has little chance of developing a good relationship with his children
- Even with his support, she may be considered the enemy
- The second wife is constantly being judged and falls short in the eyes of the children

Even if the husband is supportive, the influence of the first wife and the older children may be insurmountable for the second wife. This is what Florence and Ken faced. "I had this fantasy that the stepchildren would be available to me on some level," Florence says regretfully, "and the reverse is what took place. Ken's ex-wife remains bitter, angry and horrible. She has passed this on to the kids. Only two of the four children are willing to speak to me. I feel good about these two, but the oldest child is extremely unfriendly. She turns her back on me if possible and encourages everyone else to do the same. She will see my husband alone but will not accept me and will not speak to me. I cannot make any headway with this daughter. She bad-mouths my husband to the other children, and as young adults, they are still quite influenced by her. Holiday time is the worst. She has totally poisoned their minds. But throughout all this, Ken is a pillar of righteousness.

"There have been years without communication, but I haven't lost hope completely. The problem with Ken's children is ongoing. So while my husband shows me every day how happy he is to have married me, he has paid quite a price for our happiness. I am so sorry that there never has been any level of acceptance. I believe the real issue is their inability to come to terms with our marriage. But it is the rejection by the children that troubles me so much. I long to be included, but it is not possible."

Although a blended family is the ideal, often the reality differs. Having two children of her own before marrying a man with two children, today Gabriella and her husband, Curtis, have two young children together. "I am ambivalent about the continual togetherness of a blended family. While it pleases me to see us as one big family, I also want our children and our marriage to come first. Curtis supports everyone well enough that money isn't the problem. He has never denied me anything in order to make his children happy and they do not take anything away from me and my kids on that level. It is the emotional baggage that resurfaces constantly. It was worse before we had children of our own. Back then, his first wife was a ghost in our marriage, haunting us constantly. The haunting stopped a bit after I had babies with him.

Gabriella goes on to say, "But the connection she has with my husband will not go away. Then I say to myself, *if he would give up his kids and treat her unfairly, I wouldn't want him*. But what irks me is that the first wife calls all the time. I understand her needs because one of their children was sick with a devastating illness. Curtis suffers constantly with this. In a way it has brought everyone closer together and in a way it shows his attachment to his first family. It is a complex issue, because my husband is highly moral and good to all of his children.

"I know that our marriage is so strong because of my husband's appreciation of me. I also know that any problems in the marriage have to do with his children, to this day. In some marriages, there are money problems or sexual problems or someone cheats. With us, it is about his kids and mine from our past lives. Maybe it is the times that we live in, but I have several friends who are also second wives, married to older men with children from the first marriage. I suspect that if it doesn't work out with a boyfriend from college and the marriage fails, we end up marrying a man who has children and has been around."

In second marriages with stepchildren from both sides, one cannot dismiss the existence of these children—constant, unrelenting proof of one's spouse's former life. Asking the husband to choose between his second wife and his first family is unfair and unproductive. Experts say the right approach for the second wife is to connect with her stepchildren as much as possible and to concentrate on the big picture, that of the marriage.

MOVE ON WITH YOUR LIFE
In the case of blended families, the merging of one's past with one's present is inevitable in the form of children. For the second wife who feels overwhelmed by such a scenario, she needs to take stock and be grateful for a second chance.

Though relations with stepchildren may be fraught with problems, they also can be positive and rewarding. The realization that Helene's stepchildren adored her two young children, their half-siblings, endeared them to her and brought about peace in the household. "I stopped staking out my territory and my earlier concerns stopped mattering. It seemed in the beginning that my relationship with my husband Patrick's children was combative and uneasy. Our relationship has been rocky. Then Patrick and I had our own babies. I realized that I would end up fighting with my own children like this someday when they hit that age. I thought it couldn't be avoided. That's when I changed my attitude toward them. While I do not love my husband's children as I love my own kids, I feel very close to them. They have a mother and I know I am a friend to them.

"I'm a bit ashamed of my previous behavior and I know that my husband expected more from me. But when you don't have children of your own, it isn't always easy to accept someone else's. I admit, I was one of those people who couldn't do it readily. Not only did eventually having my own children solidify my relationship with my stepchildren, but it made us into a big family. I know how lucky I am that they like my kids, because some stepchildren would not be as open and kind to their half siblings."

GIVE TO GET
• Do not try to parent
• Be tolerant of your stepchild
• Do not make your husband choose

Dr. Michele Kasson feels the issues with stepchildren are ones of space. "While many families are blended, each child must know that the relationship with each parent is unique. With all the chaos in a house full of steps, every child must know that she has her/his parents attention, time, concern, and love. Once they are assured of this, they calm down."

An example of this maturation process is illustrated by Tiffany, who lives in a small town in Alabama with her two children from her first marriage, her three stepchildren, and the two children she and her husband share. "Parenting has become a way of life for me. When Danny and I had two kids of our own, we made it into a family. He has fathered my kids because my ex-husband has not been around. My ex-husband has remarried several times since our divorce and will call occasionally but is not there for the children. I have totally concentrated on my new life with these kids. Because our children were all so close in age, it made it easier. It is a miracle that they got along well. If there was any competition in the beginning, by the end, it worked out and they meshed well. Our own issue happens to be that of money. My husband has had problems with his ex-wife wanting more. Then she got remarried and that saved us.

"We have always made time for each other, Danny and I. With seven kids together and an ex-wife in the background, we had to push hard for ourselves. And we did. Then we made time for the children. It's quite an act, keeping it all together."

A family in which the maturation process didn't occur is a very different story. "I have been a second wife for seven years with one child from my first marriage," Adele tells us. "My husband, Byron, has three children from his first marriage. Although I am close to one of my three stepchildren, I do not consider the family to be very connected. There has been conflict between me and my stepchildren, but they are very kind to my daughter. My child adores her stepsiblings and thinks of them as family.

"There have been some amazing dramas. Byron's children have rebellious social values and attitudes. When he is frustrated with them, I become the recipient of his upset. He has much guilt about his children. What has been unpleasant for me is having the stepchildren take time away from the marriage. I suppose they resent me for taking their father away, and I resent them for taking my husband away. So we keep competing. And Byron has such guilt over them that they know how to tweak him. I try to behave as the adult, but I'm disturbed that my husband always defers to his children. I wish he didn't feel that he'd done something wrong, because then he'd have a better view of how his children really act and what they do to him, to us."

GUILT RULES THE DAY
When the husband has residual guilt about his divorce vis-à-vis his children, it is very difficult for his second wife. She feels that she cannot win, that his guilt is irreversible and a barrier to the marriage.

Guilt over children from a first marriage is a very dense and impenetrable form of regret, one that the second wife has little influence over. Her approach has to be positive; if it is not, there will be no way to build a rewarding relationship. A husband who is steeped in guilt over his children and involved in a new marriage with young children requires a wife who is one hundred percent supportive.

WINNING HIM OVER
• The second wife needs to devote her energies to the marriage
• There cannot be any negativity
• She must be supportive

Complete commitment to the new marriage on the part of husband and wife is a necessity in a second marriage complicated by stepchildren. Because Chloe and her husband came to the second marriage with such pain from their first, the blending of children was not considered a major hurdle. "When I met my husband, Dennis, he was still in deep pain over his wife's affair. Apparently they had been in counseling with a therapist to work out marital problems when his wife, Laura, and the therapist began having an affair. I don't believe that Dennis will ever really trust anyone again. My own situation was strange, too. My ex-husband only wanted custody of one of our two children. He did not want joint custody with both our children. He simply chose the child who looked like him and insisted that he live with him. Of course that hurt the other child and now the children are divided. It has had a negative impact on both children."

"So, when Dennis and I came together, we had been through a lot. We decided we simply would not let the children interfere in our commitment to each other. It wasn't even close. I have no issue with Laura. I know that she caused my husband big problems, but I am friendly and let the past go. In this marriage, we are together and our relationship comes first. Even though I am not their mother, I do a good job when we are with all of the kids. This happens twice a week. There is no competition because it isn't set up that way."

Often in a blended family, everyone is competing for attention, the stepchildren and the spouses alike. If each person receives enough attention, as occurs in Chloe and Dennis's family, they do not need to compete as much. Of course, as is true of any marriage with children, it is better if there is an established routine. When there is a schedule to follow, everyone feels more anchored. The less that is left to the last minute or chance, the more easily the relationship flows. Blended families do better when each child understands his/her schedule and adheres to it. For stepchildren in particular, changes are not very welcome and cause greater feelings of instability. For the second marriage, it is better if the schedules are followed as precisely as possible.

Patti's husband, Brad, divorced his first wife because she had an affair. "His first wife is married to her lover and my two stepchildren spend a great deal of their time with our family, which includes my two children from my former marriage. Basically, I am surrounded. All of our children, ages eight to thirteen, are here on weekends, holidays and during the summer. Because there is so little stability in their mother's home, the stepchildren prefer to be with us. Brad is very involved with his own children and with mine at this stage. Yet in my heart, I must admit I would have preferred to have no stepchildren. It is the most demanding role in the world. I think that being a second wife is not at all the same as the first time around. It becomes a thousand times more difficult if there are children in the package. I know that my husband feels more obligated to his first family than to his second because of his children. In his mind, he left those children, he abandoned them.

"At times, I have been so bothered by his torn feelings that I have been ready to walk out. The idea that I felt this way was enough to get my husband to pay attention. This is our life now and we have to come first. He's been making a major turn around. And while I know how he feels about his kids and how I feel about mine, I need our marriage to be placed before everything else. There is the burden we both face of having these extra children. The fact is that for each of us, our stepchildren are not ours but emotionally connected to us all the same.

Neither of us has final say about the other's children, but we'd do anything in the world for them. We are very lucky that all of the kids get along. That's the most important part."

A stepmother who loves her stepchildren still may find fault with her husband's way of dealing with them. Some second wives who have their own children from previous marriages do appreciate their husbands' roles as stepfathers, but resent how their husbands favor their own children from their first marriage. Second wives who feel this way, many experts feel, are experiencing their own struggles for the new marriage, not an effort to short-change his children. They are struggling for the validation of their new relationship; they want this relationship to rule above all else.

AMBIVALENCE
Many second wives form attachments to their stepchildren and still resent the husband's attitude that his children come first. The second wife is trying to validate the marriage; because of her insecurity, she may see the children as obstacles to this.

Some second wives are determined to choreograph the marriage and children/stepchildren. She wants it all. In the meantime, her husband is often unable to separate his present life from his past. He remains responsible to his first wife through the children, which unnerves the second wife. Often in these cases, the second wife has difficulty coping when something goes awry with her stepchildren and her husband is in contact with his first wife. She sees the first wife as using the children to cause friction. It is always an easier situation when everyone is content: the first wife, the second wife, the husband, and the children.

Major events, such as weddings and the birth of children, often bring out repressed feelings on the part of stepchildren. When Delia's stepdaughter was preparing her wedding, she leaned on both her mother and stepmother for guidance. "I felt good about this initially, but as the time passed, I began to feel uncomfortable. I noticed that my stepdaughter had these fantasies that her father and her mother would somehow be reconciled because of her wedding. It was strange because her parents had been divorced for years, since she was in kindergarten. I said nothing because I didn't want to cause any problems, but it was unsettling. Then it actually came time for the wedding and my stepdaughter insisted that there be family photographs which included the bride, the groom, my husband, his ex-wife, and the bride's sister—as if they were still one happy family.

"What bothered me most about all of this was that my husband went along with it. He was virtually out of touch with his ex-wife because the children were grown. The wedding definitely brought them into contact. And I felt like the first wife had this secret goal of getting him back. That blew my mind. I suppose my husband's attitude was what harm can it do for an afternoon, and why not make his daughter happy on her wedding day. I felt hurt and excluded by his behavior and it definitely came between us. Later, we straightened things out, but this was an ordeal. At times, I wanted to leave the wedding altogether. Second wives really do tread on slippery turf."

A husband has to be sensitive to his second wife's feelings during family affairs. When a child is being confirmed or bar mitzvahed, gets married, or has a child, the original family may be brought back together. The child might fantasize of things returning to what they once were, of their parents being together again. Such fantasies will only serve to hurt the child when they are not fulfilled and leave an excluded second wife feeling angry and embarrassed. As a responsible parent, the father must dispel his child's fantasies, and as a loving husband, he must not allow his second wife to be ignored or left out of family events. His loyalty to his new wife, who not only represents his present and future but who should be considered a member of his family, is necessary and appropriate.

FAMILY AFFAIRS
Celebrations such as a stepchild's wedding, confirmation, bar mitzvah, inevitably bring the first wife into the picture. The husband must be aware of his second wife's feelings and keep her involved, while maintaining cordiality with his ex-wife. His attention to his second wife and to the present, not the past, is what counts the most.

If dealing with stepchildren who are not adults, the issue of parenting naturally comes up. When a second wife and her husband have different ideas of parenting, problems crop up which are intensified in the stepfamily. "My husband and I see his children differently," Honey admits. "I think they are spoiled and greedy. He feels that his monetary donations are a way of making up for his absence. My husband, Scott, finds it easier to say yes than no to his kids. I think if we had children together, we would fight over this as well. I see it as too indulgent and not a method of making up for lost time or a divorce.

"What bothers me is that when my kids are here, he barely tolerates them. But then again, when his are absent maybe mine remind him of what he is missing. Then there's the misery, the misery of giving to someone else's children while his own are not available. I do relate to what he goes through.

"On top of this, Scott's own children are exposed to different values and different rules in their mother's home. That is something he cannot overcome. What he offers the kids is not what his ex-wife does. I wish he could somehow work it out with the children or with his ex-wife, but that's a hopeless cause. She will say black if Scott says white. Money is the only common denominator. I feel his conflict and I feel my own. I sometimes wish that all of the children were here together. It is the closest thing I know of a perfect world, because he's happy and so am I. Our schedules with our children are such that we can't arrange it much. When it happens and we are all physically present, I'm relieved. Then I wait for the weekend to be over because it's also exhausting. Everywhere there is conflict and yet there is also great joy."

Dr. Burak warns us that differing styles between two sets of parents can be difficult for children. "The kids have to switch gears from one parent to the other. There may be conflict in the new marriage over how the kids should be treated, because even the stepmother and her new husband have unique styles. And the fact that she did not have these children from day one makes it more complicated."

CONFLICT
• Blending of families takes time and consideration
• When there are two sets of steps, it requires great skills
• Putting the new marriage on hold is not the answer
• Hostilities arise from everywhere—kids, parents, exes

The discord and battles of blended families are inevitable when one considers what divorce and remarriage mean to children. While the new couple might be madly in love, most children of their parent's previous marriage are devastated by their new marriage, hoping against

hope that their parents will be reconciled. Blended families require pro-
cessing. A period of adjustment often ridden with antagonism is par for
the course. A second wife who can see past the early stages of dishar-
mony and turmoil, who has no shadow of doubt about her love and
devotion to her husband and his to her, will have the reward of a committed and rich marriage.

REWARD
• Introspection and insight win the day
• Even teenagers grow out of it
• Challenge builds character
• Children come to love and accept you, him, and each other

Of the second wives interviewed on the subject of stepparenting, the majority felt positively toward their stepchildren and blended
families. However, several wives openly disliked their stepchildren
and/or were hostile toward them on some level. About half of the second wives expressed a sense that their husbands were there for them, in
the midst of clingy first wives and the complications of parenting children after a divorce. Others felt that their husbands could not be supportive of them because of the distraction of their ex-wives and children from the first marriage.

A study quoted in the book, *Stepparenting*, by Jeanette Lofas
reveals that 52 percent of divorced fathers in the United States pay full
child support, 23 percent pay partial child support, while 21 percent
pay none. Since divorced women with children have a 73 percent drop
in their standard of living and divorced men have an average of a 42 percent rise, the requirements of the second wives who have been single
mothers and marry men who have been single fathers may be very specific. Two-thirds of the interviewees openly discussed how important
finances were to their blended family.

The prominence of the stepfamily/blended family in our society today cannot be denied. *Psychology Today* reports that there will soon
be more children living with a stepparent than with both biological parents. In a remarriage that includes stepchildren, the partners should
agree ahead of time that the marriage stands on its own, but the copar-
enting/stepparenting is a big piece of it. Forming the stepfamily/
blended family entails the cooperation of both the second wife and her

husband. The stability of their unit depends upon the strength and uni-
fication of the adults who are in charge. Once the coparenting has a
beneficial routine and an equitable structure for all the children, there is
less enmity. The second wife/stepmother who forges a positive relationship with her stepchildren is wise and practical. She realizes that the
validity of her marriage cannot be undone by the stepchildren and that
her relationship with them can be a rewarding one.

CHAPTER SIX

MANY TIMES MARRIED

Laurie, an occupational therapist, was married for seven years and had a son when she became divorced. "Three years later, I became a second wife to a man who had been married without children. I look at my first marriage, and I can see what went wrong. My ex-husband was in law school, and I was the one to hold it all together. Our son, plus all of the responsibilities were mine. Then Harry began to have an affair. Yet that isn't what actually separated us. It was the marriage itself that failed. I ended up taking care of his lover's child while she was having an affair with my husband.

"My self-esteem was low. I was so alone and there was no sex in the marriage. So, I began an affair, too, even though I had a child of my own by this time. I mean, how much more committed can a marriage get than a mortgage and a son? I really did it for the sex, because there was none in the marriage by then. Still, I was so miserable. And there was this other man who found me interesting. My lover made the affair easy to go along with because he pursued me actively and was single. After a while, I was able to let the affair go and face the fact that it was time to be divorced.

"Soon afterward, I began to date Phil, who became my second husband. Phil's ex-wife had remarried right after their divorce and had a few children. I was very curious about her. I saw her once on vacation. She was with her children and her new husband. I had this incredible urge to talk to her. I wanted to know what her marriage to my husband was like, how the sex had been, and how close they were when the marriage was good. I was very curious, but I never approached her. Had I not seen her at this place, I might never have even conjured up images of them.

"Both Phil and I are bound to make our second marriage wonderful after what we've been through. What bothers me is how each of us was treated in our first marriages. It makes it all the more special that we are together now."

As in Laurie's case, a past history where trust and devotion had been lacking can result in a present and future marriage where both partners are totally committed. A personal evolution occurs when a second wife has been through an ordeal in her previous marriage. She cherishes the new marriage that results in a health partnership and takes pleasure in giving and receiving love and affection. Yet it is hard for some individuals to recognize their shortcomings and the problems that lead to the downfall of the first marriage. For them, breaking old habits and patterns is difficult and they find that their second marriage seems a lot like their first. In any case, statistically, the chances that a woman will not only be a man's second wife but will be married a second time herself, are quite good.

Women who have been second wives more than once are now an every day occurrence. It seems for some, ironically, that this is one's fate. A seasoned second wife has accomplished a great deal, having met a unique set of standards and perhaps surviving the ghost of a first wife. There may be stepchildren to contend with along with her own children. There may be two sets of her own children and two sets of steps. In this modern day phenomenon, the many times married second wife is a veritable one woman show. Daniel J. Levinson tells us in his book, *The Seasons of a Woman's Life*, that women in their late thirties and early forties are in search of an "egalitarian marriage enterprise." In this set up, both partners would "share in domestic rights and responsibilities on more equal terms."

According to *The Janus Report*, it is estimated that one out of every three marriages is a second for one or both partners. Because men tend to be lonely and unanchored when not married, a woman, after a divorce or widowhood, will find a man in a similar position, ready to commit again. Many men yearn to repeat the pattern of a home life that is lost with the dissolution of a marriage. In circumstances where both partners have children and a history of their own, there is often a necessary shifting of priorities in the new marriage. Forging a blended family and a new life is an ambitious undertaking, but the rewards are many. The down side of second marriages is that both partners bring "baggage" from previous marriages and former lives that may create stress and strain. Such a union between two people who have suffered disappointment occurs in dire hope of another chance.

George S. Stern, President of the American Academy of Matrimonial Lawyers, represents an equal amount of female and male clients. "Most of my clients remarry because people get lonely and tired of the dating scene. What is interesting is that often the mistakes of the first marriage are repeated in the second and probably the third. The habits we carry from family and society, along with our religious and cultural differences and personality traits, can cause a first and a second marriage to fail. It is usually when people are able to marry another kind of person and not the same type as their ex-spouse that things improve in the second marriage."

Sidney has three daughters from her first marriage and is presently married to a man without children. It has been successful because she learned from the mistakes of her first marriage and found in Luke, her new husband, a different person than her ex-husband. "I was fine about marrying someone who had been married before, but I drew the line at someone who had kids from that marriage. It was enough that I'd already been a second wife to my first husband. Luke's first wife was not a problem for me, not a story that mattered. But I wanted him to be fairly free of burdens. His marriage dissolved over the issue of having children. She wanted kids desperately and he refused. He knew that she wasn't right for him and he didn't want to further complicate things. Then we got married and now we plan to have children. I know that our marriage is right for Luke. For me, bringing my children to this marriage worked even though I couldn't have done it with someone else. I know that seems hypocritical, but when I watch my friends dealing with children coming from both first marriages, it is a nightmare. And having these children really lets him off the hook. Although we were planning a family, if it doesn't happen, that's okay.

My daughters are crazy about him. This marriage makes Luke very happy. He is so different from my ex-husband. My daughters and I benefit from his kindness. And for some reason, I don't worry about the future. Having lived through a divorce with kids and remarriage, I know my own strengths."

It seems that a many times married woman may not subscribe to the conventional definition of marriage, specifically that it lasts forever. Rather, she may put the concept of marriage only in the present. A woman who wants to become a second wife repeatedly is a new phenomenon. "Lots of women today live in a fantasy world," says Dr. Ronnie Burak, "and believe that if they just find the right man, it's going to be better this time. Unfortunately, how a woman's next marriage works out has more to do with who she is than who the man is that she finds."

Linda has been a second wife three times. "My first marriage lasted seven years and my second marriage lasted for thirteen years. Now I'm forty and my husband, Charles, and I have two children together. Although my husband had no children with his first wife, I'd always felt connected to her. I did not want to be, but I was. Charles and I had many arguments about her. I never felt so threatened by an ex-wife before. Of all my marriages, I look at this one as the most complicated in terms of the past. I remind myself that I am mature. I've been around. Eventually, I fell in step with my husband, more in step and bound to him than his ex-wife was. We have two children together and have gone way beyond what their marriage was about. We both really want this marriage to succeed."

THE CHALLENGE OF BAGGAGE
- Neither of you has gone scot-free
- You understand each other's issues
- How many times can one really be a second wife?
- Optimally, neither partner is easily daunted nor discouraged

Experience teaches and ripens all of us, but for those in the roles of second wives it is essential. My research brought out that a second wife who had already been a second wife has learned how to listen to her husband and is less dissuaded by the usual intimations. In many cases, her self-confidence is impressive. She is able to contour the marriage to please her, all the while keeping her husband satisfied.

Dr. Donald Cohen views the many times married second wife as practiced. "She knows that she has been around, so has her partner. In this sense, there is no question of self-esteem. They are on equal footing. Neither the often married second wife nor her husband is threatened by the past."

THE PERPETUAL SEARCH
Some women who have philosophical views of marriage become many times married second wives. These women define the latest marriage as the one that fits best and suits this stage in her life.

There are famed second wives who have had previous marriages. One notable public second wife, Jacqueline Kennedy Onassis, who married Aristotle Onassis in 1968, took on her role with dignity and grace. The marriage was viewed with great curiosity by the eyes of the world. When Steven Spielberg, director of *Saving Private Ryan* and *Schindler's List*, married actress, Kate Capshaw, both were previously divorced. Both brought to their marriage children from their previous marriages. Their marriage has not only endured, but both partners extol its happiness.

Other examples of famous second wives abound, some successful, some not. Ali McGraw was married to producer Bob Evans before she became actor Steve McQueen's second wife in 1973. His first wife, Neile Adams, told the press that she approved of his choice. McQueen had fallen in love with McGraw on a movie set, where they both had leading roles in the current production. After they were married, he would not allow her to work on a project without him. Both McGraw and McQueen brought children to their second marriage. One of the most well-known examples of a love affair between an actress and leading man resulting in marriage remains Elizabeth Taylor's relationship with Richard Burton. Not only was she his second wife twice, but she has been married a total of eight times.

Many times married second wives recognize the importance of common values in a marriage; an idea they may not have focused on the first time around. Unfortunately, the first marriage usually occurs when a woman is young, naïve, and full of romantic notions. She may not be considering how compatible she and her fiance are or whether they truly share common goals and values when she is choosing a wedding dress and planning her dream day. The second time around, she is seasoned and has a better idea of who she is, who she wants to be with, and how to make a marriage work.

BETTER CONNECTIONS
Contrasting a previous marriage sheds light on the present marriage.
The idea is not to attempt to change one's partner but to compromise.
Working toward a common goal, after a negative experience, makes
for better connections and success.

Michelle has been a second wife twice. "Both my husbands
came from another culture and both were ten years older than me. Even
though both men are older, my current marriage is so different than my
first. We have two children together and that changes everything. I knew
my husband, Ivan, and his ex-wife, Natalie, because I worked at a small,
family owned business and Ivan was my boss and Natalie worked with
us. I was young and married at the time, but still he flirted with me. I
think that my ex-husband, who was my husband then, was having an
affair. Ivan initiated our affair as a way for us both to get out of
unhappy marriages. I began to see there was another world out there. I
would not have thought of leaving my first husband until I met my second. He gave me the courage to go.

"I know how upset Natalie was when she learned about the
affair. She did not want to get divorced. Ivan was not a great husband
to Natalie, I know this. I don't think he ever really loved her. Ours was
a love affair. But the whole story was that she couldn't have children.
Maybe in the back of his mind he might have wanted the option. Maybe
that was partly why he left. Both of us had been through difficult times,
having been married before. And despite the fact that our affair is not
something we are proud of, it brought us to the right place. How can
either of us compare what we had before to the richness of our children
and the full life that we now share? What I also realize is that ours is a
more social life and that Ivan had a quieter life with his ex-wife. He likes
to go out with me, and we are surrounded by people who are bright, successful, and interesting. But when it's over, he likes to be comforted at
home. I know that Ivan needed some of what his ex-wife gave him, but
it wasn't enough. I fill in those gaps. For him, being married to Natalie
was existing, but with me, it's really living."

Although society often prides itself on puritanical ethics con-
demning infidelity, affairs are rampant. While most would agree that it
is not right to cheat on one's spouse, infidelity may indicate deeper
problems in a troubled marriage. When a marriage is joyless, often it is
an affair that provides the catalyst for a spouse to divorce and begin

another kind of life. However, there is a downside, even for the individuals having the affair. For the two lovers who intend to leave their marriage and become spouses, trust becomes a recurring issue. The second wife who once had no qualms as his lover, begins to judge her husband differently. His credibility and her fortitude ebb away. After all, she thinks, if he did it with me, he could do it again with someone else.

AFFAIRS AS WAKE UP CALLS
An affair may prove to be the only means for some people to leave an unhappy marriage. The question then becomes, can the same players in the second marriage be trusted?

"In a situation where both partners have been married at least once before, the issue of trust does not extend only to affairs. The question becomes, if this man has left a wife or two already, he is capable of doing it again. How can I truly be safe here?" remarks Dr. Ronnie Burak. "And of course, it is problematic in a society where couples do divorce, remarry, and divorce again. Both partners have to know one another extremely well and believe that this marriage is the final one."

TRUST AND THE SECOND WIFE
• If he did it to his first wife, will he do it to you?
• Was it purely a matter of circumstances?
• Did he ever do it before?
• Do you believe you satisfy each other?

If this brand of second wife is in search of love at all costs, it is passion that she seeks out and craves. When it falters, she moves on. Having survived at least one poor marriage, such a woman is motivated to find true love. Instead of becoming cynical with age this second wife may become a romantic with a very practical side. She believes that she is entitled to have it all and that she is able to find someone who will meet these requirements.

This view of entitlement may have positive results. Eileen left an unhappy first marriage to begin again as a second wife. "I was very aware of my husband Lionel's past from the start. I had been married too, but had no children. We met within a year of our divorces. His ex-wife, Davida, was remarried by the time that we got together. If Davida had been single, I know our relationship would have been very difficult.

I don't pretend for a minute that Davida didn't have some kind of hold over my husband and I give her credit for taking care of her own needs. I admire the fact that she went on immediately with her own life. And of course, I am always aware of how Lionel feels about me. My husband compares me to her and is so grateful for the life we have together. He is not jealous of my ex-husband and we never talk about what could have been; we talk about how lucky we are to have found each other. But I know that if I had ended up with the wrong partner again I would have become very fragile and withdrawn. I think that I have blossomed in mid-life by finding the right partner. I know that I needed to be loved and romanced as Lionel loves me and it works."

If a woman's ego is beaten down by her marriage, as much as she yearns for independence, she may be too insecure to feel good about another relationship. For most people, especially women, divorce is a loss of hope and stability and may cause them to lose their faith. A woman may then give up on any chance for a new start. On the other hand, a second wife who is expecting a new life and planning it, will seek out a partner who encourages her. She can focus on this new relationship without getting mired in her own past mistakes. This woman is self-assured, strong, and will undoubtedly finds happiness.

INSECURE
The more marriages that someone has, the more insecure she may be when she gets involved with the next partner. For her, absolutes no longer exist and there are no guarantees.

VERSUS

SECURE
The second wife who comes with her own set of life experiences is a better listener and is more aware of what her husband needs. She is curious about the ex-wife but not intimidated by her. She knows what she wants and goes for it. She is bound to make a success of her next marriage.

In my research, I found that many times married second wives speak of being more appreciated by their husbands and of tolerance levels that did not exist in their previous marriages. This breed of second wife is not intimidated by comparisons made to their husbands' first wives. Rather, they see what the strengths and weaknesses were and feel that they have won. The self-confidence of a second wife of this type covers all aspects of the relationship, from sex to friendship. It is a support system that was often lacking in the past. In return, the seasoned second wife offers unrelenting love.

One such seasoned second wife, Rhonda, tells us, "With my husband William's first wife, everything was guided along and there was no time to stop and consider anything. William is more in love with me and he can be himself in our marriage. If he decided to stop practicing law to be an artist—which is a hobby of his—I'd be supportive. I don't believe that his ex-wife could have handled it. She would have questioned William about a choice like that, because everything in their marriage was for show. I am not like that. And he carefully sought me out for this reason.

"My husband has become less immature through his divorce and his subsequent dating. I think by the time William met me he really understood what counted for him. We rarely speak of his past marriage or of mine. I do remember being very disturbed in my past marriage that my husband had been married before. In this marriage, I could not care less. I once saw a picture of William and his first wife and I found it incomprehensible that he was with someone so different than myself. You could almost tell from the photograph that her values and mine were not the same. In a strange way, this made me all the more comfortable with my place. I know I give William what he needs."

Just as there are many times married second wives who find themselves with men who have not yet faced the problems of their first marriages, there are second wives with ghosts of their own. A second wife who does not reveal everything about her first marriage may be wise. While she may tell her husband the most important things that happened, the subject should be put to rest after that. In many marriages where both partners have been married before, there is a required healing process. It is very rewarding when the two partners can be a part of this evolution for each other. Viewing their new marriage on another plane is the solution.

REALISTIC EXPECTATIONS
- **Do not bring past injuries to the present marriage**
- **A whole and healed psyche makes for reality**
- **Strength comes from experience**

Rebecca is married to Arthur, who has two stepchildren and two biological children from his first marriage. "Arthur was so certain about marrying me and I had been a second wife twice already, with one child and one stepchild. I know that there is commitment here, because we have had to wade through the muck to get there. Both of us have been in unhappy marriages and had lots of complications with children to add to them. There were numerous times when the children could have brought insurmountable problems. But both of us promised that nothing would come between us and what we share is an amazing attachment to each other.

"Sometimes our life is a zoo and we are crazed with all these kids. Other times we are alone and our life is romantic and tranquil. I know we both need a lot of sex and passion in this marriage. Sex was missing in my former marriages and I was so tired and so busy holding things together that I didn't even notice. With Arthur, I've been taught to really appreciate our physical connection and to see how magical it is. What doesn't matter is that we have taken vows before or that we've made mistakes before. What matters is that we have gotten it right this time. It isn't one sided; the marriage works for both of us."

SUCCESSFUL SEX
Sex is extremely important after a marriage where sex might not have existed. An emotional connection leads to a better sexual connection. Sex becomes unencumbered, free of inhibitions.

Although many women who remain single have had multiple partners, it may not be quite as obvious as when a woman has been married several times. The new husband's confidence could be threatened by his new wife's past. He may be plagued with doubt as to the strength of their relationship. Sex is a valuable expression of the new marriage. The husband profits when he believes in his second wife's commitment.

SEX AND TRUST
If the second wife is the experienced one, her husband may not trust her. Then the sex is not as open and free as it should be because he does not feel secure and stable. He may become jealous and suspicious after the marriage, plying her with questions such as, when are you coming home, where have you been?

Another scenario that surfaced is that for the many times married second wife there is a choice of living one of two ways, my interviewees revealed. The past has brought the second wife into the present and she has a keen resolution to make it work. When a marriage or even two has failed, a woman's self-esteem may be on the line. She may begin to doubt herself and her ability to be successfully married. Or she may become stronger and more self-aware, able to discard a relationship that does not suit her needs. In the optimal case, when she remarries, it is with the understanding that she is there for the right reasons.

Liz had three children from her first marriage when she remarried. "I put up with a terrible marriage before I got divorced. I ended up marrying a man who also had three children, along with a difficult ex-wife. Robin lives less than an hour from us. I've had plenty of interaction with her over the years. I even knew her in high school. My husband, Jeff, is several years older than we are and I remember when Robin used to go out with him. By the time he and I got together, Robin was already with someone else. There was a custody/visitation issue and my husband got custody of the kids. Jeff foolishly changed his mind and gave Robin custody, thinking she'd be a good mother. The problem was not only her mothering, but her jealousy of my husband and me. What Robin envied, although she had a relationship, was our solid marriage and the money that had come to my husband after they divorced. Things got much worse when Robin broke up with her boyfriend.

"What I did was ignore Robin and try to be very patient. I had learned this in my first marriage and the training helped me in my new marriage. Eventually, things became less volatile.

"Because our children were all the same ages, the discrepancy in how they were raised was quite apparent. I am very religious and Robin had no religious belief at all. However, over the years I've mellowed toward her. She has mellowed toward me too. We are all in our fifties now and the children are grown up. Today, twenty years later, I look back on those weekends with six kids, ages five to ten, and I can't believe that I got through them. As a second wife with six kids between us, I know that it takes exceptional people to undertake what we did. We never had what one has in a first marriage together, the quietness and the building of a life. But we have had stability in the relationship and financial security because we both worked. There is no real reason to complain."

To Liz, after twenty years as a second wife, her husband's first marriage seems less formidable although their common ties persist. Now, it manifests itself in the form of the stepchildren's children. Both Liz and Robin are thrilled to have babies and young children in their lives. The grandmothering has become a common denominator and there is less negativity toward one another.

TIES THAT BIND
When the children are small and the first wife is a constant shadow, the second wife does not anticipate a future of stepgrandchildren. When the day comes, she realizes she and the first wife are inextricably tied through the children. But time has softened old anger and hostility has lessened or disappeared.

Some women I interviewed complained that before they reached their fifties or sixties and became stepgrandmothers, there was a struggle to hold their second marriages together. Continually, it was being tested by visible ex-wives and the trials of stepmothering. *Psychology Today* reports that it requires three to five years for a blended family to acclimate to new members and a new environment. During this transitional phase, the second wife often endures the first wife, whose personality and beliefs are reflected in how she treats her children and her ex-husband.

For Beth, her husband Dan's first wife's state of mind greatly affected her stepchildren and even her husband. "When Dan's first wife, Nadine, broke up with her second husband, we all shuddered. Nadine called my husband at the office and wept. Dan liked it much better when she was happy and set financially. Then Dan's two children arrived on the weekend, hysterical because their mother had made them so crazy. Nadine had dragged them into her drama. This was a lot of interference for me, even though she and her husband eventually got back together.

"In addition, my own story was complicated. First, I was divorced from the man who had been my college boyfriend, without any children. Then I remarried and was widowed. My husband who died had been married before and had one child from his first marriage, but she lived with her mother. Maybe because I was widowed it was easier for my current husband. There was no one lurking, offering unsolicited opinions and interfering. Things were so tense with his ex-wife I sometimes didn't think we'd make it. The stress did not bring out the best in my husband.

"Despite how I felt at the start about his ex-wife, I began to see Nadine's issues with him. Dan could be stubborn and he was not the best listener. He didn't always do what was best for his children and paid her support late, which really bothered me. After a while, Nadine called the house and made arrangements directly through me for the children. She and I had similar thoughts about what the kids needed on the weekends and how to handle their schoolwork. It became much calmer once he wasn't involved.

"I tolerate his first wife for my husband's sake and for the sake of his children. I wish her the best, because I really do know how difficult it is to have a marriage which, from it's first day, must cope with children. She has the same problems I have with my husband with her own new husband. It goes on and on. We all need to help each other."

"What happens eventually is that the families become blended and people have to work very hard at making these relationships work," explains Dr. Michele Kasson. "And when people make the effort, they will reap the benefits of cooperative relationships. Over time, the first wife's hurt and disappointment from the loss of the first marriage and the anger toward the ex-spouse and new partner can be resolved. The second wife may begin to see what the ex-wife felt in certain instances. Each woman may implicitly recognize the similarities and differences of her relationship with the same man. The second wife gains knowledge that the first wife possessed earlier."

I found that the empathy the second wife has for the first is usually cumulative. A big part of it has to do with how the second wife treats the children. After a second wife has spent enough weekends with her stepchildren, she knows how trying it can be. Peace at any cost becomes a mantra, and to this end, she wants her husband to deliver payments to his first wife on time and to be amenable to the first wife's requests, within reason. At the same time, the second wife hopes this woman will find a partner and develop a new life of her own.

RARE EMPATHY
- The second wife recognizes the first wife's frustrations with her husband
- She appreciates how the first treats the children
- The second wife acknowledges how difficult the children can be
- The second wife wants the first wife's new marriage or relationship to work as much as she does her own

Cecelia, at thirty-five, is the mother of two children, one from her first marriage and the other from a long term live-in relationship. "My first husband, Russell, was married before and had a young child who I took care of. I had to deal with Russell's ex-wife because of their child. Jody was selfish, irresponsible, and inconsiderate. One summer, when their son was very small, only four or so, Jody left him for six weeks at our house and never even called. While I did not think of their son as mine, I felt a responsibility toward him. Russell's marriage to the boy's mother had never been good. He stopped trying to fix their relationship once I fell in love with him. I understood what had happened with Jody and I saw how their child suffered for her behavior. I think Jody lost her confidence when Russell stopped paying attention. Then I lost my self-esteem when he did the same to me. In a strange way, I was becoming like Jody. That was what he did to us. By then we had a baby. I thought that at least he was doing well at work. But even that was a lie.

Cecelia had other issues as well. "My parents had been alcoholics, and I stupidly believed that since Russell was not on drugs or alcohol that he was clean. Jody once told me that she too had chosen him because she came from an alcoholic family. What neither of us realized was how destructive he was to women. When I left him, I found a man who was a drug addict. That was how low and lost I was. We had a child together, but I knew not to marry him. I pulled away and slowly built myself up. I found a stable partner, who I married after I was able to make the commitment to be stable and strong myself.

"My current husband is wonderful, but he has his own past problems also—his unhealthy obsession with his ex-wife, his guilt ridden over-indulgence of his daughter, and his constantly interfering mother. He has had a life of pain and his marriage was torture for him. We both come from too much bad stuff. But I love him. I believe that I can make him happy."

Another downside of a loaded past is that it is not easy to go forward so encumbered. If Cecelia is ambitious and she and her husband share a commitment to go forward together to preserve their new marriage, they can make it happen. Yet before she remarries, any doubts that exist for a second wife who has a history of stepchildren, children, and exes, ought to be considered seriously.

LOADED PASTS

When there are so many players from the past imposing on the future, it is up to the second wife and her husband to set the boundaries. If the second wife is uncertain about any aspect of the marriage, it will take its toll. Self-exploration before the second marriage happens is the best defense.

Marie knew what went wrong in her first marriage yet found herself facing the same problems in her second. "Both ex-wives have detested me. The first thought that I had stolen her husband. I was divorced and he was not when we met. She said that I gave him the impetus to do it. The truth is, he was already planning to end the marriage whether she knew it or not. She was very bitter. After we married, he traveled a lot and I hardly ever saw him. Between that and his ex-wife, our marriage just couldn't survive. On the other hand, in my situation with my current husband Frank's ex-wife, she did not even want to be married to Frank. She remarried immediately and then wanted to be free again. She divorced again and remarried again. I understood her in some strange fashion. And there have been moments when I've been with the children—his, mine, ours—and I've thought of her. I can identify with her complaints. I know that Frank was never home at night for her. I had that complaint about my first husband and Frank promised me it would be different in our marriage. And since his work had changed, I believed him. But it turns out that Frank also travels and is not home at night with me. I cannot believe I am alone again at home with the children."

RED FLAGS

Women who come with a history often end up with men with complicated histories. If only women would listen closely to these men, they could decide intelligently before they become the man's second wife.

The second wife who lacks clarity after her divorce will inevitably choose the wrong partner for the wrong reasons and is apt to repeat her first mistakes. In Marie's case, she found herself reliving her first marriage: home alone with the children, her husband never around.

The savvy many times married second wife is one who has already disentangled herself from one failed marriage, committed to not making the same mistake twice after all she has endured. She has looked within herself and knows what she wants. While she may attract a man with a similar tale to hers, she is able to decipher if he is truly remarriage material or not.

WHO CONFUSED SECOND WIVES CHOOSE
- Men who need them
- Men who have and need power and status
- Men who appear to be unlike their past mates

WHO THEY END UP MARRYING
- Men who dominate
- Men who want mothers for their children
- Men who on the surface seem different but underneath are very similar to their first husbands

Five years ago, Nina was remarried. "Not having stepchildren was the saving grace of my marriage. I knew that with my own child to bring into the marriage, it was too demanding if he also had children. His ex-wife, Connie, lives here in St. Louis, two streets away, and that is enough for me. Connie did not want to give up her marriage to my husband, Leo, for anything. One of the biggest issues between Leo and Connie was the fact that she wanted to, but could not get pregnant. The pressure was tremendous, and after a while, he couldn't take her complaints and demands. She wanted a child, she wanted things her way, and he wanted out.

"She and I are the opposite, although we are the same age and are both athletic. I believe this marriage works because I do not pressure my husband; instead I make life easier. I don't push him on the subject of my child unless he wants to spend time with us, and I don't make financial or social requests. The one thing she wanted besides having a baby was to have status. Connie is an accountant and she quickly remarried another accountant. I know that my husband could not give her what she wanted. On the other hand, I am very happy with our lifestyle, and he loves the fact that I already have my own child so the pressure to have children is off. This is a second marriage where both of us have our needs met. Not a day goes by without him expressing his gratitude in some way. And for me, I take the faults of my first marriage and see that this marriage doesn't have the same problems. In other words, I have learned from my mistakes. And so has my husband. The key in a second marriage is to not end up with the same type of person as the previous spouse, but a person who is better suited to you. I'm thrilled that we were both married before, it means we come from a similar place."

In midlife, one's self-awareness is heightened; a second wife takes the sum of her experience and puts it to good use in her new marriage. A previously married second wife offers her partner a second chance with an acute sense of commitment and desire for success. Maturity and self-knowledge create the right ingredients for a successful second marriage. Regardless of where one has been, it is never too late to start over, to have a second chance. When there are more factors involved, the second wife operates from self-awareness and self-confidence.

Of the many times married second wives interviewed, three-quarters felt they had made the right decision in marrying the men whom they are married to. The emotional limitations of the past marriages did not plague their new marriages. Only one-quarter of the interviewees hesitated on the issue of trust with their husbands and expressed any doubts. As many times married second wives, they saw themselves immersed in repeat performances of their previous marriages. Yet they did not want to be divorced again, hoping instead to work on the marriage and solve their problems.

The National Center for Health Statistics reported in its research study that the average age of men divorcing after the first marriage was thirty-five and for women it was thirty-three. The average age for men divorcing after their second marriage was forty-two and for women it was thirty-nine. Thus, for the many times married second wife, her second marriage represents the second half of her life. The young married couple who did not make it is long gone and the woman has since had the chance, hopefully, to mature and become self-aware and self-sufficient. Her children are not babies and she has survived a divorce. The new marriage is not about children or careers, but about the couple and companionship. She is prepared for life and ready to commit to the man she loves.

PART TWO

ENTERING THE ARENA

CHAPTER SEVEN

INEXPERIENCED WOMEN/ SEASONED MEN

Nell, who is thirty-nine, is a second wife to Joel, a man twelve years her senior. "I wanted to know every detail of his first marriage, but Joel was reluctant to discuss anything. He wanted to put it all behind him. I was dying for information, to the point that I began to ask his relatives about his first wife. They described his ex-wife, Patricia, as attractive and confident—someone who never hesitated. I wanted to know more and couldn't uncover it. I had this confessional attitude about my former lover and his first wife, but my husband didn't approve of that. Once the divorce was final, my husband asked Patricia to give up her name, but she wouldn't. Joel wanted her to give back his grandmother's ring for sentimental reasons and he offered to pay for it, but she refused. I couldn't imagine what this woman was like, based on so few facts.

"There were no children from Joel's first marriage and no lingering attachment. But it bothered me that his first wife was more accomplished than I was when I got married. What was noticeably different about us was our education. Patricia was in finance, like my husband, and very well educated. I think it haunted me and made me feel inadequate. I understood their attraction to each other, but I also knew they made each other miserable. This information empowered me. I knew Joel made a mistake and didn't want another. He is competitive and success oriented; he needed to win me and keep me."

The acute sense of being a second wife does not dissipate with time, according to my research. In certain ways it is a painful, lifelong label to which second wives have acceded. While many women begin their marriages as fresh brides with equally fresh grooms, second wives never had that opportunity. Instead, they walk into a role that was designated. There is no choice but to be the second bride, the second wife. Whether age is a factor in how being a second wife affects a woman is an unresolved question. A young and vulnerable second wife may be very surprised by the repercussions of her husband's first marriage. Most women, whether young or mature, have certain reservations, particularly when it is their first marriage and his second.

If her husband's first marriage was without children, it is obviously more ideal for a first time second wife. However, it is the history of the first marriage, which had once succeeded but ultimately failed, that casts a spell upon the new marriage. One second wife reported that on the day her husband proposed, he requested that until he had announced the engagement to his ex-wife, he didn't want anyone else to know. Not even his future second wife's parents were to be told. Although this second wife felt hurt and confused, she held fast to the knowledge that she was going to be his second wife—*wasn't that enough?* she asked herself.

In a society that perpetuates the goal of marriage, even as we fall short at the task, the concept of being successful, even the second time around, is notable. If a man has been married for a number of years and then divorces, there are long term habits and a history with the first wife that have formed. The second wife might have to contend with her husband's attachment to his first wife's style. His ability to adjust well to his new life and the second wife's optimistic manner are valuable to the second marriage.

WHO WAS SHE?
• His high school sweetheart
• His college sweetheart
• The first woman he met in the workplace
• Someone who was there at the right time
• An infatuation

Almost every second wife I encountered has a perverse curiosity about the first. The never married second wife is even more intrigued with her predecessor than seasoned second wives. Information helps the second wife feel comfortable with her own status in the new marriage. If the first wife was a girlfriend from high school, college, or graduate school, she and her husband might have grown apart with time. If she was a working woman, competition over career success or paycheck size may have driven them apart. If their relationship was based more on lust than love, then the marriage may have worn thin for lack of substance. In any instance, when he entered his first marriage, the husband was younger, less worldly, and less self-aware than he is now going into a second marriage. Whether she is a younger woman or a contemporary, the second wife who has never been married is fresh and filled with hope—which her appreciative husband benefits from.

WHO IS SHE?
- A younger woman
- A contemporary
- Someone from the workplace
- Someone from his past
- The one who offers a new life

Second wives fear that if they are similar to the first, they are interchangeable. If they are opposites, the role of second wife is less threatening. Second wives who were never married before may feel more jealous of the first wife than those who have already had a wedding and/or children. The never married second wife is stripped of any opportunity in which she is first.

As Alicia tells it, "When I was planning my wedding, I was well aware of the fact that my husband had gone through the entire process already. When my future brother in-law suggested that his daughter be a part of the wedding party, I refused, on the grounds that my guests would mistake these children for my husband's. Randy was ten years older than I and could well have had children that age. In retrospect, I recognize my viewpoint was one of a very young, callow girl who was catapulted into the arena of a second wife. When we walked through stores looking for silver and place settings, I wondered if this was what Randy had done the first time around.

"To make it worse, my husband had not cleaned out all of his ex-wife's belongings from the house they shared and in which he still lived when I met him. We lived there for the first two years of our marriage and then I couldn't take it anymore. I wasn't feeling any better about it, because I kept finding Sara's stuff. It was as if Sara moved out, leaving her belongings, knowing how aggravating it would be for the second wife to discover things like her manicure set, her nightgowns, and her stockings in a bottom drawer. After I found her yoga books and books on how to make a marriage work, I began to wonder what had gone wrong. I blame my husband for not paying more attention to my needs in this regard and for taking it for granted that I could handle Sara's residual presence. An older woman in my place might have known what to do. I was too inexperienced. I only knew that she should not have left evidence and he should have cared about it for my sake."

SIGNS THAT A FIRST MARRIAGE IS FAILING
• No longer are there shared goals
• The intimacy is missing
• One partner suffers a mid-life crisis
• Career choices conflict, physical separation may ensue
• An extramarital affair evolves
• Financial differences escalate

The psychological divorce happens in many cases long before the actual divorce occurs. Many husbands hesitate to facilitate the official divorce because of the children. In retrospect, some ex-spouses may admit the marriage did not bode well from the start. Whatever joint decisions are made in terms of life objectives and motives, in a failed marriage, they ebb away. A lack of intimacy is another sign of a marriage gone awry. If the marriage lacks intimacy and common goals, it will be on shaky ground. Career choices can drive the relationship further apart logistically or emotionally. Often an affair ensues because the marriage is not satisfactory. When the husband divorces and marries for a second time, he has most likely thought about his needs. Either he has been in therapy or has done enough soul searching to find someone who complements him. If he is marrying a second time, he believes in marriage despite the fact that his first failed. Sometimes, if he is childless, he chooses a younger second wife to have the family he yearns for.

THE MAN WHO CHOOSES A NEVER MARRIED SECOND WIFE
He is often older by a substantial number of years than his second wife. He wants a trophy. He married too young the first time, without understanding his needs. He is now ready for a second chance. He does not have, yet wants a family. He believes in the institution of marriage.

Cynthia George, divorce attorney, views the never married second wife as having to contend with her husband's past. "While it certainly does not apply to everyone, there are many younger women marrying older men. The woman may be thirty and he fifty. He's been through a nasty divorce and she's never been married before. He's got all the money and she's got nothing. This man wants a prenuptial agreement to limit his exposure if he goes through another divorce."

The divorce rate today is over fifty percent, with eighty-five percent of divorced men destined to remarry. Forty percent of all marriages in the United States, according to *American Demographics*, involve formerly married individuals. In many other countries, there are similar trends. This translates into a large population of second wives. For those second wives who have not been married before, looking at their husbands' pasts as merely part of the man's history is expedient. This history should to be accepted just as a husband's health or his family of origin is accepted. It is the second wife's confidence in the marriage that keeps it from being threatened by the past.

"The never married first wife definitely suffers the consequences of the 'ghost' more than a second wife who is also divorced," observes Dr. Michele Kasson. "For the second wife who has never had a husband before, it is a constant irritant that her husband had a wife before her."

One never before married second wife, Felice, at the age of thirty-six, has been married for eleven years and has two children with her previously wedded husband. "I have insisted that my husband, Deryk, answer my questions, so I know the positives and negatives of the first wife. My husband describes his marriage to Dina as a mistake from the beginning. He married her because he thought it was the right time to be married. If there was a checklist, she certainly got checked off properly. I learned all this from the start. I wanted to know how Dina and I were similar and how we were different. I do not come from the same background as my husband and we are not the same religion. But

I do think that, physically, his ex-wife and I resemble one another. In the beginning, I thought a lot about her. Then I realized Deryk hadn't stayed with her. We moved beyond her in years and had children. She became less of a threat.

"By the time I met Deryk, he was well over Dina. He explained that she was a cold and envious person; I'm extremely warm and outgoing—just the opposite. There was one incident several years ago when Dina wrote to my husband and explained that she was divorced again and had a child. She was wondering if he was divorced, and could they get together. I resented that she wrote to him; it was very nervy and intrusive. I made this clear to Deryk, but he simply found it amusing. I'd like to think he wrote back and said he is blissfully happy with me.

"I don't care about Dina anymore. I have put her out of my mind. Perhaps I'm wrong, but I think she is the last person on earth I should worry about. There are enough women who would like to be with my husband. He is handsome and successful. I can only concentrate on us; the marriage, the children and day to day life. Deryk becomes annoyed when I make any reference to her, so I don't. It all happened years ago. It may have even helped our own marriage that he tried marriage before and failed."

The never married second wife who achieves a sense of contentment in her place in the marriage does well. Unfortunately, this does not happen overnight. She must try to view the first marriage as a learning lesson for her husband that has made him a better spouse for her. She should also avoid comparisons to his first marriage and ex-wife, focusing instead on her own unique character and the marriage they now share. The husband has influence here—if he reassures and shows her that she is the one who is important to him and that he is happy in the marriage, she gains confidence and the force of the first wife lessens.

COMFORT LEVELS
The state of the second marriage says it all. For a second wife who is extremely confident about her relationship with her husband, the ex-wife is much less of a presence.

"The children and the life I have carved out with my husband makes our marriage strong and steadfast." Michaela reflects, "There have been many occasions during our marriage when I knew why and how I was selected, when I thought that I had brought Roger everything he had dreamed of and more. There are photographs where we stand as a family, the children are in the front line and we, the parents, as anchor, stand united. I know that no one else but me, as his second wife, has brought him these rewards, giving him family.

"I believe that my husband was more than ready to make another commitment and stay for keeps. With me, Roger understood what mattered, what he was looking for. I've been buffered by his experiences and what he learned from them. I never think about his ex-wife, because I'm the one who brought about change."

I learned from my interviewees that having children, especially when the first wife and husband did not, is a solidifier. Now the second wife is elevated to a more superior role than any first wife could have been. The children become the focus of the marriage and the husband is thankful for his wife and family. The never married second wife realizes her accomplishment.

SHIFTING GEARS
After much angst, an event like the birth of a child will trigger the second wife's status to a more secure position. She and her husband will have achieved the ultimate of a connection.

The assurance that the absence of children from the first marriage makes the next marriage less encumbered for the second wife is not always so. Some women have found that first wives still make demands upon their ex-husbands. "If a first wife continually contacts her ex-husband when the divorce is over and finances are settled, there is an unresolved conflict," Dr. Donald Cohen remarks. "How he responds is the key. If he jumps every time she calls, then the marriage is not really over although they are divorced. Boundaries need to be established."

Diane's husband Dwight's ex-wife was getting divorced again and embroiled in a custody battle. "Kara called him constantly. I finally said that I was sorry she was in such turmoil, but that I resented her demands and the energy she required from my husband. Dwight gave her money, which was difficult for us because we have a child and I'm not working at present. When I confronted him, Dwight really didn't have a convincing explanation. My take on it is that he feels so guilty about asking her for a divorce seven years ago that Kara can still wring him out. I am very disheartened that he respects her needs over mine. I've been in therapy for this, but still feel badly. It's quite obvious to me that he feels obligated to her. There's no real solution here since Dwight hasn't figured out which wife he is most responsible to."

Priscilla, who has been married for sixteen years and has three children, describes her husband Jonathan's ex-wife as someone who called whenever she needed help. "If her tires need changing or rotating, the phone rang constantly with Maggie's requests. Her calls were never pleasant. She had an abusive boyfriend and she'd call my husband and asked Jonathan to defend her. The wrong thing was that he would drop everything and go running to her aid. I couldn't stand it.

"Finally, I laid down the law. I told Jonathan that he had to make a choice. I demanded that we were not to be a part of her life and that there was little hope of our having a healthy marriage as long as Maggie kept calling. Thereafter, she carried on one too many times, and even my husband had enough. Although I'm relieved that her interference is over, I resent that my husband couldn't make the break in a more dignified way.

"On Maggie's part, what altered her behavior was when our children were born. Maggie saw that my husband had a family, something they did not share, and she never bothered him again. Before that, I was always conscious of her. Then my images of her began to disintegrate. I was no longer worried about her. And I realized that she was never his friend. I am his friend in every way. I began to see how safe we are together, because we are connected by friendship and trust. He needed that after Maggie's manipulativeness. Everything he offered her, she refused. Jonathan offered kindness and a family life. She wanted none of it. I got what she tossed out. I'm happy that he was married before. I see it as insurance that he now knows what he wants."

A second wife may feel inexperienced in comparison to her seasoned husband, regardless of how often he tells her the relationship works for him. Nonetheless, he may tend to be less romantic, maybe because he has done the romantic route already. The ghost of the first wife lingers inexplicably. The second wife reminds herself of what she has to offer. If the husband compliments his ex-wife in any fashion, i.e., terrific cook or brilliant stockbroker, the second wife is thrown off balance. Conversely, if he complains about his first wife's deficiencies, the second wife feels reassured. She sees that he has learned what he does and doesn't want from his experiences in his first marriage. The fact that he attained this self-awareness and chose to get remarried gives her confidence in herself as his spouse and in their marriage.

CONSIDERATIONS OF HER FIRST/HIS SECOND
- She feels she has missed something sacred by being second
- He is not enamored as she is of romance
- The first wife does not just disappear
- The second wife is the new hope

A famous second wife who recognized her husband's disappointment over his first marriage is Nancy Reagan. Ronald Reagan's marriage to actress Jane Wyman ended because they were incompatible. He was in tremendous pain once she left him. In his role as a divorced man with children, he was not looking to marry again. Nancy, who had not been married, was able to see his wariness and insecurities as unwelcome gifts from his first wife. As he got to know Nancy, Ronald Reagan realized that he could embark on another marriage and find happiness. Although a never married second wife, Nancy Reagan proved herself to be a supportive and devoted second wife long before her husband became President and she became First Lady.

Often it is when a second wife is very young that she fails to comprehend her husband's concerns. A new second wife hears her husband speak of not being able to afford another mistake, and the concept is alien to her. Many young second wives interviewed see their relationship as invincible, and the potential of happiness monumental. Frequently, the thought of making mistakes doesn't cross the young second wife's mind. This may make her blind to problems in the relationship. However, in many cases, this works in her best interest. If she is positive about the outcome, her attitude may have an influence.

"For the first five years of my marriage, whenever I visited my mother-in-law, I poured over stashed away photographs of my husband James' first wife," Andrea confesses. "People who knew Grace described her as striking or outstanding. I only met her once and it was civil and as pleasant as could be expected. We had a mutual friend and ended up at the same party. In retrospect, it was actually good for me. I was able to learn more than I needed to know. I saw her new husband, her children, how she mothered and interacted with people. I understood why my husband had married her and I understood why they were no longer married to each other. As the years have passed, I have come to wonder about her, wonder if what bothers me about him had bothered her. I believe that she resented me, while I initially feared her. But ultimately she was the enemy and I didn't want to identify with her. Besides, she did things that hurt, like sending him cards and calling him. I didn't get it. Wasn't it over, weren't they divorced? Weren't we married?

"The night that Grace announced her engagement to her boyfriend, we opened a bottle of champagne. James was euphoric and quite relieved. There was no money involved with their divorce and no children, but the residue of having made a vow to a life together that later came undone was enough to make him feel responsible. His friends were divided over me in those early years. There were those who felt loyal to Grace, if only in theory, and saw me as the younger trophy wife. Eventually, we staked out our own territory socially and this made for great success. I did not choose my husband because he was a father figure or because James offered a certain lifestyle. Yet I know that when people met us they saw the disparity in our ages and wondered what the attachment was. I explained to close friends and our children that I wanted a life partner and he was the embodiment of all I ever wanted."

Several events, according to the second wives with whom I talked, cause them to stop obsessing over the first. If the first remarries or moves far away, the second wife rejoices. When the first wife has a family with her new husband, this is another cause for celebration. When her marriage develops its own history, the second wife again feels the positive effect.

WHAT SEALS THE SECOND WIFE'S ROLE
• The first wife remarries
• The first wife moves a great distance
• Her own marriage grows stronger
• A child is born to the first wife
• A child is born to the second wife

Above all, the most important factor that helps eclipse the first wife is the second wife's self-confidence. If secure in herself and her marriage, the second wife can avoid fixating on the first and instead see her for what she is: a piece of the past. The second can acknowledge that there was a first while recognizing that she is now in first place. This is not always an easy process.

For Dee, it was difficult to shed the ghost of her husband's ex-wife. "Once, while I was pregnant, we ended up at the same party. I finally understood how Ilene felt about me. I had always suspected she wanted Christopher back. At this party, she made it very clear to me. I was in my eighth month and felt so unattractive and Ilene was quite glamorous. She used the situation to her advantage. She actually flirted with my husband. Then Ilene invited him for a candlelit dinner, and he refused. I was infuriated by her gall, but I also knew then that I was his prize.

"Christopher and I have always been passionate and I know that he cherishes me. Just when I was feeling so good about our marriage, this woman tried to creep back into the picture. I even began to wonder what their sex life had been like. Then I pulled myself together and remembered that he and I have a whole future together."

"Although the second wife has the husband, there is a often competition with the ex-wife," explains Dr. Michele Kasson. "The second wife asks herself, am I better than she is? And then the new wife assuages her own insecurity by reminding herself that she is prettier, younger, smarter, sexier, or whatever. As long as she is confident, she won't feel threatened by this other woman. If, however, the second wife is unsure of herself, the competition persists."

It is normal for the second wife to harbor curiosity about her husband's relationship with his first wife and wonder how she measures up. But these thoughts should not affect the marriage or become all consuming. For the new wife who feels confident, the first wife has no impact on the life that the second wife and her husband share.

Her own insecurities over Jake's first wife caused problems early on for Stephanie. "Jake and I fought over his son, who lived with us. This was really a way of fighting over his wife. I often wished that Jake's son lived with his mother. I really resented her and hoped that she would remarry and get a new life. I remained strong through those rocky first few years until my stepson was on his own by remembering that I was the opposite of her. And I told myself that Jake had left the first marriage; it was our marriage that was important now. With time, everything settled down. But my insecurity took a long time to dissolve.

"I don't know why it all seemed so dire at the time. I regret how I treated my stepson at the beginning. I suppose that our age difference had a lot to do with it. I was twelve years younger than my husband and inexperienced in dealing with children."

Unlike Stephanie, Janet didn't let thoughts of her husband's first wife bother her. "I never felt a moment's insecurity about Dick's first wife," Janet recalls. "I view her as a lovely person and I don't believe that she is bitter about me. I never wanted to be the first wife, and I never thought that I had lost out by being second. My husband had been to one place already and I was a new place, virgin territory. Everything we do is new to us, our home, the life we share, our world together. I look at Dick's first marriage and since there are no children, I view it as a big mistake, as if he merely visited with this woman and then just left. His first marriage was another relationship, except they had a party, which was called a wedding.

"Our marriage was of another order altogether. We planned from the start to build a life together, to travel, to start a family. Whatever happened with the first marriage must have really affected Dick. He is extremely dedicated to ours."

When a second wife does not feel she is competing with her husband's first wife, she trusts her husband implicitly, which stabilizes the marriage. Her message to her husband is such a positive force that any dealing he might have with his ex-wife either ends or has very little meaning and has little or no effect on their marriage.

UNTHREATENED SECOND WIVES
- Give up the competition
- Forget exclusive rights to the relationship
- Toss out his past and any mistrust
- Build stability—it works both ways
- Avoid entanglement between husband and his ex

Brett is a second wife who has managed to be confident in her relationship despite her husband's threatening first wife. "We had an office romance and it was the catalyst for my husband's divorce," Brett confides. "My husband, Larry, left his marriage to marry me after we met at a convention. I understand why his ex-wife, Donna, loathes me and how furious she was. They had two young children and Donna poisoned their minds against me. Even though Donna has a successful career, remarried, and had more children, she was bitter toward me for years. She and Larry would fight and scream at each other. There was so much negative energy. I was gracious because I'd won. I had gotten him. I became the mediator between them. I actually intervened sometimes because of the children, but it made me anxious. I realize that they should never have been married. He hated her world and sought what I offered. I know that the life we share is the one he ought to have had from the start.

"In this marriage, our compatibility in lifestyle is a factor. We are quite similar in our tastes and interests. After the marriage he had, he really appreciates this. All things considered, breaking up a marriage leaves you feeling dirty and, in spite of the great things I get in the relationship with my husband, I know why Donna has hated me all these years. I don't deny the choice we made, but it bothers me."

Sonya admits she wanted very much to be a second wife to Robert. "I no longer wanted to be his girlfriend. We had dated for several years and I wanted the constancy and permanence that marriage represented. Robert's children had seen so many women come and go. I wanted the solidity of being his second wife and the credibility with the children. His ex-wife, Renee, was always a problem, but she's finally moved away. Although my husband did not want to have any more children, we compromised and had one. The way I see it, he has three children and I have one. I love his children, but they are not mine. And now, after twelve years, his children with Renee are grown. There are no longer as many issues. Renee was never a terrible person, but she had a different view of the world. In fact, there is little about my style that coincides with hers."

According to my interviewees, in a never married second wife/ stepmother scenario, with the children living with their mother, there is very little fantasy. This breed of second wife knows these children are not hers and that mothering them is not the right way to go. She is cautious and careful in how she deals with them and many times the connection to the stepchildren succeeds because it is about friendship and not parenting.

NEVER MARRIED SECONDS AND THEIR STEPS
• Stepchildren are never your own
• Strive to be their friend, but not their second mother
• Do not overstep bounds

In addition to dealing with stepchildren, the stigma of being a younger second wife is unfair. People often question what the motivation is when an older man falls in love with a young woman and she finds solace and happiness with him. Friends' tongues wag, relatives gossip, and many disapprove. The questions they toss back and forth include: Is he grasping for reminders of his youth? Is she looking for a father figure or a sugar daddy? What could they possibly have in common?

Notorious, younger second wives abound in the present and past. Joe DiMaggio's love affair with Marilyn Monroe began partly because of his unhappy marriage to Dorothy Arnold. Although Dorothy Arnold claimed she only wanted what was best for her ex-husband, she stated it did not include a blonde who was more glamorous than she. She was furious that DiMaggio took up with Marilyn Monroe. To retaliate, she attempted to end his child visitation rights and increase his child support payments. What was ironic was what these two women had in common: marriage to a man who could not succeed at it. Twice DiMaggio chose women who desired careers and had strong wills. What would have worked for DiMaggio was a wife who prized domestic routine, putting him first and her own needs second. While he battled both wives' aspirations versus his desire for a combination of beauty and traditional domesticity, it was Marilyn Monroe's celebrity status that raised the stakes.

Plentiful are the successful marriages between older men and young first-time second wives. Some older men see a young woman as someone to mold into their ideal dream wife, whether that is a house-wife, a replication of their first wife without her faults, or someone completely different. Beware a husband who hopes the second wife will have the same style as his first. This may extend to places where the first liked to vacation, stores she liked to shop in and restaurants she liked to frequent. Second wives who listen closely when their husbands talk about what went wrong in the first marriage may profit from the information.

HUSBANDS WHO DO REPEAT PERFORMANCES
- Did you discover that even the suite at the resort is from his past life?
- Does he tell you what to do even after admitting this attitude was the demise of his first marriage?
- Has he never addressed what went wrong the first time?
- Does he admit that intimacy is an issue for him?

Often closely associated with the younger second wife stigma is the belief that she is looking for a father figure in her older husband. If this is the case, the second wife risks outgrowing her husband as the years pass. Unless the projections are kept in equilibrium, the relationship will not survive. The second marriage with a significantly younger, never married second wife may become a parent/child situation for a period of time. Eventually, the second wife needs to break free and stake out her own role as a wife and individual.

Tanya has been a second wife for twelve years, and is seventeen years younger than her husband, Kevin. "I understood my motivations from the start. I saw the whole package immediately. He had been divorced for over fifteen years when we met and he was ready. His ex-wife saw me as similar to her, a younger version of herself. I think she flatters herself. We are not alike. I was too secure to wish that Kevin hadn't been married before or that I was the first woman who walked into his life. I know that his ex-wife begrudges me the material things I have. But I've given my husband a new chance.

"When we first married, I looked to him for advice and support, but now I'm very independent and strong. I knew that he was older when we married, and I was happy about that. But as time marches on, the difference in our ages is becoming more apparent. I'm in my forties, and he's in his sixties. That's a big gap that didn't seem so big when I was younger and yearning to be with an experienced older man. The lifestyle he was able to offer appealed to me from day one. I still love my husband, but out relationship has changed. We are equals now. It is no longer him providing for me or taking care of me—we take care of each other."

Like Tanya, Elisabeth initially sought shelter in her role as a second wife to Carl. "I needed to be taken care of. My father had died when I was very young. I thought that my husband would provide me with what was missing. Instead, we lived above our means. There were cars, endless trips, jewelry. I had viewed him as a father figure and I was devastated when this image didn't work for me any longer. What I began to see was that Carl had a pattern of being with younger women and pampering them. He had severe emotional problems and the pampering gave the recipient a false sense of security.

"Carl and his ex-wife, Wanda, had lived together for a long while before they finally married. We did the same thing. Wanda and I were even similar in looks: tall and dark. What was different was how he took care of me. He did a better job with me than with her. But we broke up so many times during the marriage and he cheated on me, just as he'd done with her. They'd have these big scenes and then they'd reconcile. Carl expected me to do the same, but I was not like that. Carl was in the music business. I began to take comfort in material things, such as the house he poured money into. It was supposed to be in my name. That was the security that he had promised. But Carl lied about the house being in my name. I began to understand how his first wife felt being lied to and cheated on. I began to be sympathetic.

"I left Carl when he refused to put our home in both our names. I saw that he was treating me exactly as he'd treated his first wife. I was devastated. We went back and forth for a long while. I started to know exactly what Wanda had gone through. It was a revelation for me. He was incapable of being an adult. Any stability I thought I had was a farce."

It is never wise to go looking for a father in your husband. Trust and marital stability come from common goals and values. While you can share these with an older man, you cannot expect to share them when you see him as a security blanket and he sees you as almost his child. This type of relationship puts him in a superior position, a fact you will likely discover and be unhappy about as you mature. In addition, a man who chooses to get involved in this type of relationship likely enjoys all aspects of it, including the power and superiority that come with this position. The more the young wife matures and grows, developing self-confidence along the way, the less she needs such a relationship. At that point, the marriage beings to unravel. The husband who displays dysfunction in his second marriage likely carried the behavior over from his first marriage. If this is the case, the second wife empathizes with the first wife. This new empathy and understanding provide even more clarity enabling her to recognize the marital problems and consider her options. She then asks herself: *Are these problems fixable or should I move on?*

AVOID DYSFUNCTION
As the second wife matures, she develops confidence and a sense of self. She wants to be on more equal footing with her husband. Yet he wants to continue to be her "daddy." A marriage based on misplaced emotions and distorted relationships is doomed to failure.

Another problem that a never before married second wife faces is an ex-wife whose past and/or current manipulative or cruel behavior continues to affect her husband. The second wife sees the damage this ex-wife inflicts but since she is inexperienced, she may not know how to handle the situation.

Marcia's husband refused to marry her for six years because of his miserable first marriage. "Although I had hoped to be married sooner, I respected Dean's ordeal. My husband described his ex-wife as a woman who was the greatest con artist on earth. I had such a difficult time proving myself to him because she had screwed him over royally. Phoebe was several years older and a manipulator. At their wedding, she announced her pregnancy, blowing his mind. I know that he postponed marrying me because of his experience with her. I hate Phoebe for what she put him through.

"On the other hand, I think that the second time around, there is more energy and more of a commitment. I am still curious about Phoebe. I would love to be a fly on the wall when she and my husband meet. I would love to hear her and watch how she manipulates him. I wish I could help him. I wish I could undo what she does to him. It bothers me terribly that they are connected because of their child. I get through it by reminding myself that I am the future, the choice, and the new life."

Vivian is another second wife whose husband's ex will not let go. "I recall the year when I became relatively secure," Vivian reveals, "the year my husband's ex-wife remarried. There wasn't room in our child-laden world for this phantasm. Jillian, my husband Glenn's first wife, was in her own territory with her new husband by then. Still, Jillian approached my husband for specific reasons, such as work related questions. Later, there was a crisis in Jillian's life: her second divorce. When her role as second wife tumbled, she leaned heavily upon my husband. I think she wanted him back. By then, I knew Glenn's shortcomings. What I have always wondered is if she and I could have met before I was married, if we could have been honest about who Glenn was to us and who we were to each other. But I knew that Jillian's loyalty could never extend to me. I know this because when I announced that I wanted a divorce, that first wife of my husband's, the woman he had promised me years before would never be in the picture, was the first person he ran to for solace."

When either the first wife or husband leave behind unfinished business, the concerns of the first marriage appear in the second. It then becomes a triangle between the first wife, the husband, and second wife. The first wife/never married second wife/husband triangle is worsened because the second wife is so absorbed with the image of the first. The husband's connection to the first wife may or may not be through children. In either case, the responsibility of the husband is to sever his ties to the past and concentrate on his present and future.

With that, his second wife will feel more secure and it is only then that she can go forward.

THE TRIANGLE
The husband unwittingly creates a triangle by keeping in touch with his first wife. Whether there are children involved or not, he must put his past behind him and make his second wife his number one priority.

Of the never married second wives interviewed, they related that their anxiety manifested itself in the following ways: feeling threatened by the first wife's career, being upset by similarities to the first wife's appearance, annoyance over the interference of stepchildren, and dissatisfaction with their husbands' attachment to their former wives. Sadly, less than one-fifth of the interviewees felt completely confident and had no interest in their husband's first marriages or their first wives. However, there may still be hope for the remaining four-fifths of the interviewees; only two of these anxious, unsettled wives reported leaving the marriage.

The several areas that most perturb the never married second wife are: sex, stepchildren, finances, appearance, status, and romance. The most prevalent disturbance expressed by the never married second wives is their level of insecurity over their husbands' first wives. Furthermore, husbands who are unaware of their new wives' acute sensitivity and fear only exacerbate the problem by increasing their anxiety.

All second wives have to develop self-confidence to succeed in their marriages. Based on what the interviewees revealed, this is especially important for the never before married second wives, who overwhelmingly admit that they are lacking in that area. It is vital for them to develop this confidence if they ever hope to move beyond their insecurities over their husbands' first wives. If a second wife views her husband's previous marriage as a life lesson that has ultimately strengthened him, made him a better person, and enabled him to know what he really wants in life, she can relax in her role. After all, with what he has learned, he chose to marry and plan a future with her. He must also keep his eyes open and be aware of her insecurities, assuring her that regardless of his past, she is the only woman for him now. With this kind of love and support, they can weather any storm, emerging happy and triumphant.

CHAPTER EIGHT

DOMESTIC VIOLENCE

Lisa did not accept the fact that there had been violence in her husband Will's past marriage when she became a second wife. "Will's first marriage had appeared to make sense. Will and Lindsay had been together for years before they were married and they came from the same background. Lindsay was very pretty and I thought that the marriage had disintegrated because of her desire to raise a family. Will really did not want children so finally they split up. What I didn't face was that he was physically abusive. I was sixteen years younger than my husband and I was too sheltered to understand what the abuse meant. Lindsay had retaliated with abuse, but I could not. At first I felt sorry for Will, because he told me that his ex-wife had almost cut off his hand with a butcher knife. He ended up in the hospital with hundreds of stitches.

"As our marriage went on, I learned that my husband was a very angry person. I believe that he and his first wife provoked each other. At first, our marriage was not based on violence. Will never touched me, but broke things when he lost his temper. I did not have the same violent reactions to his behavior that Lindsay had, but Will's outbursts continued. As time went on, I began to wish that I could fight back as Lindsay had. I wished that I could be violent, too. I began to understand why she tried to cut off his hand. It started to make sense to me. Once that happened, I knew I had to leave.

"Today, I am divorced from Will. Being his second wife was a no-win situation. I believed that he would take care of me. He was older and my father had died when I was very young. I saw my husband as a father figure, but he was not. I was the opposite of safe with him. I became filled with fear, just like his first wife. The violence was not about us, the wives; it was about him and his need for control."

The topic of abuse is too important not to be treated in depth and thus is not really a subject within the scope of this book. Nevertheless, it must be mentioned since abuse in the first marriage often occurs again in the second marriage. If the husband has a pattern of abuse, it may prevail. When a first wife leaves such a situation, she remains fearful of her ex-husband and is often unable to admit to having been abused. A woman who has the courage to leave may feel ashamed, isolated, and emotionally dependent. In the cycle of violence, according to the experts, there is tension, an explosion, precipitated by drugs or drinking perhaps, and then remorse.

DEFINITION OF DOMESTIC VIOLENCE
When a person uses physical violence, threats, emotional abuse, harassment, or stalking to control their partner's behavior.

Violent men act out of a need for control: physical, emotional, and even financial control. Dr. Michele Kasson, psychologist, explains why violence escalates. "People take their difficulties out on the person closest to them. It is easier to not take responsibility for one's problems and to blame the person to whom you are attached. For a woman who is emotionally or physically abused, there is a loss of confidence. She is afraid to stay, afraid to leave." Abuse pervades social classes. Although we are most likely to hear of cases among the poor and uneducated, white collar professional men are equally responsible for abuse. In a "Jekyll and Hyde" syndrome, the abuser is at times wonderful and kind to his partner and at other times, cruel and intimidating. Over two-thirds of domestic abuse violence is committed by a spouse, according to the National Domestic Violence Hotline, and one in three women will experience at least one physical assault by a partner during adulthood.

A second wife who finds herself with an abusive husband usually is shocked and in denial for a period of time. According to researchers, it requires tremendous courage for a woman to pick up and leave. A classic case is that of Nicole Simpson, who tolerated acts of violence at the hands of her husband, O.J. Simpson, before her death. Although she cried out for help many times, O.J. was still seen by the world as a hero. While her death has raised the consciousness of the American public in terms of domestic abuse, it is still prevalent and problematic.

ABUSE AND THE ABUSER
Once a pattern of abuse is established, it is repeated. Denial on the woman's part perpetuates the problem. Domestic violence exists as an unacknowledged epidemic in our society. This is because men are able get away with it.

Emotional and physical abuse of women has existed in our society for centuries. Today, it is reported that a woman is beaten every eighteen seconds in America and that women who leave their abusers are at a seventy-five percent greater risk of being killed than those who stay. Although in the past there has been little protection available for abused women, as evidenced by cases of repeated abuse, stalking, and even murder, currently there are actions a victim and the police can take against the perpetrator. For example, an order of protection can be filed against the abusive husband. Once issued in one state, the order is valid in every other state. Although protection orders may help decrease the risk of continuing abuse, they cannot entirely eliminate such abuse. Action taken by government officials includes implementing programs that have taken aggressive steps to reduce domestic homicides. In certain cities, for example, if there is evidence of abuse, the batterers are arrested and put in jail. In addition, there are non-profit and government funded services for victims of abuse, including toll-free nationwide domestic violence hotlines that are available twenty-four hours a day and can provide battered women with information, guidance, and support.

NO REPEAT PERFORMANCES
The second wife who is abused may be unable to break the cycle of abuse. She will then leave one abuser for another.

Despite the help that is available to victims of domestic violence, the phenomenon of wives who remain and suffer at the hands of their husbands/abusers can often be attributed to fear. These women fear for their children and for themselves. In addition, some women may not be able to break the cycle of violence. With nine out of ten abused wives coming from abusive childhoods, it is likely that mistreatment is all they know and understand. They may imagine that they do not have a choice in the matter. With so many painful feelings and unresolved issues, these women possibly cannot handle or be a part of a healthy, loving adult relationship until they seek counseling or therapy. Without getting help and escaping the violence, these women may even become abusers themselves, especially if that is all they know in their personal relationships. Although there exist cases in which women are the perpetrators of domestic violence, it is rare that they initiate such abuse on their husbands. Statistics show that this is a problem in which women are overwhelmingly the victims.

STATISTICS (From the Bureau of Justice, 1995)
• 90-95% of domestic violence victims are women
• 95% of domestic violence perpetrators are men
• Wife beatings result in more injuries that require medical treatment than rape, auto accidents, and muggings combined

When Leigh became a second wife, her husband Paul's first wife was living abroad with their daughter. "I knew no details of the break-up of the first marriage and I never asked him about it. When we were first married, I did notice signs of abuse and I chose to ignore them. By the time I was pregnant, I knew there was a problem. This was eighteen years ago, when no woman admitted that she was abused, physically or emotionally. I kept wondering what I had done wrong to live in this private hell. I kept going through the motions of being happily married to the outside world, but I was sick inside. I began to really understand what Paul's first wife had endured. I even had dreams of her. I wanted to contact her somehow, but knew I couldn't do that. When my son was six years old, I asked my parents to help me out financially and I left the marriage. I had my parents' support to get me through, but it was rough. I had no real skills to go to work. I became a secretary and climbed my way up through this corporation.

"For years, I felt like I was living the same life as Paul's first wife, leaving my home and beginning over again with a young child. I thought how we were both victims of the same man. Escaping him was what we had in common. I knew why she had taken her child across the ocean. I also felt I could not get far enough away. I knew what she had gone through with him because I had tolerated the same thing. Not only was this man verbally abusive, but he drank and did drugs. Both of us, his first wife and myself, had children at risk. I think that I was somewhat stronger than she was, because I stayed here and stood my ground while she fled the country. I took legal action against him and got sole custody of my son. My ex-husband was denied visitation rights to our child. I raised him on my own, just as the first wife had done with their daughter."

While control is a major aspect of domestic abuse, it is not necessarily an indication that abuse is occurring. "If someone is controlling and can strike a deal, and the control doesn't impinge on the other persons' freedom, then there is no abuse in the relationship," states Dr. Michele Kasson. "However, if the control leads to the other partner's inability to function as she wishes, then the treatment becomes abusive because one's decisions and actions are controlled by the partner." This is exactly the situation with which Ellie was confronted.

Ellie feels that the behavior of Jim's first wife contributed to his need for control, thus setting up Ellie and Jim for the conflict that ensued after they married. "I know that in Jim's first marriage there was a great deal of abuse. But when he became my husband, he was paranoid and out of control. I sometimes watched Jim's and his ex-wife's little boy after work. But when Jim would get home from work, he'd be insanely jealous from the moment he walked in the door. He'd go crazy, screaming and shaking me. He'd think that I was cheating on him when I was supposed to be watching his son. He'd check the bar for dirty glasses to see if I'd been drinking with and entertaining some man. He was crazy. I believe that his ex-wife must have cheated on him or maybe he'd suspected that she had. I began to see how hellish life could be with him and why she'd left. Still, she was no bargain. She called constantly, yelling and making demands, and dumped their son on us at a moment's notice.

"I began to shrink from his touch, so he forced me to have sex. It was rape. That was how bad it was. Boy, did I stop loving him. She had done the same. Jim did not want to get separated or divorced. He begged me to reconcile. Then I got pregnant. When I saw how he mistreated his child and ex-wife, it sickened me, and I realized I was afraid to have children with him. But still, it wasn't enough to encourage me to leave. I guess I felt tied to him since I was carrying his child, even though I feared for myself and my unborn baby. Then I miscarried. It was a blessing in disguise; that's when our connection was broken and I found the courage to leave. I knew it was finally over. Slowly, I put the pieces of my life together. I remarried and became a second wife again, this time to a man who is so wonderful and kind. I really know the difference."

A second wife may be successful in discouraging her husband's abusive behavior if he was only abusive with his first wife and if he and his second wife share a dynamic different than the one in his first marriage. However, in the case of a husband who has been a habitual abuser, the prognosis is more pessimistic. Even if his second wife does not respond to it as his first wife did, the abuse might persist anyway—if it is too deep-rooted to stop.

Nevertheless, though it is difficult, some past abusive behavior patterns can be broken. Adele's situation with her husband has worked out positively. "My husband will get upset when I order for myself in a restaurant, because he still remembers his ex-wife's docility. He liked being in charge and I suspect he'd like to be in charge in our relationship. But the price that he paid for his ex-wife's docility was her eventual anger. She was from another culture and he was drawn to her uniqueness. She was displaced and wanted to belong. I had a similar story except that I was much younger. My husband saw this as my weakness and consequently his strength. He had an ex-wife whom he had controlled and a new wife he thought he could control. His concept of romance, if he had one, was satisfied with each of us. But finally I could not stand the control. I knew that she had not been able to stand it either. What worked in my favor was that I had an established career. I was self-reliant and didn't need him to support me. Plus, I had a lot of self-confidence, so I knew my worth and what kind of treatment I wanted and expected. So I stopped taking his in-charge attitude. In the end, we sorted it out. Today, he has truly come around. I think he wanted me enough to try."

WHEN HE CHANGES
• A new partner elicits change
• A new partner demands change
• The husband is no longer able to repeat the same pattern

If the first and second wife differ in their styles, their reactions to situations will not be the same. "What determines the success of the second marriage," observes psychologist Dr. Michele Kasson, "is the energy level that existed in the beginning of the romance and set the tone. This strengthens the bond. If the husband reverts to his old style, the new wife may empathize with the first wife, but she may also forge ahead with confidence."

Sara and her husband, Jerome, do not have the volatile relationship he had with his first wife. "I do speak with Vicki, my husband's ex-wife," says Sara, a second wife for eight years. "We are in touch, politely, because of their children. I eavesdropped one night when she and Jerome spoke on the phone. They were arguing over money. Jerome explained why he couldn't increase the money and Vicki became verbally abusive. I know that she was like that in the marriage. So was he. This is what they brought out in each other. I am not like Vicki and I would never be her friend. On the other hand, I know how it must have been for her in their marriage. She has affected me. We waited to have children because of her children. My husband needed the space. My way of parenting is so unlike Vicki's. Then I see how her children love mine and vice versa and it hardly matters that she and my husband were at each other's throats."

The relationship shared by the husband and second wife may be the opposite of the first marriage. This is especially true if in the second marriage, a partnership of equals is established that demands change. In such cases, the husband recognizes that he cannot behave as he has in the past marriage, and there is an acceptance and respect for his new partner that alters his response for the better. This occurs when the husband finds a second wife who is healthy for him. Together, they cultivate a new domestic world where the focus is shifted from control, power, and dominance, toward common goals like commitment, mutual respect, sharing and acceptance.

CHAPTER NINE

THE REBECCA SYNDROME: WIDOWERS' SECOND WIVES

When Justine, at the age of twenty-seven, married her husband, Joseph, who was forty-three, she took on the responsibility of his four young children. "I knew Joseph's first wife, Darlene, and we were friendly and fairly close. I knew how she mothered her children, because we lived in the same town and worked in the library together. Joseph and I met when Darlene became so ill that I came over to help with their four children. After she died, I continued to help. I think what attracted my husband to me was how similar I was to his first wife. My view of how to raise the children was the same. However, in terms of our view of marriage, we were not alike at all. It is a very different marriage than his first. I think this is because my husband has actually grown as a person since his wife died. And I believe that I bring out good qualities in him. We have a more open relationship than he had in his first marriage.

"Marrying a widower is not the same as marrying a divorced man. I know that I am the only mother figure for these children. I absolutely feel that they are my children. I cringe at the word 'stepmother' because I cannot imagine anyone loving these children more than I do. When I married Joseph, I married his entire family. We have the same religion and goals, but at times I'm overwhelmed by having married a widower with young children.

"Before the wedding I was so concerned about the children's transition that I didn't take my own adjustment into consideration. Now, three years later, I realize that I healed my husband by becoming his second wife. I see the age difference between my husband and myself as a way of giving him a second chance. But for me, I jumped right in, putting him and the kids first. I regret that there are many stages that my husband and I cannot share because they are already established. This includes, of course, the children and his career. He is a physician, and at his age, he has built a strong practice. What I see as the best result of my efforts is that both my children and my husband are no longer in pain. This is very gratifying, so how can I think of the sacrifices?

"I am embraced by the community for what I've done for this man and his children. But I still feel compared to his first wife by people I meet. It has taken all of my determination to be respected. I feel the ghost of the first wife; she is never completely gone. I chose to fill her absence. But she did exist and she created a marriage and family before me. We all want to be someone's number one."

Widowers and widows alike do not choose to be widowed. Rather, it is thrust upon them, and they are tossed into an abyss, a lonely single universe. It is often not only a partner for whom the widow or widower longs, but the very structure of marriage. Experiencing the death of one's partner and facing the prospect of growing old alone is most dismaying. For many who are widowed, the lonely future propels them toward a second marriage and the security that it provides.

Statistically, second marriages amongst widows and widowers are the strongest of remarriages. There is the desire to abate the loneliness and to live a coupled existence. Widowers tend to seek out widows, because the common experience brings them closer and places them on equal footing. Yet there are many widowers who marry again and find themselves with women who have been divorced or never married before. These women take on a tremendous amount of emotional baggage. Not only is she a second wife, but one who may be constantly compared to the first. The idealization of the dead can be formidable to contend with, and for the second wife who is inexperienced this role is particularly daunting. This exact scenario is depicted in the famous novel *Rebecca* by Daphne Du Maurier. It is only at the very end of the story that we are told by the unnamed narrator, who is the second wife, that her husband did not have a happy and loving marriage with Rebecca, his first wife. Throughout the entire story, the second wife believes that her husband is grieving for his beloved deceased wife. At the same time, everyone she encounters never fails to remind her how beautiful Rebecca was, what a wonderful hostess she was, how sophisticated she was, and so on. The second wife is then stunned to discover the truth, having been haunted thus far by the ghost of the seemingly perfect first wife.

A Widower with Children and the Young Second Wife

"In a second marriage to a widower with children, the couple doesn't have the time to develop separately from the children," Dr. Ronnie Burak comments. "These marriages start off on a sad note. The ghost of the first wife becomes more glorified in death; this woman could do no wrong. She is an indomitable force for the second wife, because the feelings that the husband has for his first wife are positive." Unlike in a divorce, one cannot be angry at their absent spouse because she died. This woman did nothing wrong; there was no infidelity, no betrayal, no broken vows. This makes it more difficult for the second wife; she is competing against someone whose relationship with her husband ended with lots of love.

BEFORE BECOMING SECOND WIFE TO A WIDOWER
- Are you secure enough to disregard constant comparisons?
- Can you take on someone else's children full time?
- Do you want to have your own family?
- Can you deal with stepping into someone else's shoes?
- Are you willing to navigate a new life for this man and his children?

Another noted second wife who married a widower is Maria Von Trapp, immortalized in *The Sound of Music*. Schooled to become a nun, she was sent from her convent in Austria to teach Captain Von Trapp's children. At first she thought the captain was aloof and distant, and as the twenty sixth teacher to be hired to care for these children, she was determined to succeed in her role. What Maria saw in the Captain was a broken man who had lost his wife and whose career was on hold. Several weeks before she was to return to her convent, the Captain unexpectedly proposed. Only twenty years old, Maria was aware of the overwhelming responsibilities of being a mother to seven children and a second wife to a man with a high profile. Singing became an important part of the newly formed family. Music, encouraged by Maria, became the core of their united lives.

SECOND WIVES OF WIDOWERS WITH CHILDREN
- The instant family is the name of the game
- A strong ego is required by the second wife
- The ages of the children are pivotal in establishing a working relationship
- The memory of the first wife is not taboo and should be cherished

Widowers' wives have no time to dreamily contemplate the idea of family. They need the fortitude to quickly build a new structure. While younger children may be easier to win over, in truth, whatever age the children are, these women need to become immediate mother figures. Often, older children may resent her presence and fear that she will try to replace their lost mother. When the second wife/stepmother is loving yet encourages the children to cherish the memory of their mother, it eases the tension all around. The family begins to take on a different, but promising spirit.

SECOND WIFE AS HEALER
- She helps him to let go of the past
- She builds a new family relationship
- The loneliness dissipates for the family
- She brings a new purpose and focus to her husband's life
- She represents a second chance at happiness

According to Dr. Donald Cohen, "For the second wife of a widower who has never been married, it is important that she has had enough life experience. If this woman is evolved and secure with herself, she will be able to be a positive force as a second wife. She cannot forget that she is, by definition, competing with the shadow of the first wife. She must accept this and move on to create a new family structure."

Widowers' wives come face to face with the ghost of the first wife in almost every instance. It is quite a feat to feel her equal. The widower's wife has to fight hard to maintain her self-esteem. The husband does not always notice his wife's struggle because he is preoccupied with his own issues, which may include his own residual grief and concern for his motherless children.

THE GHOST PERSISTS
Everywhere the second wife turns, there is a reverence for the first. The second wife may feel inferior and that she can never make up for her husband's loss. She may begin to doubt herself.

The second wife who marries a widower may feel particularly threatened if the husband has not dealt with his grief. If his marriage was happy, the second wife ought to respect this. Even if the marriage was not a happy one, she needs to help her husband come to terms with his loss and help him heal. The never married second wife who is now a widower's wife is rigorously challenged. Her dependence upon her husband might meet with resistance because of his own preoccupation. It does not bode well for the situation if she is insecure. In the case of a second wife who is ready to be a widower's wife, her stability and security enable her husband to work out his problems without having the added burden of her leaning on him.

HALF-DEVELOPED SECOND WIVES FOR WIDOWERS
If a never married second wife has little knowledge of life, she will look to her widower husband to fill the void. Because he has been through so much, he will be less likely to respond. Instead he requires support. She cannot be supportive of him if she lacks self-esteem and self-confidence.

VERSUS

WHOLE SECOND WIVES
Wherever her life has taken her, she is prepared for the demands and expectations of being a widower's wife. This woman is stable and tenacious when it comes to caring for her husband. She buffers his pain and moves him and their marriage forward.

Leslie, a second wife who was never married before, married Justin, a widower, out of sympathy. "Four years ago, I felt sorry for Justin and ended up marrying him. I was too stupid to realize that one major reason he was marrying me was because his three babies needed a mother and a home. I was very curious about Justin's first wife, Lori, who had died of an illness. I asked a lot of questions, but I never got any information. There were constant comparisons to the first wife. I know that I was fortunate in a sense, because the children were too small to remember her and he was clearly smitten with me. After the shock wore off that he was widowed, he was thrilled to have me. That was when I saw that I was a necessity.

"I remained curious about my husband's first wife. I realized that I am a much different type of person than she was. I don't look like or act like her at all. But I felt as if I lived in Lori's shadow because I lived in her house. I felt she had some presence or something, although I understood the loss. I felt I deserved to live in a new house and to begin a new life, because I was the one living with Justin and mothering his children.

"After I had a baby, I realized that his children were not mine in the same way my child was. They joined me in loving the baby, but they were very attached to their father from the start. What was certain was that I was responsible for all of them, his and ours. Because Justin had been widowed, he was very ready to be a terrific husband to me and to make it work. I basically stepped right in. I never felt that he loved anyone but me. I was his savior and that gave me confidence. I see myself as having saved them all."

SECOND WIVES AS RESCUERS
• Are prepared to take on the world
• Realize that young children need them full time
• Are aware they may carry their husbands emotionally for months, perhaps years
• Accept that only they can rebuild a life for them

Aside from her role as her husband's savior, the second wife of a widower with children has many issues to confront as she is thrust into motherhood. "Children who do not have a mother are not the same as children of divorce," Dr. Ronnie Burak reminds us. "The stepmother is taking on a full mothering role to a child sadder than a child of divorce. This second wife is also the caregiver to her husband, because he is so needy after the loss of his first wife. Unlike in a divorce, there is no conflict between the first wife and the second, but there is still competition. The widower's wife, as she pulls the family together, competes with the former wife because she was so loved and revered."

According to the women I interviewed, often after a child is born to the second wife the balance shifts. The life that is created by the new couple is in the forefront. The blended family in the case of a widower has another significance for the second wife. There is no first wife to deal with nor are there custody arrangements to be followed. Her commitment is steadfast to both her stepchildren and to her own children.

The widower's wife who is new at marriage may be in shock over the day-to-day responsibilities of mothering. Unlike other second wives who are involved in a joint custody situation, she is constantly caring for these children. The second wife must remember how desperately these children need her, especially when she is feeling overwhelmed. It is up to this woman alone to guide her husband and the family back to a happy place. It is a daunting task not to be entered into lightly, and may not be for everyone.

THE ENTIRE PIE
For a woman who has never been married and marries a widower with children, the adjustment to her new lifestyle may be overwhelming. The children and daily grind makes for an unpracticed situation. The second wife often has little time for reflection.

For Kelly, there was always the specter of her husband Max's first wife. "I absolutely had a 'Rebecca' complex. Max's first wife, Jacqueline, had died so tragically that the knowledge was always with me and I could not escape it. I had never had children and I became a cross between a friend and a companion for my stepson. I know now that when you go into a family situation where there are no prototypes or rules, you must try to do what is loving and kind. But I had to learn this because I really didn't know my role and I was so spooked by the ghost of Max's first wife.

"Once we had our own child I felt much better. I so desperately wanted my marriage to be the best ever. In my heart, I wanted Max to forget about Jacqueline," Kelly confessed. "I wanted to be the love of his life. I was young and very paranoid. What I have learned is that in reality we can have more than one love of our lives and that forgetting a dead love is not the answer. Letting go is. His first marriage took place in a different time, another place altogether.

"The fact that Max and I are the same religion made a difference. I know that Jacqueline was not the same religion as he was and that it mattered to my husband. I felt secure about working through this issue, but in other areas I did not feel as solid. A chronic problem in the marriage is my husband's guilt. I can feel it even though it isn't verbalized. People said that Jacqueline and I seemed similar in personality. I thought that he really missed her, that he was pining for her. It took a long time for Max to admit that his marriage to Jacqueline had not been a happy one. I felt she was canonized, mystical, some kind of legend. And legends grow. Then I learned the truth: she had not made him happy. I was astonished to hear that. What I wish was that I had been aware of the reality from the start; it would have saved me years of feeling less important than she was to him.

"I came to understand my marriage in time. I know that I eased my husband's suffering and gave him a second chance. He has told me that I make the house bright and bring it to life. Gradually we have built our own world and have broken free of the past."

It is only fair and thoughtful for a previously married husband, especially a widower, to inform his wife of the condition of his previous marriage and how he felt about his first wife. It is this information that puts the widower's new wife at ease and helps the relationship to take on its own rhythm and qualities. If there are in-laws or family friends who are not tolerant of the second wife, the husband ought to be aware of this. "Living in the shadow of another person's history is a daunting task. The second wife must be clear with her husband about how she feels about her responsibilities and she must, above all, trust herself," Dr. Donald Cohen explains.

THE HUSBAND SETS THE TONE
- If he shares information, it saves your imagination from running wild
- The second marriage must be set apart from the first
- His love and care for you will put the past to rest
- He protects you from any family or friends who make you feel uneasy or judge you

"My marriage and role as a second wife is based on practical knowledge and my commitment," says Marjorie, the mother of two. "For the last six years, I have been married to Noah, a widower, who has two children from his previous marriage. It was amazing that our collective children were exactly the same ages, nine and eleven. Noah and I met soon after I was widowed. Our children got along on the surface from the start, but there were definitely undercurrents. After a while it became clear to everyone, because both of us were widowers, that we were one big family. It was never difficult to have four children, because there were no other parents involved. When we married, the children were young and I spent the first two years on winning his children over. I understood that I had the love of my own children, so I worked hard on his. These children now consider me their mother and my children see my husband as their father. For me, the focus has always been on making this family function well and not dwelling on the past.

"Noah and I do not discuss his first wife. From what I gather, she and I are not similar. He says he is much happier since we have been together. I have given him confidence and a second chance. I am very content in my second marriage. My husband is kind, tender, and terrific with the children. From the start, Noah and I have made time for ourselves. I do not compare what I have now with what I had. Life has many chapters. This marriage has succeeded because we have brought energy and determination to the relationship."

NO PLACE FOR THE PAST
• Build a life together
• Concentrate on the children
• Be grateful for what is
• Do not dwell on historical events
• Do not make comparisons

"The widower's wife takes on the entire family; she is in the role of mother, not stepmother, for these purposes," Dr. Ronnie Burak, psychologist, notes. "This definitely applies when there are small children. The widower's second wife has to be quite secure with herself and not jealous of the first wife's memory. It is only with this frame of mind that she will succeed."

"I had dated several men who did not have children and were divorced before I met my husband, Eric," Jessie explains. "I was widowed with six year old twin daughters and I was anxious to be remarried. After three years of dating, including two very serious relationships, I met my second husband at the gym. Eric had been widowed as well, and his kids were ten years older than mine and in college by the time we met. He had raised them himself and he was lonely and tired, as far as I could see.

"Maybe it was that we were both widowed, but Eric and I really understood each other's lives. We dated intensely and became engaged after several months. That was when everything changed. The pressure was on. He wanted me to sign a prenuptial agreement and his children were no longer so wild about me. I was confused by all of the changes and my own children were not as infatuated with him anymore. We forged ahead and got married, kind of ignoring everyone's behavior. It was a long haul, but three years later, I'm living proof that a second marriage between widowers can work out. In the case of two widowers getting married, you have to adore your partner and blindly love and care for each other's children."

The second wives I interviewed agreed that when children fill the widowers' and their second wives' lives in a successful second marriage, the adults tend to function in the present and future rather than the past. They do not compare life before and after but put energy into building a shared life. The children of the widower may be intimidated by the second wife/stepmother but eventually will come to appreciate her. The potential for one happy, blended family is greater in the case of widower's wife than in cases of divorce.

BLENDED CHILDREN

For the children who have lost a parent, competition with and jealousy of the new wife/mother figure will dissolve with time. This requires constancy and strength on the second wife's part. A complex family unit may be unwieldy at first, but has the potential to grow and blossom.

While there may be sensitivity and intimacy in a second marriage, there are also high expectations for a fulfilling life beyond the children that might not have existed in the first marriage. Nevertheless, with a widower, there is a tendency to idealize what has been lost. Yet there is also the realization that a second chance and new life is before him. Sex is a very important aspect of this new marriage for a widower. While the puritan ethic of married sex prevails, sexuality may be one of the motivating aspects to seek out a second marriage. Rekindling her husband's sexuality is something a second wife can do. At first, the memory of the first wife may hover or prevent the true expression of sexuality. "If a widower has residual guilt, the sex will not play out as it should," reveals Dr. Michele Kasson. She explains that sex can be very exciting in a second marriage, because it is explorative, and yet there is a comfort level. The discovery of a new partner's sexual style is a motivator and, with a widower, more so than with a divorced man, freedom from his past must be achieved in order to enjoy his present and future.

When Caryn remarried Jack, her fears about his sexual history with his first wife created a tumultuous path. "I am younger than my husband by ten years. I married Jack several months after his first wife had committed suicide. My husband told me that his first wife, Dawn, had emotional problems and there were difficulties during the marriage. But I do believe that Jack was in love with her. I'm not sure he understood how serious the situation was. He was quite taken in by Dawn's good looks and breeding. I know there was definitely a sexual element to it. And our marriage is also very sexual. In fact, it is very important to both of us. My husband told me that his marriage was passionate and had lots of sex. That was why I could feel her presence when we first slept together. When I realized our sex was good in its own right, I began to relax. I know that we are totally committed to each other. There is no joy in Jack's life like what we share.

"Jack's first marriage seemed golden to the outside world, but I have learned it wasn't. I had also been married before to someone the outside world perceived as golden. When I remarried, Jack and I entered the marriage with complete knowledge of what we wanted out of life. It gets better and better. We come together emotionally, sexually, and in terms of our values."

In many second wives' stories, finding out or imagining the sexual history of their husband and his former wife can be troubling. Often the new wife feels that her sexual performance is under scrutiny and that she is being compared to the first. For the widower's wife in particular, this aspect of the previous marriage may undermine the new marriage. It is important for the second wife to concentrate on the here and now. There is nothing she can do to change the past, nor can she compete with her husband's deceased wife. Instead, she must be herself and establish a strong sexual bond with her husband. This sexual synergy between partners is particularly crucial for the second wife of a widower.

SEX AND THE GHOST
If sex is strong and satisfying between a second wife and her husband, the ghost of the first wife dissipates. The ghost lingers if there is no sexual synergy in the second marriage.

Judith is a second wife who identified strongly with her husband's deceased first wife. "Susan's strength was similar to mine. We are not alike in looks but in our determination. Susan had a temper and would flare up, but I do not react that way. What is similar is that she was a very positive person and had a high powered career. I also have a career that is important to me. In both instances, there is stability in my husband Nick's life that is provided by his partner. My husband is attracted to this. She actually paved the way for him to have a relationship with me. I sometimes think that our marriage would have pleased his late wife.

"Nick was ambivalent about my career in the beginning. I think that my working reminded him of his first wife and this time around he might have wanted someone more available than I am because of work. I also know that he is accustomed to my schedule and I think that gives him a sense of continuity. There is no question that I'm doing something his first wife would have done. I think about Susan and I feel like she would be proud of his choice."

As in the case of Judith and Nick, if the first marriage was successful, and the husband was compatible with his new wife, he will likely choose a second wife who is similar to his first. The emotional turmoil of losing a spouse can be assuaged by the familiarity of a similar partner in the new marriage. Ideally, the closeness that forms between the two new partners is based on mutual goals and understandings and the husband's realization that even with similarities, his new wife is a unique individual. The second wife flourishes when she and her husband share common beliefs and values.

SAMENESS ATTRACTS
The more common the base that is shared in a second marriage, especially after there has been a loss as in the case of the widower, the stronger the bond. If one's goals and values are shared, the couple will thrive.

Several months before Melissa's wedding to Keith, a divorced man, his first wife died, and Melissa took on the responsibility of raising his three young children along with three of her own. "The safety net of their mother had disappeared. The most difficult part of the entire package was not having enough time to be with my husband. I worked long hours at a plant and now had six young children. I had little energy for my husband. I had expected Keith's children to be with us on a part time basis and having them full-time was an adjustment. I had vaguely known his wife, Monica. I knew that she resented our plans to marry even though she was the one who had wanted the divorce. Monica didn't want Keith, nor did she want him to be happy with anyone else. In a sense, I knew her unhappiness could not have been one-sided, that my husband can be a difficult man. On the other hand, she couldn't have it both ways. She remarried, had a baby immediately, and died of cancer. It was a tragedy.

"To complicate matters, despite how much I loved my husband, he was a loner and a drinker. But I was determined to make it all work. Everyone had suffered enough. I ended up raising six kids by myself. What I have come to realize is that my husband is happier with me than he ever was with his first wife. This gave me courage. In retrospect, twelve years later, I look back on our beginning and understand what a huge undertaking it was. But I loved him, and having had one bad marriage, which he also had, I knew how to always give him the care that he required. For years we weren't able to even take a vacation—with the children or alone—because of finances."

Caring for stepchildren who have lost their mother is a monumental task and not for every second wife. Before assuming the responsibility, a woman must take inventory of her own capacities and limitations. While the rewards of raising children are innumerable, the rewards of a happy, healthy marriage can be even greater. Such a marriage requires time and effort. Marriage to a widower with children demands special nourishment. This may mean day, overnight, or weekend trips for the new couple on occasion. At the very least, regularly scheduled "dates"—out of the house and without the children—are essential.

BUILDING A SPECIAL LIFE TOGETHER
For a stepmother of children who have lost their mother, the parenting is constant and without relief. To keep the marriage alive, it is important to spend time alone with your partner and to give constant energy to the marriage. Making time for each other in a complicated world is essential.

A Widower and a Second Wife in Her Later Years
There are many cases of second wives who marry widowers at a later stage of their lives. This woman has been through enough in her own life

to be able to discern what her desires are. Their children are grown, and companionship is the primary motivation. While the issues of stepparenting are no longer of major significance, there are adjustments to be made. In a society where we commonly live into our eighties, becoming a second wife at the age of sixty is still a relatively long-term commitment.

"When the children are older and the marriage happens later in life," Dr. Donald Cohen, psychologist, observes, "the role of the widower's wife is to be respectful of the family history and to understand that these are not her children. They should be seen as an extension of the first marriage and the second wife should feel warmly toward them in this capacity."

"My first marriage lasted thirty-two years," says Hillary. "But I never imagined that if I married again, I would become a second wife to a widower. I married Rob, who was widowed at the same time that I was. We fell in love, and since our children were long gone and there were no ex-spouses, it seemed very easy. What else could we want? There was one person who was not happy, however, and that was my husband's son, Caleb. I think he saw me as having too much influence over his father. Between his mother's death and my appearance on the scene, Caleb was the one who had exerted influence in both investments and in his father's lifestyle. Financially, Caleb controlled his father.

"Our marriage was quite wonderful and we enjoyed a unique lifestyle. His first wife had controlled their social life and was much fussier than I am. We moved to California and retired. I was the opposite of his first wife in every way and I think Rob liked that. What I know was that we helped each other get over our grief and build a life together. Neither of us dwelled on the past. We had a natural and independent marriage, which I bet he did not have with his first wife. Rob was thirteen years older than I was, and his health began to deteriorate. I took him to a doctor in Los Angeles and Caleb kidnapped him from there. The hospital staff told me that Rob's son took him home and that Rob would be living there from then on.

"I received divorce papers from the son soon after Rob and I were separated. I was devastated; it took me a year to get back on my feet. I kept thinking how his wife would have wanted us married and happy together, and that it was the children who rejected our happiness. By then my husband was very ill and Caleb had manipulated his father's money. All I wanted was my husband back. I wondered what right his son had to control his life.

"My role as second wife failed because my husband was vulnerable and I had no control of the situation," Hillary said sadly. "His son was too old to be involved in our marriage in any manner. He had no right to make decisions and it was only Caleb's fear about his father's money that made him interfere. I have mourned Rob's loss and regretted that things could not have worked out differently."

"When people are older and remarry after widowhood," notes Brondi Borer, divorce mediator, "it is very wise to sign a prenuptial agreement. It is experience, not age that is the factor. There are many obligations to the prior family that must be recognized. A co-mingling of funds is a situation fraught with potential pitfalls. For this reason, if people remarry in their fifties or sixties, a prenuptial agreement is still the right decision." An adult approach to a second marriage in midlife would be to make provisions for children, any illness, and all finances ahead of time. Such a preventative measure can help a couple avoid what Hillary and Rob experienced.

PROVISIONS FOR SECOND MARRIAGES
Regardless of age, spouses need to make provisions for:
• Finances
• Illnesses
• Caretaking of children and grandchildren

Becoming a second wife as one grows older, rather than when one is young, has another appeal. The motivation after sixty, according to the women interviewed, is that it staves off loneliness. Companionship is extremely important to women who are older second wives and when they marry a widower, it is a shared need. The fear of facing ill health alone or the threat of being disabled is very real for both partners, particularly after they have witnessed the deaths of their spouses. The later life second marriage should not be interrupted by grown children and the marriage, like a marriage at any stage, should be respected for its wholeness and entirety.

SECOND MARRIAGES IN LATER LIFE
• Put this relationship ahead of any other
• Do not let your children influence your lifestyle
• Be grateful that you have each other
• Respect the past but live for the present

Sally, who was born in Europe and lives in Detroit, is a second wife at the age of seventy-two. "My first marriage lasted thirty years. I was a widow for ten years. When I became a second wife, it was to a man who had been widowed for several months time and found it difficult, as many men do, to live alone. But I was ready to marry again, too. I was lonely and no longer young. The man I fell in love with and married five years ago is ten years older than I am. I knew if I wanted him, I'd better hurry up. I think I was too lively for this man in the beginning. He had been married to a woman who was very sick for a long time. I was such an extreme change. But we both required friendship and love. A second marriage in later years is about caring and warmth. Sex belongs there too, but it isn't such a priority at my age. If we hadn't cared so much about each other, we would not have remarried.

"We have always talked about our spouses. It has helped us. I pull out all of the photos from both families and so does he. One cannot and should not forget the past, especially if it was a happy one. My first husband doesn't deserve to be forgotten any more than my husband's first wife should be forgotten. Yet we are very happy to have found one another. My husband told me that he would have died if he had not married me."

Another sunset years marriage is Blair's, but her reflections on it are very different from Sally's. "I became a second wife to a minister," Blair tells us. "My husband, Edward, and I had been widowed at the same time. I remember his wife and I admired her greatly because she was able to keep her career going to raise a family and to aid his career as a minister. Yet after Edward and I married, I struggled to keep it all together. I almost wished it was simpler like my first marriage, where we were busy raising young children and seeing them off into adulthood. There were actually less shared interests in my second marriage but such a need to be together. But if anyone tells you that just because you are both widowed, sharing a second marriage will work, it is not necessarily correct. For me, there were huge adjustments of lifestyle.

"I waited for three years for our marriage to become what I imagined and hoped it would be and it never happened. Finally, after the fifth year, I decided to leave. It took more courage to leave than it did to marry Edward. I was devastated by the failure. What I sought in this marriage wasn't feasible. And I secretly began to wonder if his first wife had found marriage to Edward satisfying. Today I am happy to be alone. I am a firm believer in second marriages but the love has to be strong and steady."

Unlike Blair, Daphne's adjustment was successful. Daphne was fifty-five when she met her husband, Marty, and remarried. "Both of us were widowed and came from happy marriages. My husband had two children and I had three, but they were all grown. We were in California at the time and Marty made the decision to move to the northeast. It was a good idea, because it gave us the opportunity to start our own life, away from where we had lived with our former spouses.

"We go west three times a year to see our children and grand-children, and on occasion they will come to visit us. But our marriage is at the heart of our lives. Marty and I are so pleased to have found each other and to be so compatible. It wasn't easy with our histories and our commitments to just pick up and leave, but we did. We felt that all the kids were married and had their own children and we were still vital enough to do something exciting. We did what people cannot do in a first marriage, we put ourselves ahead of our children. And," Daphne smiled, "it has worked out beautifully."

It is notable that for many widows and widowers the success of first marriages can be incorporated into the second. The mutuality of experience and the timing can bring a couple very close. When both a second wife and her husband are widowed, there is a comfort level that exceeds any other second wife scenario. Shared interests, commitment, and the appreciation of having found another partner is what drives the marriage. There is more satisfaction and fewer issues to be resolved. Still, neither the second wife nor her husband is as flexible as they were earlier in life. To be happy, both partners need to be in harmony and accepting of the other.

INTIMACY AT ANY AGE
Marriage is a unit formed by two people who love and cherish one another. Intimacy is a large part of the sharing and connecting. Regardless of the age of the second wife and her husband, intimacy must be preserved at all costs.

Of all the widower's wives who were interviewed, half are happily married and have adjusted well to the demands of caring for stepchildren and/or enhancing the husband's solitary existence. In some instances, the widower's second wives reported being quite unhappy in the marriage and a few of the older widower's wives are divorced from their spouses. One interviewee expressed her opposition to caring for a widower's young children, but very few women were haunted by the memory of the first wife.

As evidenced by the interviews, the dedication necessary to make a go of a second marriage to a widower is not like any other. While there is no ex-wife to interfere, the memory of the former wife may haunt the second wife, especially if the first wife is idealized after her death. Also, when marrying a young widower, a second wife may find herself an instant mother.

In some ways, the role of mother is easier to handle when marrying a widower rather than a divorced man. After a divorce, the children are often hostile and unaccepting of their father's new wife. For the children of widowers who are in need of a mother, acceptance of a new wife occurs more quickly and openly. In other ways, the role of mother for the second wife of a widower is more difficult than after a divorce. Children of divorce often spend most of their time or half of their time living with their mother, while the widower's children live year round in the same house as their father and his new wife. In this arrangement, a second wife may feel overwhelmed by pressure and stress, especially if she has never had children.

In later life, children are usually grown and ideally do not interfere with the new marriage. These marriages usually work well because both partners are older, wiser, and know what they want. They are also at a stage in life where they have similar goals and hopes. Yet they are also less flexible than they were when they were younger, a fact they must be aware of to avoid pitfalls.

No matter what obstacles the second wife of a widower faces, there are a few key ways to make her new marriage work. She must be independent and strong and thus able to be supportive of her husband. He may need to lean on her if he's still working through his grief or other issues. She must ignore and not fear comparisons. When a second wife feels insecure, she need only look to *Rebecca* for some perspective. In the book, the second wife eventually learned that Rebecca was not as wonderful in life as people made her seem after her death. If she had known all along the truth about Rebecca, she wouldn't have tortured herself or felt so haunted. No one can change the past. If a widower's former wife was the perfect woman or a fiend, the second wife must remember that she is a different person and the new marriage is different, too. The former wife's memory should not be obliterated, but the focus should be on the current relationship and the future they plan to share.

CHAPTER TEN

FANTASY MARRIAGES: POWER WIVES AND TROPHY WIVES

"As a young girl I was introduced to a successful older man and I knew what he expected of me," admits Rena. "This marriage was very purposeful on both our parts. I was chosen because I am a tall, thin, model type and he admired that look. I represented the physical attributes and life that my husband craved. He, in turn, offered financial security and the security that came from his knowledge of the world. I am absolutely his prize and he is my protector. I wear sheer and wild clothing for him and he likes to see how other men react. I know that his first wife was nothing like this; in fact, she was boring and plain. I am such a departure. They were of the same culture and religion while I am not. This is another benefit for him, another fantasy fulfilled. He was pushed into his first marriage when he was too young and they did all the things they were supposed to do together. This second marriage is a kick for him—he's having the time of his life.

"At first I reveled in the lifestyle that my husband offered me. I had left my first husband for him and was intrigued by the lavish things he could afford. There were clothes, jewels, restaurants, and nothing domestic was expected of me. He doesn't like me to do anything ordinary at all, not even boil water for tea. There was no glamour in his first marriage and he craves it

now. I'm always available for him and his first wife wasn't. On
the other hand, I don't think that he controlled his first wife and
he definitely attempts to control me. He is obsessed with me,
but it is a part of the relationship. It is only when I attempt to
break free in some way that there are any problems.

"I found there was no comparison between our marriage
and my husband's first marriage, which was non-sexual. How
can I feel threatened when it seems to me that she did not exist?
He tells me repeatedly that I am the first. He never mentions
her. What has happened, however, is that I'm breaking my mold
as a trophy wife. I am becoming a power wife. Recently, I landed
a job in advertising and I'm climbing the ladder quickly. I'm
finally able to choose my own clothes without having to consult
him. I was totally dependent, and that had to change. My husband is adjusting to my new found status."

Power Wives

When a woman attracts a man who is narcissistic to varying degrees,
whatever brand of narcissism he has, she is a reflection of it. In some
ways, a power wife is the antithesis of a trophy wife. Although both
types of second wives illuminate their husbands' fancies, the motivations
are quite different. The power wife has achieved success on her own,
without the benefits of her husband's accomplishments. She is professional and confident. The careers these second wives have are varied; she
may be a politician, a surgeon, an investment banker, an artist, an actress.
But she has forged her career and cultivated power on her own. If life is
a pie, the marriage of a power couple is a large piece of their pie, but
not the entire pie. This second wife's career and position is unquestion-
ably a priority and her success defines her to a large degree.

The power wife/second wife attracts a man who has achieved a
great deal on his own as well. It appeals to him that this partner in many
cases, is equally or more successful than he, while his first wife was
dependent. When we think of power wives, several women come to
mind: actress Nicole Kidman, married to actor Tom Cruise; actress and
exercise guru Jane Fonda, married to mogul Ted Turner; anchorwoman
Connie Chung, married to television host Maury Povich; and news journalist Claudia Cohen, the second wife of financier Ron Perelman. In
these instances, we see both partners pursuing their paths and joining
together in a personal merger.

Each of these women commands her own fame and recognition. What appeals to the husband is his second wife's success. Secure in his own success, he is not threatened by hers, but proud of it. These couples share the limelight and enhance each other.

"After a divorce, many professional men—doctors, bankers, lawyers—remarry women who are in the same profession and considerably younger than they are," Brondi Borer, divorce mediator, acknowledges. "These women are nothing like the first wives who stayed home, had children, and got their husbands through the lean years by emotionally supporting them. The second marriage is about an intellectual peer who is a kind of trophy—an intellectual trophy. She and he are on the same level academically and intellectually. Powerful men really like that and the women find a power merger has its perquisites."

In a power marriage, the wife may fulfill one role while the husband fulfills another. If she has a high powered job and he is artistic, this works. If both partners have high powered jobs, they become a power couple. A highly visible power wife in the political arena is Elizabeth Dole, whose second marriage to former senator Robert Dole has endured changes. And the interesting combination of liberal James Carville and conservative Mary Matalin has enlivened several national shows.

Though in power marriages the wife is powerful as well as her husband, she often identifies with his strength because she wants to be with another person with high energy. "It is dull and boring for a woman who is not ambitious and hungry to be with a man who is and vice versa," says Dr. Ronnie Burak. "In a case of equals, the excitement is shared. Women who are powerful are very involved with their careers and travels, as are their husbands. If they are not with a man on the same kind of schedule, the relationship doesn't always evolve."

There are instances when the balance between the power wife and her husband shifts. This is not new. In the past, for actresses in Hollywood, the lure of fame and fortune was sometimes threatened by a traditional marriage. When talented Elizabeth Ashley married actor George Peppard, who had a popular television series in the 1960's, she allowed her own career to dwindle because he wanted a conventional wife. Ashley gave up several plumb parts in films to please her husband. When they divorced, she sought to reclaim her career after a long hiatus.

If mutual respect exists and both partners carry out and respect each others' interests, change is less threatening to the marriage. Losing oneself in a relationship, especially a power relationship, is never healthy and ends up causing major issues between the two partners. This is especially true when they paired as a power couple.

HOW TO SUCCEED IN A POWER MARRIAGE
• Build a relationship in which you both give each other space
• Respect his wishes without losing yourself
• Carve a life for yourselves that suits both your needs
• Keep him interested in your career
• Keep interested in his career

Jude, a physician, has been a second wife for seven years and is now contemplating divorce. "My husband, David, is fifteen years older than I am and got a divorce from his first wife because of our affair. The entire episode took most of my adult life. We were together secretly for seven years before he actually began to get divorced. During this time, I hung in, built my career, and waited. He was not in his first marriage for any reason but the children. I knew that and so I did not resent his ex-wife as much as I resented his children. I was not concerned that he had done all that he had with someone else, I just wanted to move forward with him. What happened was that during the time he was getting divorced, because he is someone who is out there—a player, if you will—he became very educated about divorce laws and practices. He kept the divorce lawyer on call because he was so guarded even after we were married.

"My husband liked very much that I was a doctor and had done so well. I was definitely a feather in his cap. In his first marriage, David was his ex-wife's trophy and Phyllis flaunted him. Then he had a chance to make me into the power wife and he flaunted me. Had he not done so well on his own, he might not have tired of being her toy. But once he achieved his own success, my husband wanted someone successful on his arm. It was suddenly reversed. I grew tired of being the one shown off to the world. I craved closeness and a less public life. Had I continued to play it his way, we might have survived. I suspect he will want another kind of wife altogether in the future. Perhaps someone very beautiful without brains. A trophy wife. Who knows."

Maryann has repeatedly gone for older, respected, and successful men, and then married one. "I know the life that Austin and I share is very threatening to his ex-wife, Ashley. She begrudges me the material things I have and resents my young children as well. She knows, as well as I do, that my husband is content with me. My strength and independence is maddening to her. I know that Austin married me for this and that Ashley's abilities are of a very different sort. We are in the same field, but with very dissimilar approaches. I have been very successful while she has not done as well. What my husband has repeated in marrying me is that he is taking on a partner who works and who has a degree. I'm motivated and successful and always moving up. I provide Austin these things, but also give him more. Ashley was not able to. I realize he was looking for a certain type of person and he thought he found it in his first wife. But she was only that type on the surface, and he wanted more. He found it in me. How lucky we are to have a life together and to have the same goals."

There are instances where a power wife is substantially younger than her husband. Whatever her age, the fantasy of having a wife who is powerful in her own right does not work for some men and women. It works when both partners are committed to the partnership. The lifestyle may be materially driven and sexually intense, but whatever it is, the husband is enamored of his second wife and her achievements.

Bridget has had three older successful partners. "To them, I am the departure, the second wife worth striving for. I am younger, professional, successful, and quite attractive. I come into the picture for these men after they have had boring first marriages with wives who stay at home. I do not look for a romantic marriage, but one where lifestyle counts. It is odd that I have been a second wife to men like this three times. But mostly, I see that they want me for what I bring to the table. If it only counted that I have looks, I would not be happy. But my husbands cannot believe that I am successful in my work, run my own business that makes a substantial amount of money, and I still look good. For powerful men, this is a bonus. Men still believe they can only have one or the other, achievement or sex appeal in a partner. I contradict the theory. But I'm not after constant romance and intimacy. And I pay little attention to their children. I have one child, in his teens, and he is the one who counts. Yet I put the marriage ahead of all of the children, his and mine. It is the only way to succeed. A man who wants me will want my full attention and what I can bring to his life. I make him feel important."

"A marriage to a power wife can be a relationship of equality," Dr. Michele Kasson remarks. "These people meet because they are on the same level in the professional world. Each person, the woman and the man, is doing her/his own thing and they find each other. The power wife can be very independent. She is often unlike the first wife."

Betina is fifteen years her husband's junior. "I am totally aware of why my husband left his marriage to marry me. He definitely needed someone who did something. We live in a little town in Eastern Pennsylvania and the fact that I have a job and make my own way is a big deal to him. He boasts about how I own a restaurant that is very popular and still take care of his older children and my own little ones. It is a lot to handle, but I feel confident. He tells everyone how capable I am and how I still look sexy and beautiful even with all that I do. It adds energy to the marriage. His career is important to him, but not in the same way that I take my job so seriously. He works for the government in a fast paced sales office. Basically, when we get together, we spend quiet time and relax. We have begun a new life together and he is really delighted with the marriage. I feel his pride and his lack of criticism. Since I never had much praise before, I am thrilled to have it now. I am not afraid of growing old with my husband. I know that we will change, we will not look as good. Somehow none of it frightens me because we are together and I feel I am his prize."

Most of the power wives with whom I spoke are not as threatened by their husbands' past marriages as other kinds of second wives may be. While the power wife may have narcissistic tendencies, it is also healthy that the marriage is incorporated into her life. In the best scenario, she handles the role with aplomb, and the connection to her husband results in teamwork. If both partners seek the same ratio of career, social success, and intimacy, then they are well suited to each other.

Trophy Wives

The trophy wife may be younger than her husband, and is the kind of woman whose looks and sometimes social position demand attention. Whether she is forty to her husband's fifty or thirty to his forty, she looks better than other men's wives and he takes pride in showing her off. This husband does not want the same kind of wife as he had in his first marriage, someone who probably raised the children and ran a household. "When the husband finds a second wife who is younger and prettier than his first, it is because he believes that he deserves something better. This is a form of narcissism," says Dr. Michele Kasson.

The husband seeks an attractive and/or socially prominent woman who functions as a "trophy." She, in turn, gets an older, wealthier man who admires her and her attributes, which he shows off to the world. The trophy wife as his second wife is invested in the marriage for her fulfillment: that of financial and emotional security. In many cases, she is disinterested in her husband's first wife because she is preoccupied with her own state of well-being.

In most but not all cases, "the husband holds the purse strings," says Christopher Rush, private investigator. "The second wife gets quite a lifestyle. This second wife has a big house, foreign cars, and hired help. The first wife may or may not have had it; it depends on when this man became wealthy."

Things become complicated if the marriage is so superficial that it is unhealthy and without depth. In any marriage, first, second, or third, if there is no foundation, no matter what the understanding, any unexpected stress will take its toll.

Dr. Ronnie Burak believes that most women who are notably younger than their husbands want to be taken care of. "This is a woman who is fearful of being alone and might come from an overprotective family. The subtle message growing up was that she is not able to make it on her own. Her mother is a study for that and has always been dependent upon a man—in this case, the father."

One trophy wife with whom I spoke typifies many of these qualities. "I am very confident of my role and I'm too secure to wish that my husband hadn't been married before or to think about the fact that I am not the first woman who walked into his life," Lucia, a California blond who is twenty years younger than her husband, explains. "I have never looked at myself as a certain kind of wife, some kind of label. My focus is on this marriage and the life I have given to him. I see that I make him happier than he could ever have been without me.

"By the time that Greg and I met, he had become very successful and had lots of money. The first time around he was not settled or established. I know that his first wife, Betty, views us as similar, that I am simply a younger version of herself. It isn't so; she deludes herself. And I know that she has done some nasty things, such as sending her daughter, my stepdaughter, on our honeymoon. On the other hand, I'm the one he's with—what more is there to say?

"I was very taken with Greg, and he saw me as glamorous and very sexy. I was once a model for *Sports Illustrated*. We went to bed immediately and that was that. I'm very sensuous and an artist. She was a social worker and so unlike me. Once I became pregnant, she backed off completely. Even pregnant, I knew that my husband was quite taken with me and my style."

A controlling husband usually is a part of the dynamic of the trophy marriage. This second wife does not delude herself in any way. She knows what the trade-off is and since her husband is enamored of her looks and style, she relies on his persistent affection. The trophy wife, having found her stage, is usually pleased with her situation and quite amenable.

CONTROL ISSUES
She may give herself over to the controlling husband willingly, because she sees this as part of the deal. In return, she attains the lavish lifestyle she strongly desires.

The issue of control also comes into play if the potential trophy wife is asked to sign a prenuptial agreement. "When older men marry younger women, the younger woman should not resist the prenuptial agreement," recommends Brondi Borer, divorce mediator. "It simply means the husband has to preserve his obligations made before the marriage. She should respect his first family's needs. However, some young wives see it as the ultimate control."

For Meredith, her position as a trophy wife comes from her patrician looks and social connections. "I have been married three times, and in each marriage I was a second wife. I always seem to marry someone who likes who I am on paper and not who I am in my heart and soul. I come from a successful family. I know that my ex-husband's first wife was from an excellent family also. So I suppose it's a pattern with him. With my present husband, Charlie, his first wife was not from money. He really sought a socially prominent wife. I think that his ex-wife hates me because I have him and did not need him financially or socially. The whole package that I represent drives her crazy. I've learned to ignore her. I know that together my husband and I click. He needs someone who can introduce him to a social life, who can entertain and see and be seen. He appreciates it and I keep it going. I don't deny that we are both into society living."

"In a marriage where the second wife and husband are egotistical, neither recognizes the other's egoism. This is affirming for the second wife. The trophy wife is validated by the way that her husband treats her," states Dr. Michele Kasson. "This is about interpersonal power, and the feeling that she is better than the first wife. The feelings of superiority are very important to her."

"I did not tell my husband that I had two plastic surgeries when

I became his second wife," confides Wendy. "One to lift my eyes and the other to enlarge my breasts. I didn't want him to know, because I thought he would judge me. I knew that he was enamored of my looks and he kept saying to me that he couldn't believe I had two children who were in college. I think he wanted a beauty and was relieved to find someone who not only looked good but already had children. The pressure was off. Meanwhile, I kept quiet about all of this self-improvement because I was afraid. I didn't even tell him that I colored my hair. For him, I know that I was his trophy of sorts. I wasn't a classic trophy, because I'd achieved a lot with my career as an illustrator. I enhanced him with my looks and my artistic talent.

"He is a business man who really wanted someone beautiful on his arm who knew the things he didn't. At these social functions, I was able to talk about art shows and films while he could be his linear self and think of business all night long. The marriage fits both of us. But I am very guarded when it comes to my vanity. Perhaps if we had been married longer or if we were more like best friends, I'd be able to talk about it. Right now we are in a honeymoon stage, with lots of romance, sex, and going out together where he can show me off. This marriage works for me because I like the fact that he is so pleased with me and is so successful. We are tolerant of each other's hectic schedules, yet when it comes to a business function, I'm there for him."

WHEN THE BALANCE SHIFTS
Once a trophy wife realizes the limitations of her role, she may struggle to break free. As the initial superficiality wanes, the marriage is hopefully left with a deeper connection.

The marriage becomes precarious when the trophy wife begins to feel stifled and less valuable. At this juncture, one of two things happens, either the relationship begins to have some substance and credibility even while the wife is trying to reinvent herself, or it falls apart completely. As with any attachment, if it is only superficial, it will not last.

DOES IT WITHSTAND THE TEST OF TIME?
If the marriage evolves from being based on a special attribute of the second wife to a partnership of equals, then it can succeed. If a man wants only a second wife for the vicarious thrill of her looks and status, then the marriage probably will eventually wither.

Arm Candy

"Arm candy," the phrase for the latest type of escort/girlfriend/trophy wife, refers to a beautiful woman who is considerably younger than her man. In fact, the husband is so much older that often he is like a father figure to this woman. The woman is impeccable in terms of looks and style. It is fairly obvious to the outside world that her main attribute is her ability to be shown off. Usually these women rely on their looks and often times are or have been models. This second marriage feeds into the husband's conceit more than a "power wife." The connection this wife and husband share is questionable since they are not beginning on an equal playing field. One could wonder if they are truly suited for each other. This woman reaps the power of her husband's monetary success, while he objectifies her.

"If a woman's father was estranged or living away from the family during her childhood, the woman may seek out a father figure in her adulthood." According to Dr. Ronnie Burak, "This may manifest itself in marrying an older, more stable man. In these instances, the marriage changes as the woman grows older and her dependency on an older man is no longer necessary."

For Kayla, her trophy wifehood is about a certain kind of lifestyle. "Gil appreciates how attractive I am when we're out in public. I like playing the role. I know how to do it and he likes that. Gil always tells me how good I look. He is involved with how I dress and likes sexy designer clothes. He buys me jewelry and then I have the power because I show it off to the world. Our marriage is a second chance for him, no question about it. We also include a family life. But it is the glamour and romance that he prides himself on. I know he never treated his first wife, Marilyn, like this. I think that Marilyn knows this and resents it. She was not a glamorous wife. And I am. Still," Kayla confessed, "Marilyn is in my head and is never really gone. I hold onto what I do for him that she could never have done. The most successful factor in my marriage is the age difference and my husband's past experience."

FEEDING TROPHY EGOS

If a husband feeds his trophy wife's ego and she feeds his, their union is a success. She may be there for the money and he for her looks—but if both partners are satisfied, they may be very happy. Money or social status can be aphrodisiacs. Their needs are thus being met in this type of union.

Being chosen for one's looks becomes a pressure as the years pass. The second wife who is keenly conscious of her position may worry that she could be replaced. Again, the marriage requires substance to keep it alive. Success is achieved when the husband and wife carry each other, and both partners are pleased with the outcome.

AGING SECOND WIVES

If you are chosen for looks instead of deeper attributes like ability or intelligence, the union becomes precarious as the years pass. For the woman who ages gracefully and is complete within herself, the marriage works beyond the peripheral layer. Maturity and/or striking a deal is the answer if nothing profound is established between the two partners.

Another potential danger zone for these second wives involves the area of finances. Cynthia George, a divorce attorney, has had many interactions with second wives who are so-called "trophies" where there are issues of control and money. "In my practice I have represented second wives on their finances in a prenuptial agreement. Often the husbands want their prenuptial agreements to limit their exposure if they go through a divorce again. These are the issues that women face. They believe that they will be taken care of financially, particularly a younger second wife. Then their future husbands say that their money is off limits. These husbands view their money as separate from their wives. The second wife is forced to negotiate as if planning for a future divorce."

On occasion, wives who begin as trophies mature into women of substance and their relationships change. Camilla, a two time second wife, chose both times to marry a man who would give her a certain security. "I was raised to be married and I fit the bill nicely. I was young and very appealing—that was the initial draw for my husbands. But my present husband and I have gone way beyond that. I know that he is proud to have me by his side. The fact that I was a model means less and less. I know that something like that cannot sustain a marriage, especially because his first wife was also very alluring and beautiful. I sometimes become afraid that my husband goes from one pretty woman on his arm to the next. That is why it is so important that we have more than that in our marriage. Still, I know why he first sought me out. I'm not nearly as sure as I was in my first marriage that I'm indispensable. I think that's why his first wife gets to me. Deep down, maybe I worry that I'm next."

Despite the fact that a maturing relationship has the chance to grow into a fully developed one, Christopher Rush, private investigator, warns against the young wife/older husband trophy marriages. "Repeatedly I see a second wife married to a man in his late forties to late sixties where the woman is there to stay as long as she needs to. She divorces him because she can get some money at this juncture, because she is younger and wants to live a life she desires. If the man is retired, this woman's lifestyle may be curtailed because he is now not at the office and is watching her more closely. That's when she looks for a husband who is closer to her age. If she becomes a second wife again, it is with a man who is more her style. At that point, financial security will not be as much of an issue as she is financially secure from her first marriage to the older man."

When a second wife is married to a man and the marriage lacks dimension or is shallow, the marriage is at great risk. The ability to grow together is limited, if the superficial aspects of the relationship are all encompassing. If a man marries a model only for her looks, regardless of how exquisite she is, the day-to-day grind of life will soon overcome them. If there is no team effort, and no real substance, there is no real attachment. This is true of all marriages. If, for example, a couple gets married because of their similar career goals and focus only on money and success, but do not share an emotional connection, their marriage is likely to fall apart. If there are no shared interests, no common views on life, the marriage may not succeed, despite an initial understanding of why the partners are together.

TRUTH OR CONSEQUENCES

If a couple finds that they fill shallow needs, the union can work for each person. Yet if one partner's views change or desires no longer mesh with the other's, it is not easy to hold on.

"Amongst second marriages, it is the ones where the partners are together for show that have the toughest time. If both partners are able to bring something of quality to the marriage beyond the image, then they have both—the trophy and the bonding. If there is nothing but a seduction, it wears thin," explains Dr. Michele Kasson.

Sharon became a second wife when she was in her mid-twenties. Eighteen years later, she has certain regrets about the life she has led. "I know that my husband has always loved me, but it has been a rocky road. His first wife was his age and they grew up together and had a family. When I met John, he was already successful and had become well-known in his field. Valerie was bitter about the divorce, but I was too immersed in my life with my new husband to pay much attention. From the start John and I had this ideal, fairy-tale life. He wanted me there for every company event and to host his dinner parties. There has been a lot of entertaining and travel from the start.

"The other issue for me has been his temper. In private, John can be very cruel and it frightens me. I know that many women would want this life, but it is very lonely when we are at home. We have four children, two sons and two daughters and they are the joys of my life. When my husband joins us for dinner or is with us on weekends, I am always uptight. I worry that John will go on to the next wife, a younger version of me, perhaps, someone similar but fresher. I work hard to please him and my goal is to remain his second wife. I never forget that I was chosen to be on his arm and the life we have shared shows me how quickly he can forget or become disinterested. It isn't easy and sometimes I lose faith."

Sharon's fear of being replaced causes her to constantly strive to please her husband. Other women who find themselves in similar circumstances may use sex to do the same. Yet she must be aware of her husband's sexual desires and needs in their marriage. Oftentimes, he isn't all that interested in her sexiness when they're not in the public eye, and her attempts to use sex to hold onto him will subsequently backfire.

"Sex, in these instances, can go in several directions," according to Dr. Ronnie Burak. "If the woman is beautiful and he's all about money, he wants someone at his side to be a sexual object. Then sex is a big part of the marriage. If she is very powerful herself, this is also sexy to a lot of men. Yet their sex life may take a backseat to their hectic schedules and they may simply be exhausted much of the time."

A trophy wife or arm candy can be sexually gratifying for her husband and speak to his ego. Many men of a certain age feel they need this kind of woman in order to be aroused. For the "trophy" woman, her sexuality really depends on the private deal: does her husband want her or does he just want her to be sexy in public?

SEX AND THE TROPHY MARRIAGE

How the intimacy plays out in trophy marriages varies. A man who has been around may or may not be very interested in her sexually. It might be that the second wife has chosen an older man because she does not wish for the sexual part of the marriage. Or sex may be at the very heart of the union for her.

A typical scenario with trophy marriages that do not fare well concerns the husband's perpetual search for affirmation. It could be that once he is where he wants to be in life, he no longer needs whatever kind of ego satisfaction in the form of fantasy his wife provided. He has shown her off to the world and the relationship is neither novel nor exciting. If the wife is substantially younger than her husband, this may continue to make him feel young. Or, as the relationship cools, he may go on a desperate search for his next wife in an effort to continue feeling youthful.

CHANGING FLAVORS
When the trophy wife loses her appeal to her husband, it is possible that he will seek out another woman. Because he feels defined by her effect on others, a different woman may fulfill him at different stages in his life.

Charlotte is a second wife for a second time, and in both cases, she views herself as someone who enhanced her husband. "I met my first husband when I was twenty-three years old. Clint had two sons and an ex-wife who looked remarkably like me. He wanted to be married immediately and so we were. That was how it was with him, he always called the shots. I knew that my role was to be a happy, beautiful wife, to give him children, and to look terrific wherever we went. We had three daughters together and then he died. I was in my mid-thirties with three young children and I was very frightened. Because Clint was so well-respected in our hometown, people were kind to me. But it wore off and I finally decided to move across the country.

"This worked out and I met someone else. What is so surprising to me is how similar Alfred is to my first husband. He had been divorced for several years and has grown children. So again, I am married to a man who is fifteen years my senior and has a strong position in the town we live in. I think his wife was tired of his inflexible nature. I suit his needs, because I have been trained to be this kind of wife by my first husband. I know that I am to organize our social life and make sure that we see his clients and travel whenever he wants.

"For me, there have been trade-offs. In both marriages, I was denied the chance to be my husband's equal partner. Always, I had to look good and be perfect, even while I was raising the children in the first marriage. It seemed ideal in some ways. I just wonder if another type of man exists, and if there would be less pressure from him. For my husbands, I have been expected to take care of everything, to be constantly available, personable and a knockout to show off to the rest of the world. What I had wanted is a best friend, and I don't believe that the brand of men I've married can be like that. The upside is that I am very well taken care of financially. I am secure and I know that Alfred adores me and protects me. I work hard at keeping my looks up and being socially connected because I do not want him leaving. I do know that men like my husbands are willing and able to get a newer model."

Men like Donald Trump, who go from one beautiful, accomplished wife to the next, are becoming more visible in our society. In the past, this occurrence happened more commonly among movie stars and socialites. For a husband who chooses a woman as his ornament, when she loses favor and he is ready to go on to the next, there are a myriad of problems down the road for his flavor of the month.

In addition, plucking a pretty face out of a crowd to wear on his arm may lead to unexpected outcomes. Just because a woman is pretty does not mean that she will quietly perch on a man's arm and do his bidding. The shortsighted man who looks for such a woman may be in for a big surprise when she shows some spunk and rejects his demands for submission.

SERIALLY MONOGAMOUS HUSBAND
A man who seeks out a second wife to adorn him may not have the commitment level to stay married. His inability to make a substantial interpersonal relationship is what draws him to this second wife from the start. The union is not about how to relate to someone, but about the prestige he derives from the relationship.

Many of the women interviewed felt a sense of entitlement in their roles as second wives in power or trophy marriages. Consequently, some were disappointed and disillusioned when things didn't turn out exactly as they imagined. Many of the trophy wives disclosed their fear that their husbands would eventually seek out a newer, younger, prettier model and divorce them. This fear is not surprising considering these women were chosen solely because of their physical attributes. After interviewing these power and trophy wives, I have found that it is important for a woman stepping into either of these roles to realize that such unions are fantasies for them and their husbands. In theory, the marriage may seem like a dream come true, but in practice, these relationships may be far less appealing. When the motivation to begin these marriages is strictly to have superficial and material needs met without any emotional connection, the relationship will ultimately be unfulfilling and come to an end. While a large part of a relationship can be the satisfaction of each partners' needs, it requires love, respect, and commitment to be long lasting and rewarding.

When a man seeks out a "trophy" wife and a woman willingly fills that role, their motivations to do so are often borne of issues like poor self-worth and an inability to have meaningful relationships. Such a relationship cannot help but be based on negativity at the outset; however, there is still a possibility of it developing into a rich and rewarding marriage. If the couple grows together, shares their hopes and dreams, and develops deeper feelings for each other, their relationship can flourish.

Like the trophy couple, the coming together of a power couple may be based on negative motivations. If a man chooses a power wife to enhance his image and feed his ego, his superficial needs must change at some point if the marriage is to be truly meaningful, enriching, and successful. However, the union of a power couple may also be borne of positive forces for both husband and wife. When a man marries a power wife because of an emotional connection and shared goals and values, and sees their union as a loving partnership of equals in which each enhances the other, the marriage has the advantage of a positive start.

Although the average age of men divorcing for the first time in the United States is thirty-five and the average age for women thirty-three, as documented in a report by the National Center for Health Statistics, this is not applicable in the case of fantasy marriages. Usually, the discrepancy in age between these partners is notable. Neveretheless, However, the age gap may or may not have much of an impact. More important to the success of the marriage are the reasons each partner has for entering the union. In certain societies, money and its perquisites, that of a luxurious life, dominate the marriage. This phenomenon is not new, yet it becomes more pervasive in our culture with its emphasis on materialism, fame, and fortune. If one partner's or the other's expectations and needs are not being met, or the marriage is based on shallow considerations, it is very unlikely that it will stand the test of time.

CHAPTER ELEVEN

REUNITING LONG LOST LOVES

"We grew up in a small town in the Midwest and were high school sweethearts," Rita begins. "Cal and I were in love from the time that we were seventeen. When he went to college, I went to his college dances and we made a promise that we'd always be together. The problem was religion: I was Catholic and he wasn't. So we met with resistance from our families. I met someone else when I was twenty-two and married him. Cal, my high school sweetheart, also got married to someone when he was young, about twenty-four. Although our families lived nearby, we lost touch completely.

"I thought about Cal all the time. I was busy raising my children and wasn't missing him as much as I was thinking about him. I hoped I would run into him when I was out with my husband. I suppose I wanted to look good and make him sorry he hadn't ended up with me. We never did run into each other. Then I moved away. I was living halfway across the country, unaware that he was trying to find me.

"Cal would go to local bars and expect to see me or hear about me. Finally he hired a detective, but it was a friend of his who eventually found me through my sister. After twenty years of marriage, he tracked me down. By then, we were both miserable in our marriages and he flew out to see me. After that, I

saw him about once a month. I knew then I was not going to
be just his Midwest girlfriend and telephone sweetheart.

"Even before Cal showed up I knew I'd made a mistake in
my marriage. I hadn't been planning to remarry, but I knew I
wanted to leave. I just wanted to get out. After a brief affair
with Cal, we made the decision to get married. Our children, his
four and my three, were destroyed by our divorces and by our
subsequent marriage. This has been a long, hard road. I didn't
understand why my children were quite so angry when they
knew their father and I didn't get along. I was only waiting until
they were old enough to leave. I suppose I was selfish in leaving,
in taking care of myself.

"Nineteen years later, Cal and I are still blissfully happy.
I'm not convinced this would have worked the first time
around—I really do believe that children spoil romance. We
made a pact that the marriage came ahead of everyone and
everything else. The years without each other make it all the
more special to be together today."

For second wives like Rita who end up married to boyfriends of
years ago, those they knew in college or high school, there is the great
dream of recapturing one's youth and a comfort level in returning to what
was once so familiar. Often in these stories, there is the break-up of a family in order to accomplish the second marriage. The odds are that "long
lost loves" are rediscovered at quite an emotional price—even the children
realize that this is whom the parent has been pining for all these years.

The second wife who appears out of the past may be intensely
resented by the first wife. While the first wife often was a homemaker
who ran the house and raised the children in a marriage that appeared
happy to the outside world, the second wife who comes along later is
often not required to care for the house or for the children. Her husband desires her full attention. The irony here is that had he married the
same woman early on, as planned or hoped for originally, the second
wife/long lost love might very well have been in the shoes of the first
wife, filling the conventional expectations of a young wife and mother.
Instead of attention and romance, which is a major component of many
second marriages, there would have been the day to day grind—financial pressures, household chores, child rearing—of first marriages.

"Second marriages that rekindle an old romance are not without problems," notes Brondi Borer, divorce mediator. "Usually, many years have passed and both the man and the woman have older children and viable marriages. They have acquired assets as well, and with such a highly romantic second marriage about to take place, I recommend that these partners sign a prenuptial agreement. The more starry-eyed the couple, the more I recommend a prenup."

Those who become second wives to their old sweethearts can be of any age. Such a reunion might happen after a five-year marriage or it may take thirty years to rediscover one's long lost love. Once the two have found each other again, the momentum is intense and the desire to be together at all costs sometimes dominates their lives. A high school reunion, a college reunion, a mutual friend's child's wedding—these are the ways that people find each other again after forming their lives with others.

HOW REUNIONS HAPPEN
• He is travelling for business and looks his former girlfriend up
• There is a high school or college reunion
• There is a wedding or other celebration for a mutual high school or college friend's child
• One person gets the courage to call the other out of the blue

The reason the reunion of long lost lovers is so painful to their children and ex-spouses is because of the exclusivity of the relationship. The statement made in returning to a former love for a second marriage is that the one chosen instead—the first spouse—was a short term necessity, but meaningless in the long run. If this is the message that an ex-husband receives, the children of the first marriage will inevitably feel rejected as well. They may even fear that their mother laments the birth of her children with her first husband and deeply regrets that she did not instead have children with her old boyfriend.

Edwina, who is forty-three and lives in Dallas, found her long lost love after her twenty-year-old marriage fell apart. "I called Jason when my husband walked out on me, because I needed his advice on financial matters. Jason had always told me that I could count on him. Now I look back and I'm not sure why we ever lost each other. Somehow we fell apart after college and each of us married someone else. I was always sorry that I didn't marry him.

"I kept track of my old boyfriend whenever I could. Jason married first and I remember his wedding date and feeling so sad. I tried not to be alone that day and tried to surround myself with friends. Jason believed that the woman he married was better suited to him. She was older than I and had more in common with him. The families knew each other and it seemed important at the time. We both lived in Dallas and would run into each other with our spouses now and then over the years. I assumed that Jason was happy and he assumed that I was, too. Once he learned that I was separated, Jason also separated. I found great comfort in being with him. I felt the same connection with him I had when we were young, as if no time had passed at all. Nothing had changed although we now had seven children between us.

"I know that my marriage to Jason is in direct comparison to his first marriage. I give him all that was missing, all that we missed together. I realize now how superficial my first marriage was and how wrong it was for me. I also see how wrong his first marriage was for him. Jason doesn't want anything in our lives that isn't necessary. We do not want a frivolous life. And I have more confidence now because of him. I can face what went wrong for me and for him in each of our first marriages. I see our love as very adult, and yet it stems from a time when we both were so young. We feel very young together for this reason. We fantasize that we are the Brady Bunch with our kids, and that our love for each other, based on such an ancient history, provides the kids with a kind of support system. When there are problems, I just remember where I come from and appreciate him all the more. What is sad is how damaged we both are, from our past marriages and from our past lives."

After a woman spends years wondering what happened to the very special person she knew in the past, he is rediscovered and the flame is rekindled. The longing and caring has another chance. No matter what the age of the second wife who marries her long lost love, there is a sense that she is eternally young because of him. As a couple, because of all they went through before being reunited, they feel renewed and undefeatable. Together they can weather any storm.

UNIONS THAT REDISCOVER YOUTHFUL LOVE
- The long lost fantasy of love becomes a reality
- The old love never dies
- The second marriage is very precious
- Both partners feel young and alive

Seventeen years elapsed before Emily found again and married her high school boyfriend, Vincent, three years ago. "I think about his ex-wife, Michelle, sometimes and I know that she and I have something in common. Not our personalities but our interests and our hobbies. Of course, Michelle hates me so much that it is hard to believe we would have anything in common at all. I do understand what happened in my husband's first marriage. The way I see it, Michelle was abusive and it was brought on by her own unhappiness. She is an unhappy person, but I know Vince was once in love with her—not in the same way as he is in love with me. We have a whole history, a kind of secret language we speak only to each other.

"I know that Vince and I appreciate our marriage all the more for what has gone on in our lives since we lost touch. Vince and I were both in bad places and we saved each other. It is as though we never lost touch—we are that close—and it is so easy to be together. But I have a deep regret for the years we missed being together. And because of his unhappy first marriage, I make sure to make him feel secure. Emotional security is a big issue for my husband because of how he was treated by his first wife and because of his natural disposition. I feel secure in knowing I am totally loved for who I am."

"There is a shared connection, a shared community with some-one from the past," Dr. Ronnie Burak tells us. "This puts the couple at an advantage, even years later. This cushion of knowing the person cre-ates less risk in the relationship. For a person who has been living a less than optimal adult life, finding this person is very valuable. It can turn her or his life around."

Such a union came to Margaret, who is forty and spent eighteen years away from the "love of her life." "In college, my boyfriend, Tommy, and I made a pact that we'd be married and together forever. We had graduated from the same high school and had known each other since we were fifteen. Then Tommy joined the army and we were sepa-rated for a year. When he came home, either he'd been influenced by someone else, or he had changed his mind. He got a scholarship on the east coast and I stayed at home and got a job. I married for the first time when I was twenty-three, but I never stopped wondering about Tommy. My cousin kept in touch with him. They were friends and had been on the football team together in high school. He told me Tommy was sin-gle and dating constantly. It turned my stomach to hear about him. By then I had twin daughters and I was very busy. My marriage, at that time, was okay—it had its good moments.

"I heard that Tommy had gotten married about ten years ago and had moved to Oklahoma. It never even occurred to me that we could be together again; I thought the dream had died a long time ago. By then, the condition of my marriage was poor and I was thinking of getting divorced. I ran into Tommy at an airport of all places, and that was it. He got divorced, too. I moved my kids to Tulsa and found a new job in order for us to be together. We met with lots of opposition from our children, our ex-spouses, our parents, and our friends. His ex-wife was so angry and hurt. People thought we were immoral. I honestly believe Tommy and I both would be divorced from our first spouses anyway. But the timing worked so we could be together. We were married last year and all our children attended the wedding. What I have learned since we are together is that life at forty is not life at twenty, no matter who you are with. But I love him. I have always loved him."

The lure of unfinished business is very strong for the second wife who chooses to marry her boyfriend from years ago. A tolerance for each other's children is usually a part of this specific type of marriage, which is not always found in second marriages. Because there was a shared love and a shared loss in not marrying each other the first time around, the second wife's attitude toward her stepchildren is commonly one of magnanimity. With a great romance that was never consummated in marriage comes practicality and caution. The second wife is confident and realistic, devoted to her husband who was once her lover and extremely grateful for the second chance they share.

Meanwhile, the first wife is agitated because the husband and his new wife are living the life she was preparing for. She has been cheated of domestic happiness and a particular lifestyle. The betrayal of a husband leaving his first marriage for his old girlfriend is a double blow to the first wife. Not only is the life that was built around the first marriage now demolished, but the replacement by someone the first wife may have heard about twenty years earlier is enormously painful.

UNFINISHED BUSINESS

The new couple is ecstatic to be reunited. Whether their children from the first marriages are happy or not, the couple is not fazed. Their attitude is positive; they welcome each other's children. They are in awe of their rekindled love for one another—appreciative and grateful. The first wife is understandably jealous and angry.

"In some ways, I was disappointed when I became a second wife to my boyfriend from my single days," Roz laments. "I really expected this man to appreciate me because of what we had been through in our first marriages and because we had known each other for so long. I think that he treats me the same way he treated his first wife, which is financially, but not emotionally, kindly. And I do not respond as she did. That is the difference. What I do to make our marriage work is show him what he does wrong and to try to encourage him to feel and express more. I doubt his first wife ever did that and I doubt that he would have listened to her. The only reason he listens to me is because we have a shared past, we know each other. We want to be together—we wanted that a long time ago.

"I have tried to make our marriage work but it has been very hard. I knew what it would be like from the days when we were a couple. I remember how much I wanted his company and why I hang on to it now. Yet when I see how distant he can be, I have less regret for the years we were not together. I had no illusions about him the first time and no illusions about him the second. What I had hoped for though, in becoming his second wife, was that some of his negative attributes had softened a bit. I'm still looking for romance and excitement and a best friendship—just what I wanted years before. But I can feel his first wife saying to herself, 'Better you than me.'"

The potential pitfalls of pursuing one's long lost love are evident. In Roz's case, she found that some of her old boyfriend's negative attributes had—despite her hopes—not lessened with time, but were just as she remembered. Unfortunately, what comes along with the desire to reunite with a long lost love is a starry-eyed view of the past. With time, old hurts and bad feelings that might have broken up the young romance are forgotten and replaced with the nostalgia of one's youth. This nostalgia may lead a man or woman into a relationship that they wouldn't normally want, especially if they are reeling from an unhappy first marriage or bitter divorce.

"The attraction still exists between old flames," Dr. Michele Kasson explains, "and since their lives together did not work out, there is the search to try out that old flame the second time. If the opportunity presents itself, these old girlfriends/boyfriends will try to reestablish the good feelings on a more adult level, that of a second marriage since the first one never happened." If they can accomplish this while being realistic about their relationship—both the current one and the past one—the rewards can be plentiful.

"When I attended my twentieth college reunion," says Kristen, "I never expected to find my old boyfriend, Trent, unhappily married and at the party alone. I'd come with my husband and suddenly I wanted him to leave. I had no idea that Trent would be there without a wife or date. We had lost touch years ago and I last heard he had settled down and was practicing medicine in Nashville.

"That night at the reunion, Trent told me that his children were grown and that he and his wife lived their lives separately. Our feelings were so strong for each other that we immediately decided to both get divorced to be together. For me, it was an enormous decision because my first marriage worked; it wasn't lonely like his was. But I left my husband of eighteen years and I moved my two children across the country and married him. And while I'm blissfully happy and in love, I know that I caused great pain to my children and to my ex-husband. And since my divorce and remarriage, there have been some rough times. The children were difficult and my divorce was so ugly it bled into everything. But Trent and I toughed it out, and our marriage is here to stay."

WHY FIRST MARRIAGES FAIL WHEN OLD LOVES RETURN
- Reconnection of couple highlights lack of communication between husband and wife
- Memories of old goals and dreams show up in the midst of the everyday grind
- Realization that those old loving feelings never died

If a first marriage falls apart, reuniting with a long lost love holds great appeal, especially if the alternative is dating total strangers. In this case, the long lost love appears to be the second chance at happiness for which a newly divorced and unhappy man or woman is desperately seeking.

At forty-six, Dale was reunited with her high school beau, Len, after twenty-nine years of separation. "I hunted him down. Although I had never married, I had been with the same partner from the day I left my boyfriend when we were in high school until we found each other again, a year ago. I know that I remained in a twisted relationship because of the material things it included. And I was lonely. When I finally got brave enough to leave, I didn't expect anyone else to be there for me. Then I moved back to Rhode Island and I went to see my old boyfriend, just to say hello. He was divorced and we immediately fell in love again, as if we hadn't missed all these years. He'd been miserably married for seventeen years. We got married eight months ago and it feels like heaven on earth, being together again.

"Because we live in a small town, I am constantly being compared to my husband Len's first wife and people whisper about us. I do not feel jealous of her or intimidated by her. I just wish that Gina would get on with her life and stop watching us all the time. And it makes it difficult for Len, who really doesn't want to make waves. Gina is not remarried and I doubt she is dating anyone. I can feel her hating me every day. I can sense Gina's fury at us and this second marriage."

In his book, *Soul Mates,* Thomas Moore addresses the misconceptions of marriage. "People blame each other for not living up to promises made at the time of their wedding. . . . it makes sense that the marriage will be significantly different a few years into it than it was at the start."

Going into the first marriage, there are hopes and expectations that are not always met down the line. Thus these marriages may fail after a substantial amount of time because the partners no longer share the same goals. Personal change and change within the marriage are constant and unavoidable—sometimes for the better, sometimes not.

In a first marriage the partners may not be prepared for these changes, while in a second marriage, each partner is better prepared and usually more committed to the relationship. When the second wife is the former girlfriend, the marriage is strengthened by not only a shared history, but by the awareness that marriage requires open communication and constant nurturing. The "importance of caring for the soul in a marriage", as Thomas Moore describes it, is recognized.

"Although I never had a burning desire to have children," Dorothy comments, "I ended up with three by the time I was twenty-seven. Then I learned that you would die for your children, that nothing matters as much as your children. Since my first marriage was terrible, it was only the children who kept me going. Then I ended up back with my old boyfriend, Harris, from when we were young. Suddenly my priorities changed. I began to focus on him.

"Our children are all close in age, and they were all up in arms when Harris and I married twelve years ago. In retrospect, we may have made a mistake in how we dealt with them; I think we could have done better. But we did insist on family vacations where we took everyone away together. There were some hurtful scenes, but the kids calmed down eventually, although it took years. In my first marriage, money was an issue and my children were not raised with many material comforts. Harris's children were raised quite differently, so this took some adjustment. But today it is ironed out, we have grandchildren and everyone gets along. Even our ex-spouses are remarried.

"Harris and I agreed when we turned our families upside down to be together that we would not let anyone get in the way of our marriage. It takes strong people to do what he and I did, but it is worth it. We were meant to be together when we were young and it didn't work out. It took us years to find each other again. The minute we did, we knew it was right, and it had always been right. I do wonder if we had married when Harris and I were young and had children together if it would be as romantic and free as it is now."

The emotional loss that ensues during a divorce, even if it is the loss of an illusion and not the loss of the actual marriage, causes both women and men to feel vulnerable. Finding one's long lost love is a way of being comfortable and at ease. It is a way of returning to what was once familiar rather than going to a strange unknown place.

"A relationship with an old girlfriend/old boyfriend is a way of remembering an easier time in one's life," remarks Dr. Michele Kasson. "Most early romances were based on liking and friendship. There are years of common values and common experiences which can be built upon."

By recovering old feelings and marrying one's past love, it is as if life comes full circle. The emotions and attraction that were not realized because of other obligations can now be fulfilled.

LOST ILLUSIONS/RECOVERY
- The new/old love has a dreamlike quality; it is both known and thrilling.
- Whether a catalyst for the divorce or a by-product, the second marriage to a refound love is recovery of optimism
- Youthful, loving feelings are reestablished on a mature, adult level
- There is comfort and ease because of old connection

"My boyfriend, Cole, and I were destined for success, personally and professionally," Lisa realizes. "And it didn't happen. Sometimes I think this is because we were separated in our early twenties and got off track then. We both grew up in a small town in Delaware and went to the same university. There were plenty of girls after him and I guess he felt confined. I also came from a limited world and wanted to learn about people. We were so young. After we broke up, I moved to Philadelphia and got a job. I did fairly well and have worked my entire life. I never married, but I lived with someone for six years. Cole got married and had three kids so fast he never climbed the corporate ladder. Instead he took a job that kept him close to home, because his wife insisted on it.

"By the time Cole and I found each other, he had given up hope. His life was so bogged down with obligations it was frightening. I happened to be back in town, visiting my brother and ran into Cole at the local convenience store. That was all we needed to spark our relationship again. The children are definitely an issue, because they will not accept me. I have no kids of my own, which makes it harder in some ways. I know how his boys feel about me, but I want a relationship with them anyway, for my husband's sake. I just want Cole to be happy after all the pain he's been through. His ex-wife harbors such resentment she keeps the kids away from him, too.

"Through all of this, we have hung together for five wonderful years. Cole and I are a unit, and we protect each other. I look at this marriage as a positive force; as something that has saved us both. Our ages have a lot to do with it—we know enough now to weed out the toxic people in our lives and to finally realize what is best for each of us. To me, my husband is the handsomest, brown-eyed prince in the land. I've always thought that about him."

"Once people have gone through life with a partner and faced adult pressures—work, children, bills, stress—and the marriage is not strong, finding an old love reminds one of the carefree and fun days," warns Dr. Ronnie Burak. "The association with this person is of a time before adult life took over. Some couples who try to recapture that through the old love will find that things have changed dramatically. It is an awakening because the reality is not the same; real life in middle-age has lots of responsibilities."

For long lost lovers, there is a comfort level in being with someone from the past that cannot be replicated by meeting someone new.

What happens once the couple attempts to recapture those old feelings may surprise them. Life has changed since the romance they shared in their youth, and they learn that having a good relationship now is more challenging than they expected.

DAY TO DAY
- Children/stepchildren interfere with romance
- Daily life together is a tremendous force
- The new marriage is its own entity; it is resolute

"I have seen cases," Dr. Ronnie Burak reports, "where women have wanted to leave a marriage for the sole reason that they found their old boyfriend again. This is a risky venture. What may happen is that after the wonderful feeling of being in love again wears off, the new couple faces the reality of complications in life. Both of them have children and jobs in cities halfway across the country. If there are no children involved, it is much easier to pick up and leave for the sake of being reconnected to an old boyfriend. Geographic problems still prevail and one person might have to reorganize her/his life for the sake of the marriage. Yet if they have been through a lot in their first marriages, they will often be more cautious and careful with the next relationship."

"My first marriage was not right for me," Clara admits, "but I would not have left it if my husband had not wanted to. He was having an affair and I had no idea. First, I became a mother too young, because my first husband was older by eight years and wanted a baby right away. Then I became a single mother because he wanted someone else. I was just getting by, financially and emotionally, when I ran into Jeffrey, who had been an old boyfriend. We had gone to junior high school and high school together and I had always liked him. It had been a tenuous relationship as kids, where we had sort of danced around one another for years before finally getting together. Ten years had passed and then I ran into him at a train station. Jeffrey recognized me first. I was with my son and the train was delayed.

"Jeffrey and I were very cautious. First we dated, then we became an item, and then we married. He has always cared for my son, who was abandoned by his own father. Jeffrey is the real father to this child. And now we have three more children together. Jeffrey's first marriage had been unhappy and mine was filled with duplicity, so we really appreciate what we have together. I do believe that knowing each other long ago made a big difference for me. I would not have been so quick to start up with a stranger after all that I'd been through."

Having survived a punishing divorce, many people are reluctant to go out into the world and begin again, particularly with a stranger. Marrying one's long lost love is a way to return to one's innocence while obtaining the comfort that comes with the familiar. If enough years have elapsed, the reunion is that of two mature people. In such cases, the second wife now enters a marriage with someone who seeks companionship and intimacy, while the issues of career and even children have been settled to a large extent. The conflicts of the first marriage are demands often not placed on these second marriages. In stories of reunited long lost love, there is the generosity that stems from the former connection. Both partners are at the same stage, ready to go forward with the consolation and security of the past.

LIGHT AT END OF TUNNEL
- Reclaiming innocence
- Uniting of two mature people
- Generosity stemming from a former connection
- Children are no longer babies
- The marriage is the focus

Jordana and her long lost love, Troy, re-met at a soccer camp through their boys. "I got divorced within a year of our first meeting and Troy and I have been married for six years. I am so sorry I didn't marry Troy years ago. I have such regret for what we both did with our lives while we were apart. I wish my sons and his sons were our sons. Troy says that the years we were apart have helped him to realize what he wants with me and that it might not have worked out the first time. We went through hell to be married to each other. I was in an abusive marriage with a man who was older by eight years. I don't know if it was the marriage or him, but I felt like I was growing old and withered when I was with him.

"The downside of this marriage is that both sets of children have been influenced by our ex-spouses against us. Troy's first wife called me when I was first married and told me that my husband was not a good father and would not be involved with the boys. Either Troy's attitude has changed or she was not telling the truth. He is absolutely devoted to the kids. At the start, his boys were hostile and unwilling to even spend time at our house. I worked very hard to rectify this. It took years for the relationship to change.

"Through all of this, I remember what it was like before I found my present husband. When Troy and I first decided to divorce in order to marry each other, I was afraid. I did not want to break up his family because our boys were young. Meanwhile, his biggest fear, that his ex-wife would move back to Florida, has become a reality. He sees his boys in the summer and during winter and spring breaks from school. My children live with us and sometimes when my husband looks at them, I know he is missing his own kids. It breaks my heart.

"Since our first marriages were destructive, there is always the sense that we are so lucky it worked out this way and that we found each other when we were young enough to have a child. We have a daughter, who is three, and she has been the thread that has sewn our blended family together. Everyone loves her and she is living proof that we were meant to be together."

"Age may be a factor in any marriage," divorce mediator Brondi Borer observes. "But in the case of remarriage to one's former love, the couple is usually the same age and has the same frame of reference. The second marriage has the allure of being with one's contemporary. While this might not have been as valuable or as appreciated in the first marriage, when people remarry, they find it is a binding aspect of the marriage."

Second marriages are most rewarding and uplifting when the second wife and her husband have strong senses of self and when their requirements are to be found in their mate. A second wife who knew her husband in her youth is at an advantage because of their shared past and understood value system. The advantages of two people who have strong past ties marrying later are financial security and having children who are older. The couple is now able to make a strong commitment and focus on the marriage.

WHY SECOND MARRIAGES TO LOST LOVES SUCCEED
• Understood value system
• Being contemporaries
• Shared history

Of the second wives who had married their long lost loves, only one interviewee expressed doubts about her marriage to an old boyfriend. The rest reported a contentment with the man who had walked back into their lives and had become their husbands. In fact, several described their marriages in glowing terms. However, even these happy marriages are not without their problems. A couple of these second wives found the angry ex-wife to be too much of a presence in their lives. Others interviewed had complaints about their children and stepchildren's reactions to the new marriage. But practicality and realism have helped couples work through turmoil and solidify the relationship. As two of the second wives realized, ironically, the possibility that this kind of marriage, to a long lost love, would not have worked as a first marriage was very real.

Eighty-eight percent of those in second marriages say that their second marriage is happier than their first. When the second wife is married to her long lost love, the yearning for and loss of this man has been requited and seems to result in even happier second marriages than the average. In many instances, a great deal of energy and risk-taking has gone on to create the union of the second wife and her former love. It is notable that the stage of life that these partners have reached, be it late thirties, forties, fifties, impacts on how well the marriage works. The thought lingers that if they had married back then, the love they had might not have been enough to sustain a successful life-long union. There is an acute level of gratitude in most of these reunited loves for what they now have obtained. Despite any hindrance, most marriages of reunited loves are steadfast.

CHAPTER TWELVE

IN-LAWS:
EX AND PRESENT

Madeline's husband, Joshua, chose to live near his ex-wife in order to have access to his children. "I would prefer to have my husband's two children live with us and my two kids than to have to deal with his ex-wife and his ex-in-laws. That is how much I detest them. Despite the large settlement and divorce, it feels that the enemy, i.e., his ex-wife and ex-in-laws, are constantly meddling in my marriage. I don't get it; didn't Josh pay for his freedom? And even on a good day, when I am dealing only with my parents or my new in-laws, it feels complicated. My in-laws have their grandchildren and then I bring my children along. Or my parents have my children and then I bring my husband's children along. Depending on the situation, my children do not always feel that they belong. Sometimes I know that I am pushing either his kids or mine on their step-grandparents. The stepchildren are hostile and who can blame them? Still, there are these obligatory dinners on Sunday nights and I feel trapped. It isn't what I bargained for.

"Joshua views our blended family in another light altogether. He thinks it is fabulous that we have two sets of children, and two sets of in-laws. Josh believes that he is being supportive, while I feel that he is not really paying attention to the problems and my feelings. We are divided enough between ex-spouses' demands so that I want to be careful with our in-laws."

Problems a second wife encounters when dealing with ex-wives and stepchildren have been discussed at length. Yet other family members—in-laws—can also be part of the equation. The second marriage which includes in-laws and ex-in-laws—in the form of parents, grandparents, siblings, aunts, and uncles—may face a whole set of difficulties that are avoided in marriages without in-laws. For one, a second wife might not anticipate the relationship her stepchildren share not only with her husband's parents but with his ex-wife's parents and ex-wife's siblings. If the children are small, arrangements between the children and the grandparents could very well become the second wife's responsibility. If the husband is widowed, the second wife might feel she is under the examination of the deceased wife's parents. Ideally, as in any situation where the second wife is less than secure, the husband will intervene.

Troubles with in-laws can escalate when the second wife who has been married before brings her new stepchildren along with her own children to visit her parents. The husband's children may feel uncomfortable, but hopefully with time, they will develop a rapport with their father's new in-laws. It can become very sticky when the two sets of children are very close in age. There is more competition for attention and the stepgrandchildren will most likely be the losers in such a battle. For instance, if the second wife's parents decide to take their grandchildren to Disney World, even if all the children want to go, they may only invite their own grandchildren. On the other side of the family tree, the husband's ex-in-laws may want very little to do with his second wife's children. As a result, her children may feel rejected and negative feelings will abound on all sides.

Whether bad feelings and negativity permeate the various relationships involved often depends upon the circumstances that brought about the divorce and the second marriage. If the first wife was the one to precipitate a divorce and the husband has kept up with his in-laws, they may be open-minded toward the second wife. If the first wife has died, the former in-laws would, hopefully, be expansive. If the second marriage was brought about by an affair, hostility on the part of the ex-in-laws is understandable and to be expected. Surprisingly, the husband's parents may not welcome the second wife with open arms. Like his ex-in-laws, his parents also might not be keen on the second wife if the new marriage is the result of an affair.

"In-laws, meaning the husband's parents, can resent the second wife," Dr. Ronnie Burak warns. "This happens for several reasons. The time that the stepchildren spend with their father and stepmother might take away from time that was formerly designated for the grandparents. If the children are small and the visit includes the second wife, the in-laws may even be unfriendly. For the second wife this can be very painful to contend with. Of course, this all depends on the feelings that the in-laws had for the first wife."

With the ex-in-laws, including aunts and uncles, an ongoing relationship will be established with the second wife if she is the one who makes arrangements for her stepchildren. While the extended family is important for the children, the second wife needs to distance herself from them in order to not feel vulnerable and insecure. If her stepchildren are closer to adolescence, it becomes all the more difficult to contend with. Now she not only faces hostile in-laws and hostile ex-in-laws, but hostile older stepchildren.

Charlene views her interactions with both her in-laws and her husband Brendan's ex-in-laws to be uneasy for everyone involved. "I have been married to Brendan for the past three years. He has full custody of two small children, ages seven and nine. My own children are five and seven. Since all of the kids are so young, there is plenty of mixing of in-laws and grandparents on both sides. My parents, his parents, my ex-in-laws and his ex-in-laws, plus our siblings and ex-in-laws' siblings, all want to see the children. Our kids are all very close to each other and inseparable on weekends. Needless to say, I deal with these issues all the time. I make plans and do the physical delivering of the children and then collect them. It is very competitive and demanding.

"Brendan travels half of the time so I have no choice but to deal with the exes and in-laws by myself. Sometimes I think everyone actually enjoys the drama. My mother-in-law makes constant references to the first wife, telling me how perfect she was. So I finally told my husband that his mother should make plans for the children through his ex-wife. That's when Brendan told me that his mother hated his ex-wife. Sometimes I do not know who to believe. It's as if everyone is making up stories just to make things harder on me."

"What happens," Dr. Michele Kasson points out, "is that the

first marriage colors the second. If the mother-in-law did not like the first wife, then she may feel vindicated by the break-up and be nice to the new wife. And we have to remember, every parent wants to see her/his child happy. So while the in-laws might not have been able to warn their son against marrying the first wife for fear of losing him, they now have a new daughter-in-law who seems more appropriate."

On the other hand, if a mother-in-law feels some sort of loyalty to her first daughter-in-law, there will be anger toward the son for divorce. These feelings will spill over and affect the new marriage. It will be more difficult for the second wife to gain acceptance and she may feign that it doesn't matter to her, initially. However, the negative energy coming from new in-laws, combined with an ex-wife who is formidable, might be too much for the second wife. This becomes worse when her husband ignores the problem and doesn't protect her.

PROBLEM POSTURING
• The mother-in-law can punish an unwelcome second wife
• The second wife initially may pretend she doesn't care
• The first wife often watches from the sidelines
• The husband ignores the problem

As was seen in Charlene's case, a mother-in-law may play games with a second wife even if the mother-in-law didn't really care for the first wife. For example, she may tell the second wife how nicely the first wife treated her, perhaps raving about the woman. She may be sincere or disingenuous, simply to upset her new daughter-in-law. She may be doing this to wield some power and control over her son and his new wife. Such behavior unnerves the second wife and pushes her away from forging a relationship with the mother-in-law. While a healthy dose of self-confidence can help a second wife in this situation, even the strongest woman will be somewhat weakened by the negativity that an angry and vindictive mother-in-law can sling at her. If the first wife is still in touch with the mother-in-law, it further undermines the success of a relationship between the second wife and mother-in-law.

A second wife who has children from her first marriage may also witness her in-laws' disdain for her children and from the complications that arise because of their presence. There are circumstances in which the stepgrandchildren could benefit from their stepgrandparents' input. This happens only when the grandparents are open-minded and inclusive of their stepgrandchildren. If they find that the stepgrandchildren interfere with their relationship with their own grandchildren, they may not be so generous of spirit. Ideally, grandparents will put aside any negative or harsh feelings they have for the adults involved and treat their step-grandchildren—who are basically innocent bystanders—with kindness.

"I never imagined that I'd be divorced, let alone remarried," Alexis admits. "My children were fifteen and twenty and my ex-husband Bryan remarried quickly and had a baby. When I became divorced, my in-laws made it very difficult for me. They kept up with the kids, but completely cut me off. And I had considered us close. I felt that I was losing everyone, everyone around me. Then I became a second wife to a man whose parents were very involved with his two children. I encouraged this and even foolishly hoped that my new mother-in-law and I might bond. Instead, my new mother-in-law was very cold to me, outright unpleasant to my two children, and will only see my husband when I am not around."

Such behavior is difficult for any woman to take, but without her husband's support, it can be devastating, as Alexis recounts. "Bryan has not been supportive of me with his parents. Nor has my ex-husband been supportive of me with his parents. If my own parents were alive it might be less important. My new in-laws have made it clear to me that my children are not to be included with their grandchildren. I never expected anything more from them but civility. There was one occasion when one of my stepsons asked his grandparents if one of my daughters could accompany them on a day at the beach. They did and it went very well. The problem was that I met with many obstacles before this get-together actually happened."

According to experts, Alexis is not alone in her dilemma. "After finances, the greatest difficulties in second marriages are in-laws, step-in-laws, and stepchildren," Amy Reisen, divorce attorney, comments. "The family allegiance is in question; the children are accustomed to their paternal grandparents and mother taking them on outings and there is resistance when the stepmother intervenes. In these instances, the pressure really builds and causes difficulties in the new marriage."

When in-laws don't spurn their new daughter-in-law and her children and welcome them with open arms, the results can be wonderful. "My three children, ages six to nine, had no grandparents until I remarried," says Miranda. "Now they have a stepbrother who is eleven and his grandparents. My in-laws and ex-in-laws have been wonderful to my children. Perhaps it is a function of my children's ages, but they are invited everywhere with their new stepgrandparents. For my husband, Cody, and I, this relationship is quite unexpected and really exciting. We celebrated Thanksgiving with my husband's parents and my kids loved it.

"Now the grandparents feel so close that they've actually tried to discipline my children. I have very mixed feelings about this. On the one hand, I know my kids could use the discipline, but on the other hand, I'm not sure it's my husband's parent's place. But I feel that things are so open and healthy that we can talk about such issues. And I would prefer to have the grandparents involved and even somewhat overbearing than absent."

The prerogative of grandparents in our society is to come and go as they please and to avoid the responsibilities associated with raising their grandchildren. Parents are responsible for discipline and enforcing of rules for their children. However, when grandparents or stepgrandparents spend a good portion of their time with the grandchildren, baby-sitting or entertaining them, some discipline is necessary.

GRANDPARENTS, STEPGRANDPARENTS, AND DISCIPLINE
With young children, a grandparent might need to exert some kind of discipline. Yet this should be within limits and with the awareness and cooperation of the parent.

Sheila and her husband, Alex, returned from their honeymoon to find her stepson, Bobby, and his grandmother, Alex's ex-mother-in-law, in their apartment. The explanation for their presence was that her husband, Bobby's grandfather, was sick and she could not watch her grandson and tend to her husband at the same time. "I felt that this was deliberate and planned by Alex's ex-wife, which really burned me. Alex and I had put off our wedding plans until we were sure that plans for his nine-year old son were squared away. That meant that Bobby would be with his maternal grandparents and/or his mother during and for a short time after our honeymoon. Returning from a honeymoon is difficult enough, but this was really too much for me. Alex and I had a big fight right in front of Bobby and his grandmother. Afterward, I was sorry and wished that I could have been more understanding.

"But the truth is, I had been interacting with Alex's ex-wife,

Penny, and her nasty mother since I began dating my husband. His former mother-in-law has interfered and manipulated constantly. Eventually, I left my husband because Alex would not defend me. I had finally
had enough. I suppose you could say that they won. What I do know is
that I will not get involved with another man who has such baggage. I
do not mind a stepchild, but I cannot stand massive interference from
exes and ex-in-laws. Next time, I will listen intently to what a man says
about his family before I even go on the second date."

From the outset, there are many personalities to contend with
in a blended family: stepchildren from both marriages, exes, in-laws, and
ex-in-laws. With so many people in the mix, there are bound to be
problems when a husband and his second wife try to recognize and
accommodate the different personalities, needs, and patterns of each
person. For the second wife in this position, it is imperative that she
realizes her husband's level of commitment to his first family, preferably
before she becomes his second wife. Once she knows, she can decide if
she is prepared to deal with such issues. If he is too immersed in their
lives and more concerned about their well-being than that of his second wife's, the marriage suffers.

LOOK, LISTEN, LEARN
When a man tells you that he is still involved with his former in-laws
and his ex-wife, pay attention. If he puts them first, it will come
between you. Second wives require reassurance and commitment to
show that they are not preempted by a first wife, let alone her family.

Darla has carefully and unhappily watched how her in-laws
interact with her husband Colin's first wife's family. "It always irks me.
My in-laws tell me stories about Colin's first wife and her family and so
on. I can't listen and I don't want to hear it. I can't escape Adrienne, his
first wife, on some level. That, I know. When Adrienne's father died,
Colin didn't tell me he knew. Then I heard about it through some
mutual friends. When I asked him, he said he actually had known about
it, but felt it would only bother me that he knew, so he didn't want to
upset me. Colin says he tries to protect me. But I know that there is this
link to his past and I resent it.

"In some ways, Colin wanted some give and take after his marriage to Adrienne, and in some ways, he's still stuck. She wanted to take,
because she's such a taker, even after they were divorced. Adrienne

insisted that he give her a new car and put it in her name. And he did.
Maybe it was out of guilt, I don't know. Adrienne still wanted material
things and Colin still bought them for her. She wanted the creature
comforts from their early days together. He has never turned her down.
It upsets me. And when she brings her ex-family into it, I am sick. There
are no children from Colin's first marriage, so it is clearly a control
thing. There is no reason to interact or to stay in touch with them at all.

"What bothers me most is that my husband hid a lot of this
while we were dating. Once we were married, I saw that Colin was still
attracted to his ex-wife and it really bothered me. Also, it made me cling
to him as I had never done before with him or any other man. I felt like
Colin was comparing me to Adrienne and that I couldn't measure up.
Recently, I have made my needs known. I told Colin that I don't want his
ex-wife involved in our lives at all and that he has no reason to keep up
with her parents. He has agreed to this, so I'm waiting to see the results."

On occasion, there is a closeness which remains between the
husband and his ex-in-laws. Ex-in-laws who maintain a relationship
with their ex-son-in-law are often disillusioned with their daughter's
choice to end the marriage, especially if they saw him as having been a
good husband and son-in-law. This is a difficult situation with which to
deal for the second wife and if continuous, it may end up a barrier to
the cementing of the new marriage.

UNACCEPTED ENDINGS
Ex-in-laws may hold on tightly to their ex-son-in-law in hope that the
marriage to their daughter may be rekindled. It may be very difficult
for them to lose a son-in-law and the dream of their daughter's perfect life. They hang on because their son-in-law represents a stable and
happier period in their daughter's life.

"I have been very upset by my husband Dirk's attachment to his
ex-in-laws," June laments. "I have met his ex-wife Joanne's siblings, but
not her parents. I really resent Dirk's attachment to Joanne and to her
family now that we are married. He is not nice to my family, nor does
he have any attachment to them. Dirk only cares about his ex-wife's parents. It makes me furious. After his long, drawn out divorce, all we do
now is fight about Joanne's family, her requirements, and doing things
with my family as the counterpoint. I want him to be with my family

and Dirk feels very detached. At holidays, he is still at the places he went to during his first marriage.

"In the fifteen years Dirk was married to Joanne, I do not think he sat with her and their children as a family at the dinner table even five times. They weren't involved that way. Yet he harbors a fantasy of what existed and denies the reality of his past. Dirk wants me to fill a place as he dreams it was. He wants all of his friendships to remain as they were. He wants my friends and my family to be less important than his friends and his exes. He wants me to go bowling and do whatever Joanne did. But he didn't want to be with her and do what she did when they were married. It is so strange. I have begun to play tennis, because Dirk didn't do that with Joanne. No one sees her hovering over me on the tennis court. But in most of my life she is still there. I cannot tolerate her. Joanne is very hysterical and when she calls, I like to tell her, 'Oh, Dirk will be right home. I just spoke with him and he's on his way back." I like to get to her like that, implying that even though he is still connected to her family, I'm the one to whom he's coming home. I only wish that Dirk could break free of his entire ex-family, his ex-wife, her parents and siblings, and that we could move away. I moved here for him, but I cannot take the shadows everywhere I turn, shadows of more than just an ex-wife, but her parents as well."

EX-IN-LAWS WHO STAY
If the first wife sought the divorce, her parents may be very upset with her decision. Often in this case, the husband was viewed as a good and calming influence. The second wife inherits ex-in-laws who choose to retain their relationship with their ex-son-in-law.

Gwen's husband Jared's own mother, Roberta, has resented his happiness and been unsupportive of his second marriage. "When my husband was miserable and his wife was dying, Roberta was there. But now that he is happy and remarried to me and we have created a good life together, Roberta is not pleasant or supportive. She is a woman who revels in misery. Roberta speaks of the first wife as if she was some kind of saint and makes me constantly feel that I am less. I know what I've given to my husband and she knows it too. But she will not cut me any slack. She is not kind to my son from my first marriage and it has been complicated for us.

"I believe that Roberta was not as nice to Jared's first wife as she claims to have been, nor as close. I believe that Roberta was able to run her life, which she cannot do with me. She cannot boss me around and Roberta knows it so she resents my strength and my attachment to her son. I think that she feels Jared's first wife had a less intense attachment and that was better for her, easier in many ways. She is not even nice to her own grandchildren, let alone my child. She barely acknowledges our baby, which is what bothers me the most. At the heart of it is the fact that she doesn't really get along with her son and all of us are being punished for it."

"The end result is determined in these situations by what type of relationship the second wife had with her own parents. Another factor is the relationship that a second wife has with her own children and stepchildren," says Dr. Donald Cohen. "If the second wife's relationship is good with her own biological parents, her children, and her stepchildren, that will help the in-law relationship tremendously. History determines these relationships. If in the past, the in-laws' relationship with the first wife and her children was good, the same relationship with the second wife and her children can also be good. Again, it depends on the history. One should not expect the same relationship between stepgrandchildren and biological grandchildren. It can be a relationship that succeeds, but a very different one."

"In my culture, you do not break up a marriage and become a second wife as I did," Juanita explains. "Instead, the husband stays miserable with his wife and small children. The children grow up and are the only connection between these two adults who are married for life. My mother-in-law was hostile and unforgiving of me for what happened. She expected them to stay married for the sake of the children. She loves her first daughter-in-law, because they share the same limited approach to life. I came along, someone who was determined to make it in the work world and wanted her son, married or not. I can see her point of view, how devastated she was by the dissolution of the first marriage, but I cannot understand why she cannot be happy for her son now that he has found true love. I have given my husband three daughters. What this mother-in-law does is dote on the first set of children, a boy and a girl, and gives less attention to my children. She even takes the older grandchildren on outings with the ex-wife's mother. What she cannot comprehend is how hurtful it is to me. My husband tells me that his mother is not at the center of our lives, but I would have liked it if she could have been better to me. It is really a slight all around."

A husband is the one who can set the boundaries in these situations. He ought to explain to his parents and former in-laws that it is essential that his wife is treated with proper respect. He should discuss the requirements in specific terms. For example, there should be no wedding photographs of the first marriage in the in-laws' homes, and they should not talk about the first wife. It is essential that the second wife is happy and at ease. Making amends becomes arduous once the mother-in-law has been deliberately hurtful to the second wife and when the first wife and mother-in-law have an ongoing closeness. If his parents refuse to respect his wishes and don't ease up on his new wife, it may be necessary for him to cut them off from himself and his children, at least until they are willing to compromise. Even if problems continue, her husband's support and defense can do wonders to ease the stress and unhappiness of the situation for the second wife.

WHEN TO CUT YOUR LOSSES
- If the mother-in-law is repeatedly and deliberately unpleasant to the second wife
- If the second wife has attempted to make amends and has been repeatedly rebuffed
- If the first wife and the mother-in-law are still united
- If the husband cannot approach the situation and wishes it would disappear

"If a mother-in-law is not kind to the second wife, it is usually because the mother-in-law is angry that her son's first marriage broke up," Dr. Ronnie Burak explains. "Or if the new daughter-in-law seduced her son, his mother is furious, particularly if she wanted the first marriage to stay together. When she watches her son endure a difficult divorce and sees how it hurts the grandchildren, his mother will place blame upon the second wife's shoulders. Rather than face the fact that the first marriage might have been an unhappy one, his mother focuses on the loss of her idealized image of happily ever after for her son."

Selena's ex-in-laws' and present in-laws' treatment of her has been untenable from the beginning. "Maybe it is me, but I have been extremely upset by both sets of in-laws. During the courtship, my husband, Scott, told me that his ex-in-laws stayed in touch because of the children. I respected that and agreed that it was important for everyone involved. Then Scott told me that his own parents could be contentious and critical. Since I am no longer a young woman and believe that I have some maturity and life experience, I did not let this bother me at the outset. But what I have put up with is incredible. And I question why my husband does not do more. It is only when there is a real crisis that Scott intervenes.

"His ex-in-laws are very angry that their daughter's first marriage did not succeed. My husband is a physician and I suppose he was a feather in their cap. They have always been proud of him and tried everything in their power to keep the first marriage going. My mother-in-law is still close with the ex-mother-in-law. They have commiserated over the divorce and have vowed to remain friends. What I find at holidays is that my mother-in-law is purposely unfriendly and judgmental. I know that she runs back and says things about me to the ex-mother-in-law that gets back to the first wife. His first wife is another story altogether. Rosalie has remarried a man who is not college educated and not the same religion or background. Her children have a completely different kind of life than they had when her marriage to Scott was intact. I respect that it doesn't seem to matter to her. Rosalie really wanted out of this marriage and she has carved a new life for herself. This seems to irk both her own mother and my mother-in-law, who still see me negatively in comparison. If there were not two young children in the midst of this, I would not care so much about making peace.

"I actually have two issues to deal with at all times. One is my mother-in-law. Eleanor does not even want to relate to me. Eleanor only wanted to relate to Scott's first wife. This extends as far as their upbringing. They were raised in very similar environments with similar values. I come from another place altogether. I do not want to be like them, but I want acceptance from Scott's mother. My next issue is the ex-in-laws. I want them out of my face. It all has been more than I bargained for."

Children can both bring a second wife and her in-laws together and drive them apart. As difficult as Selena's situation is, there are instances in which the second wife is the one who creates the problems, making life very unpleasant for her new in-laws. As Brondi Borer, divorce mediator, explains, "There is a converse situation which comes up fairly frequently with second wives and in-laws. That is when the grandparents are denied access to their grandchildren by the new wife.

This is particularly a problem for grandparents who have put a tremendous amount of time into their grandchildren and then can no longer see them. The grandparents then may have to go to court to be awarded visitation. The courts are sympathetic and will protect the right of the grandparents to have contact with their grandchildren."

If there were no children in the first marriage, and the second wife brings children from her first marriage, depending on the age of these children, a relationship may form between the step-in-laws and the children. If a baby is born to the new couple, the in-laws usually react positively to the wife and baby because this new addition to the family enriches their lives. Now the relationship between the daughter-in-law and mother-in-law has worth, even for a combative mother-in-law.

The second wife who struggles to create a relationship with her in-laws, whether she has children from her previous marriage or not, may be ill served. Under these conditions, the first wife may have too strong a foothold, notwithstanding grandchildren, and it is best for the second wife to concentrate on the marriage without the input of her in-laws. Ironically, and depending upon the circumstances, the ex-in-laws, if there are grandchildren involved, may be forthcoming.

IN-LAW DISAPPOINTMENTS
The second wife who hopes for a good relationship with her in-laws may be very disappointed. This is particularly true if she is preempted by the first wife. It is best for the second wife to be cordial toward her in-laws and to give the relationship time.

"I was a second wife for fifteen years when my husband, Jeremy, began to change," Patsy says, describing her predicament. "He insisted we sell our house and my jewelry. Jeremy acted as if he were destitute and could not make ends meet. We had a certain lifestyle and I was spoiled, in retrospect. My husband did not talk to me about his reasoning and I was shocked at the changes. So were our two teenage children and my in-laws. My in-laws had always been very controlling, but I tended to keep them at bay. Instead, I had focused on keeping our family tightly knit and happy. Yet I always encouraged the children to be close with my in-laws despite my feelings. Then my husband came home and announced he wanted a divorce. I was hurt and shocked.

"I tried everything that I could to hold onto the marriage, but

Jeremy really wanted out. He claimed he no longer had money and that his business was going bankrupt. He then moved from northern California, where we lived and where our families lived, to Oregon. I had no choice but to agree to the divorce. When I looked to Jeremy's parents for support, despite all the years I'd known them and because of the children, they did not help. In fact, they became quite distant and ungiving. I had no one else to turn to. What I wanted went beyond my being an ex-daughter-in-law versus a daughter-in-law. I did not need them in my life, and frankly, I never had. But the children needed them desperately and I was shocked when they did not come through.

"My ex-in-laws sided with their son. He had a baby with his new girlfriend before our divorce was finalized. My in-laws carry on about how wonderful his girlfriend and baby are to my children. It was horrible for the kids. Yet I hear through mutual friends that they are just as controlling with her and treat her as badly as they treated me. My ex-husband stopped all of his payments to us and when I asked his parents to help because they are well off, they simply refused. They have abandoned my children, their grandchildren. I never imagined that any of this could have happened. But it has."

"This problem concerns how people relate to one another when a marriage breaks up," Dr. Michele Kasson remarks. "If there are bad feelings between the in-laws and their first daughter-in-law for no real reason, the chances are they will not be tolerant or warm to the second wife either. This is simply how the husband's parents treat their daughter-in-law, whomever she is."

The second marriage that is entrenched in family dynamics becomes fragile and cannot flourish. A husband who is mature enough will be honest with his second wife. He will elucidate his parents' attitude and style as in-laws, preparing her for what lies ahead and giving her reassurance that he will stand by her side no matter what happens with his parents. If he waits and lets the histrionics unfold, she will feel betrayed by his inability to be open with her and she will feel alone and lacking support in dealing with her in-laws.

ABANDONING SHIP
If the in-laws do not approve of the second wife, most likely they will not stand by her in a crisis. The second wife can be prepared for this if her husband is forthcoming.

Melanie, as a second wife for fourteen years, has resented her husband's parents from day one. "These are controlling, selfish people who revere their son and see me and the rest of the world as not good enough for him. I have done everything in my power to get them to change, to make them realize that their attitude is not only damaging to me, but damaging to their grandchildren. They do not care. Sometimes I imagine that the real reason that Alan's first marriage dissolved is because of their controlling attitude. I know that my husband, as their only son, is like putty in their hands. Alan doesn't make much money as a train engineer. I am a substitute teacher and no longer work full time because of the children. His father came into money late in life and lords it over us. When we needed to buy an apartment, my father-in-law loaned us the money. It's true that we never could have afforded a three bedroom otherwise, but we pay for my in-laws' financing dearly, in many ways.

"If I so much as buy a new dress, my mother-in-law makes a negative comment. If we get a baby-sitter to go out with friends, she has something to say about it. Not that my mother-in-law would ever baby-sit, but she judges me and my life. I have heard tales about Alan's first wife, Samantha, that make me feel sorry for her—stories of how Samantha and my mother-in-law would go at it. If I did not have two children, I would not accept my in-laws' bad attitude toward us, nor would I tolerate their behavior. I know it is a power trip for them. They tell me that Alan's first wife was too greedy for them. I suspect Samantha simply took what they offered. No one wants to pay the emotional price that my husband pays, not Alan's first wife and certainly not me. He is always defending his mother's behavior. She tells him behind my back that I am a terrible mother and then he queries me as to what I did wrong with the children. In this way, she gets between us. He will put her before, me because he was raised to do this. I exist only to service their grandchildren and their son."

It cannot be impressed enough that it is up to the husband/son to set boundaries and require that his parents abide by them in any interaction between them and his second wife. If he puts the children before his second wife and has to choose between his second wife and his mother, too, he makes an enormous error. If his first wife is a manipulator in his life, the second wife feels that her marriage is not her own.

IN-LAWS AND DIVIDED LOYALTIES
Circumstances where the second wife feels at risk are the following:
• The husband puts his parents' feelings ahead of his second wife's
• The second wife cannot forge a relationship with her in-laws and
  receives little or no support from her husband
• The second wife's stepchildren, their grandchildren, are important to
  her in-laws, but the second wife and her children are disregarded
• The first wife remains important because of the children from their
  son's first marriage, and maintains a relationship with his parents

Mattie became a second wife at the age of twenty-eight. "Ten years later, I am still baffled by my in-laws' reaction to me. In the beginning, my mother-in-law and father-in-law were thrilled to have me as their daughter-in-law. Ingrid, my mother-in-law, was very excited when I was dating her son. I think she liked the idea that I was an attorney and well established. Ingrid thought it embellished Seth. This woman dotes on her son, and because she is recently widowed Seth feels obligated to please her. We spend most of our weekends with her, taking her places and accommodating her. Seth even found her a new apartment and helped her move in. He took two days off from work to do that. When I was pregnant with our second child and we were moving, he wouldn't even take one day off. I definitely resent her demands and the fact that my husband kowtows to her. Ingrid has been very good to our two children, but never good to me. When my own mother was very sick and I had to fly to St. Louis, my mother-in-law would not help out with the children.

"Ingrid is critical of everything I have ever done. Ingrid has described Seth's first wife as selfish and manipulative. I suspect the first wife just wouldn't take this woman's treatment. My mother-in-law compares me constantly to Seth's first wife and tells me how neither of us has measured up. Whatever Ingrid attempted to do to make problems in the first marriage, she tries with me, too. She can't resist the temptation, but I do not succumb. I find her control so obvious but my main complaint is that my husband doesn't even see it. That's the problem."

"Family therapy is the answer for couples dealing with the complications of in-laws and stepchildren," advises Dr. Michele Kasson. "For those who cannot afford therapy, it is up to the husband to talk with his parents and to set the limits on what behavior towards his second wife is unacceptable. If there is no cooperation on the part of the in-laws, then the new wife should be told that she comes first."

The second wife who is bombarded by her in-laws requires a certain tenacity to make a success of her marriage. The ex-in-laws and in-laws, as mature adults, ought to be supportive of the second wife's role and helpful in terms of the children. A loving relationship in a second marriage hopefully sets an excellent example for even the most unfriendly of in-laws and gives the second wife confidence. In-laws who are able to realize the advantage of the new marriage and put the past to rest help to build a better future for everyone.

IN-LAWS & SECOND MARRIAGES:
THE NECESSARY INGREDIENTS FROM BOTH SIDES
- Tolerance
- Acceptance
- Kindness
- Confidence

Of the second wives who spoke about their relationships with their in-laws, one third of the women felt that they were compared negatively to their husbands' first wives as an intentional ploy by their mothers-in-law. They saw this as an attempt by their mothers-in-law to undermine their confidence. Another contentious issue for these women in dealing with in-laws and ex-in-laws involved the children. Sadly, almost half of the women interviewed found their husbands to be completely unsupportive and unyielding when they expressed their dissatisfaction with their in-laws. Only two women believed their husbands to be protective and defensive of them when problems arose with their in-laws. One second wife went so far as to divorce her husband over the altercations with in-laws and ex-in-laws.

With life expectancy increasing every year, more and more second wives will confront the in-law and ex-in-law situation. The solution for the second wives is to give the relationships time and make the best compromises possible. "The neotraditional marriage" which Daniel J. Levinson describes in his book, *The Seasons of a Woman's Life*, is a second marriage that integrates home life, marriage, children, and career. It is this balance that keeps the second wife from losing herself to the pressures of extended family.

CHAPTER THIRTEEN

A CHILD IS BORN

"I knew that being a second wife to a man with three children from his first wife was not an easy path," Agatha says matter-of-factly. "I wanted my own children and my husband, Theo, to accept this fact, but they really did not. He wanted me all to himself. The more weekends I spent with my stepdaughters, the more I knew I needed a life that was all mine. When I couldn't get pregnant for a year, I panicked. It wasn't only about having a baby, but having a full, satisfying family life with my husband. My youngest stepdaughter, who is ten, would ask me if we were going to have a baby. I knew that she was both titillated and angry at the idea. Once, I slipped and admitted that I wanted one, and she ran back and told her mother. Theo's ex-wife called my husband at work and said that if he had children with me, it would ruin his relationship with his first set of children. My husband was very upset by this episode and it made me know all the more how I needed to have my own children with him. I felt like I was drowning in his life. I felt like I couldn't get anywhere without his kids being in the picture.

"We had a child two years ago and it has made all the difference. My hunch was right. The balance has changed in our favor. Theo is now available to me in a way that he never was before and he is available to our baby in a way that he never was

221

to his children in the first marriage. I think it has to do with his feelings for me. Now we are a unit—the baby, my husband and I. He is in love with this baby in a way that he never was with his first family. I think that he worked hard during the first marriage to avoid spending time with his wife, so he missed the bonding with his daughters as a result. The connection with his ex-wife has lessened too. Sometimes I can actually feel how furious she is at me. She seems to forget that she was the one who wanted the divorce and the one who left. I have reached out to my step-daughters much more since the baby was born."

For so many couples in a second marriage, the idea of having a child together is the ultimate bond and way of expressing their love for each other. *The Journal of Marriage and Family* reports that 50 percent of second wives under the age of forty-six will have a baby within the first twenty-four months of marriage. What often complicates the picture is the reaction of the wife's children from the previous marriage or marriages. The concept of their mother giving birth is very hard on them. The fear is that this baby will be loved more than they are loved, that this will be their mother's special child, born of choice and a promise for the future.

The first wife suffers the consequences of this child's birth as well, because she often fears that the new baby will be preferred over her children. As far as the stepchildren are concerned, the rivalry for their father's attention, which began when the second wife entered the picture, is now intensified. In many cases, this conviction is fueled by the mother/first wife. If the second wife was married and had a family in her first marriage, her children will wonder if she will still love them once she falls in love with this new man and has his baby. When a child is born to the new family, the picture, however it is painted, is irrevocably altered. The new marriage is now solidified but the level of animosity that might stem from the stepchildren and the first wife is increased.

How the stepchildren are affected by the birth of a baby is not only about importance and status in the family, but about how the father and his new wife are perceived. Adolescent stepchildren often view the second wife's pregnancy as proof that there is sex in the second marriage. The sexual aspect of the second marriage, from the point of view of the adolescent stepchild, is not easy to accept. The stepchildren usually resent the second wife for taking over their father's life. They may view the new child as being loved more than they are because they are the products of an unsuccessful marriage, where there is no longer any sex or any love between the parents.

SEX THEN/SEX NOW
Children of the first marriage are forced to face the fact that their father and stepmother are sexual because the baby exists. The new baby represents a bonding of their parent and his or her second mate.

Children are not the only ones left to cope with the reality of a new baby in a second marriage. The first wife is also affected. "It is very difficult for the first wife who asks herself how her ex-husband can begin another family when he was not there for his first set of children," Dr. Ronnie Burak observes. "If the husband was the one to leave the marriage, it is particularly painful for the first wife. She may become furious, because it is such a blow to her and to her children. Of course, as in many situations with the first wife, her reaction depends to a large extent on where she is in her own life. If she is remarried and has just had a baby with her second husband, she will not be as threatened or unsupportive of the birth of her ex-husband's baby."

POTENTIAL PROBLEMS
• The first wife is threatened by the baby's impending arrival
• The stepchildren fear they will lose their place in the family

VERSUS

POTENTIAL POSITIVE OUTCOMES
• The first wife realizes the birth as a way to sever ties to her ex
• The stepchildren genuinely love the baby

Despite the pain stepchildren and the first wife may feel when a new baby arrives, the event often heals the scars left by a bitter divorce. "My new husband, Kevin, and I agreed to have at least one child," Rachel explains. "I wanted it because I had no children and he wanted a child because his ex-wife had been so uncompromising in the divorce. My husband ended up with a very limited visitation schedule with his two daughters and he was really heartsick over it. The baby was not to replace his children, nor was it a vengeful message to his ex-wife. This baby was to heal my husband and to give me what I longed for.

"Our marriage is based on deep feelings. Kevin has been sad ever since I met him. Until the birth of our son, I know that even with me in the picture he felt very alone. Today, Kevin is a different person—he thrives on our baby and our family life. His daughters are curious about the baby, but are distant and carefully coached by his ex-wife. We just keep inviting them over and including them, knowing it will eventually work out."

Most second wives realize that their baby's birth is a monumental event for the new marriage. It establishes the significance of the new union and puts their family at the center. For the second wife, it is a victory of sorts, proving to the first wife that there is no turning back, that the second marriage is viable. The children of the first marriage also recognize the finality and loss of the dream that their parents will reconcile. Yet the triumph is not without complications, and the advent of a new baby is complex for the blended family. Although in most blended families everyone loves the baby, the older children may view the new demands on their parent as impossible.

FURTHER COMPLICATIONS
How well the baby fits in to the blended family is complex. The dynamic of the family is forever altered. Stepchildren, especially adolescents, may resent responsibilities such as babysitting.

"Until I had my own baby with my husband, Mel, I felt that both my stepson and his mother had all the clout with my husband," says Hannah. "I have always seen our happiness as predicated upon the state of mind of Mel's ex-wife and her child. If her child is unhappy and complaining, then my husband will get on a plane to see him. Their son is ten and the hassle over Mel's visitation with him has been ongoing since the divorce four years ago. Mel's ex-wife has been remarried twice and moves all over the country four or five times a year, pulling her son out of school constantly. For this reason, my husband feels very responsible for his son's happiness. The pressure she inflicts on that child is horrific. I don't want to compete with his son, but I want a life that is just ours.

"However, I know that there is no interfering or saying, hey what about me, don't I come first? Mel would not like the demand. I have known this since we first began going out. My greatest desire was to begin a family of our own and become more established as a unit. I wanted us to have a family life so that Mel would be committed to it and not run back to his son and his ex-wife.

"I feel that unless I'd gotten pregnant, we would never have counted as much as Mel's first child does. Now Mel's ex-wife is getting divorced again, and my husband is worried about his son. He's asked me if I'd become a full-time mother to him, if need be. I ask myself, *am I ready, honestly, with one of our own and another one on the way? And do I need this constant intrusion of his past life?* It sort of wipes away what we are creating. But that is so unfair to Mel's son, who is an innocent product of divorce. I am acutely aware that this child is not my own. I have taken excellent care of him when he was with us since he was small, but he is not mine and I do not want him as part of Mel's and my daily life together. But I also better understand my husband's attachment to his son now that we have a baby of our own. All I can hope is that his ex-wife gets grounded and Mel concentrates on me and on our family."

"Typically, the husband already has a first family and the second wife hasn't any children," comments Dr. Michele Kasson. "Because the husband loves his second wife and he knows how much it means to her, he will agree to a child. This stirs things up with the first family."

Cynthia George, divorce attorney, views children born in a second marriage as causing more stress on the first wife and first set of children. "I have seen second marriages where the dynamic between the second wife and stepchildren before and after the birth of a baby can cause the second marriage to actually break up. Everyone involved, the second wife, husband, and ex-wife need to be sensitive to these issues."

The first wife could feel hurt and angry at the turn the ex-husband's life has taken. The second wife now has a family life firmly implanted in the present and future and the first wife feels her importance and power begin to recede.

EMOTIONAL TURMOIL WHEN A BABY COMES
The first wife sees her ex-husband going forward in his new family life. She feels her children will be left behind. The second wife now views the first as irrelevant. Whatever jealousy for the first family once existed, the second wife has moved on.

"If the first wife has given birth to a new baby of her own," adds Dr. Michele Kasson, "and has in fact, reinvented herself, the news that a second family is in the works has very little impact on her. Both the first and second wife now have the opportunity to be equals because they are both mothers. It is only if the first wife still wishes for her old life back that the second wife's baby is a major blow to her."

BALANCING ACT
- The husband cannot help but shift focus onto his present family
- The first wife has less clout
- The stepchild often fits in more easily, less self-consciously
- The second wife stops being so insecure

Bringing children into the second union often brings up old hurts for ex-wives. There may be scenes where an ex-wife is abusive and a second wife attempts to ignore it, because she so desperately desires peace and harmony at any price. When the second wife becomes pregnant, boundaries are even more necessary. If a second wife has an outstanding relationship with the first wife, it is another story, but this is not a likely case. For the most part, a second wife requires a family life of her own with her husband and that often comes simultaneously with the birth of their first child.

GENEROSITY AT A PRICE
The second wife's strongest desire for a full union with her husband often manifests in desiring a baby. When this is the case, the stepchildren may benefit from her joy and the advent of a baby.

After the initial euphoria of having a baby, the second wife better understands the thrills and obstacles of parenting. She may become kinder and gentler toward her stepchildren and may even begin to appreciate her husband's ex-wife's efforts as a mother. In the best case scenario, everyone in the family becomes more tolerant now that a baby has been born.

Jewel became a second wife to Harvey, a man who had two grown children, but he agreed to have another family with her. "My husband is twelve years older than I am and was married for a long time. We met at a computer convention when Harvey had just separated from his first wife and I was just beginning my career. It was a wild courtship, but I wanted to settle down and have a home and kids. I was close enough in age to his married son that the son's wife became pregnant at the same time I did. So my husband has a granddaughter and a daughter who are the same age. I expected there to be no competition and for Harvey's children to be happy for us. But this wasn't the case. They saw the birth of

our child as a real intrusion and did not like the fact that we were beginning our own family."

DISPLACEMENT
The baby is born to the second wife and is perceived as displacing the
older stepchildren. The anxiety can become quite acute. Until everyone
settles into the new arrangement, the stepchildren can be miserable.

"There is not always an immediate love affair between the new
baby and her stepsiblings," Dr. Ronnie Burak cautions. "Much of this
depends upon the age of the stepchildren and a sense of family. If they
are under ten, these children may genuinely love the baby. Adolescence
causes other issues and these children may not be as pleased. Adult
stepchildren are usually detached and uninvolved with a half-sibling that
is so much younger, but they may resent the baby for financial reasons.
In other words, they fear the size of their inheritance will decrease."

Each child in the original family, be it the second wife's children
from her first marriage or the husband's children from his first marriage,
will have strong reactions to their new half-sibling. The attachment
between child and stepchild does not form overnight.

NEW BABY/UNPREDICTABLE REACTIONS
• Judgments about the pregnant second wife which are made by the
  children can be harsh
• Adult stepchildren can be unpredictably jealous of the new baby
• The husband needs to focus on balancing between the old and the new
• Time and effort will bring positive results

"Until I had twins with my husband, I felt that I did not count
in the same way as his first family," admits Lila. "It was a real issue for me.
I know that Ned was divorced from his wife and that the children were
in a joint custody arrangement, but I felt at their mercy. I simply could
not relax about my new marriage. Then I gave birth to our daughters and
it changed everything. I became confident that I was number one and that
our girls were his priority. I look back on the two years of my marriage
before we had babies and I realize how difficult it is for a second wife to
feel special. It's as if you are up against so much. In my story, there were
stepchildren and a very angry ex-wife. There was Ned's reluctance to have
another family. And then I ended up with twins. I know he has a case of

'been there, done that,' but I haven't experienced any of it. And my ego keeps me wanting our family experience to be unlike the first time for him. I want this family we are creating to be everything to him—all of his happiness, all of his hopes should generate from us."

Alexandra had one child from her first marriage and her husband, Ron, had two when they married. "I don't know if it was a question of gender or the strength of numbers, but my stepsons always overshadowed my daughter. My daughter was in fourth grade and his sons in fifth and sixth grades when we married. I never expected to have any more children when I found myself pregnant. I honestly think I went through with this pregnancy in order to get the ex-wife out of my face and to balance our blended family for my daughter. I prayed for a baby girl and I was really lucky. Today, things are much better with my husband and we fight less over all the children.

"Our baby is our common denominator and the joy she has brought to this family negates all the trying moments beforehand. My stepsons help me in ways I never thought possible. Some nights when I'm so tired from taking care of my new daughter, I remember the exhaustion of mothering when I was married the first time. Then I remember how much I love my husband and how, after a rotten divorce, I know the difference and what I need."

While the second wife boasts that her baby's birth contributed positively to the blended family, the husband may have misgivings. Many husbands do not want to be invested in a second family but only the new marriage. Often it is the persuasive second wife who gets her way.

DÉJÀ VU
- The husband is not ready to begin another family
- The second wife wants a baby of her own
- He agrees reluctantly
- She is satisfied their family life is not a replay, but unique

Even if a husband is reassuring and excited about starting a second family, he and his second wife may still have a very unhappy first wife to contend with. Not every first wife backs off because a baby is born. Instead, she may push harder for her children to have their due. When her children complain about the baby, the first wife is extremely defensive. The second wife can assuage the upset children and invite them into the inner sanctum of the new family. Eventually, they will likely come to enjoy their new baby stepsibling. This hopefully causes the first wife's ire to diminish with time.

NO WINNERS
- The first wife may compete with the new baby through her children
- The children fuel their mother with tales of the new family
- The stepchildren reject the second wife's overtures
- The hope is that the second wife wants a large, cohesive family unit

Although it is common for a second wife's new baby to upset the first wife, time often helps to heal that wound. Since Taylor gave birth to her second child, Nyles's first wife and children have bothered her less. "There are only small issues these days. I think Dorian has come to appreciate me, because I have helped to mother her children. At first though, Dorian resented me because she is quite a mother hen. Now that I have my own, I see that. I believe that Dorian was really ticked off that her ex-husband's life turned around because he married me. And my babies took her over the top. She would have liked her children to resent me and my babies, but they do not. They are truly happy for me and their father. I have learned to roll with the punches if there is a scene. I have learned to be grateful for what I have and not to expect my stepchildren to adore me.

"What I see with my three stepchildren is that they love my babies to death. So the mix has worked out, although it was very tough at the start. Once everyone saw that there was enough love to go around, they calmed down. To this day, I see Nyles's ex-wife with her children on Christmas and Thanksgiving and most Mother's Days. She actually likes me and even calls to see how I'm doing. She is lovely to my children."

The relaxed, room for everyone, 'California approach' to blended families is becoming popular across the country. In this type of situation, an ex-wife and a second wife are not at war, but on the same side. The husband is cooperative, not only with his own children, but with his stepchildren. The first wife's second husband and her ex-husband sometimes have a drink together. Both the first and the second wife have begun new families with their new husbands. For example, in the Woody Allen film, *Everybody Says I Love You*, the California approach to blended families is evident. Goldie Hawn's character is married to her second husband, Alan Alda's character. Woody Allen's character is her first husband. The three of them are great friends and in fact, Woody Allen's character often comes to them to complain about his latest dating problem. Intertwined in the on-going interaction between ex-spouses and present spouses are assorted children from previous and present marriages.

CALIFORNIA APPROACH TO BLENDED FAMILIES
• The first wife and second wife are friendly
• The ex-husband may play golf with his first wife's second husband
• The second wife may include the first wife in family functions
• There are stepchildren and babies all over the place

Barrie's husband, Uri, has embraced her stepchildren from her first marriage. "My husband really loves my stepchildren who were quite young when I first entered their lives. Because of their attachment to me, there is an openness toward him. In addition, Uri has a child from his first marriage whom I have become close with, and his ex-wife just had a baby with her new husband. Uri and I have a baby who is eighteen months old. Uri's ex-wife has been so thoughtful in terms of her child and the custody schedule. When I came home from the hospital, she called to say she'd keep her daughter, who was eight at the time, although it was our weekend, because she suspected I had my hands full. Since then, I've seen her in another light.

"Whatever went on before between my husband and this woman is in the past. Their marriage had been in a bad state for years. The divorce was a mutual decision. The hope that their daughter would see both of her parents equally was important to them. I fought my ex-husband on the issue of custody of our children. I wanted some kind of guarantee that all the years I'd put in with his children would be acknowledged and that the relationship would be ongoing. While we are not a traditional family, there are some real benefits. On the holidays, my ex-husband and his present wife, my husband's ex-wife, her present husband, and all the children are together at our house."

As beneficial as the California approach can be for all involved, it is the exception and not the rule. As Dr. Donald Cohen explains, "When there are families that actually get together for holidays, including exes, present spouses, and the children, it should be as pleasant as possible. And it is great if this can be done, but considered unusual. Success really depends upon the circumstance. If there is a newborn baby and the daughter/stepdaughter decides to invite everyone to the christening, the exes are there with their present spouse and children from various stages. The less emotional baggage, the more harmony. It is not a bad idea to throw everyone together for an occasion like this, but there has to be a civility and mutual respect."

In total, Denise sees her husband's first wife, Marybeth, a dozen times a year. "There have never been any altercations, which is a miracle. There are no money issues and she is remarried to a totally responsible person. I respect them both. During the holidays or on special occasions, everyone is together. Both of us, the first wife and myself, have children in our second marriages. My husband, Walter, and I have never really socialized with his ex-wife. But recently when we were out in Arizona visiting my stepson, we were invited to Marybeth's home for dinner. I think this is unusual. I suspect that if we lived closer, we'd probably see them more.

"My children are now grown, but my stepchildren were wonderful to them when they were growing up. Marybeth has told me that these children were great to her daughter from her second marriage, too. So there are good feelings all around. My husband was very supportive of his children in every way when they were small and the divorce was new. It has worked out, because they have grown up to be terrific people. I feel very attached to my stepchildren and to my own children, and they are close to each other. We are very fortunate because there are so many horror stories out there. The way it has worked out is about as ideal as it gets."

Tracey believes that she benefitted from her husband Warren's first marriage in his approach to her and to the child born into their marriage. "There were stepchildren who were very upset that we were having a baby. Warren had a terrible divorce and these kids had been through a lot. There were even ex-in-laws who had an opinion on my pregnancy. There was his ex-wife's deliberate need to keep my husband attached to her through the children. So I had a baby and created our future. The kids went crazy and so did Warren's ex-wife when the baby was actually born, but I remained strong and focused on what worked for me. Then Warren's ex-wife met someone and moved away with him. They married, but he lost his job soon after. Warren's ex-wife called and asked my husband for more money, but he was temporarily out of work and we'd just had a baby. It was a nightmare. I was really worried about money.

"Eventually it all worked out, but it was an ordeal. The best part was that the stepchildren grew up to be happy, well-functioning adults. When their mother moved away, they lived with us for the first two years. They even brought their mother's dog. I was further connected to Warren's ex-wife by taking care of her dog! It was ludicrous.

But I began to appreciate her on some strange level. I saw her children as her products and I was impressed. I saw my husband's seasoned approach to fathering our child. I began to mellow about all of it."

STRENGTH RULES THE DAY
The second wife who is magnanimous sees the entire picture:
• The stepchildren are included with the baby
• She separates herself and the new marriage from the first wife
• She is prepared for financial hurdles
• She is flexible when it comes to scheduling her stepchildren
• She is loving toward her husband, baby, and stepchildren
• She allows her husband and his children space

Stepchildren will thrive when a second wife reaches out to them and involves them with her new children. When a second wife/stepmother remembers the value of her marriage and therefore the value of her stepchildren, she is successful. She does not complain about finances and is positive about the entire picture: stepmothering, mothering, and being a wife to the husband she loves. The baby and the love it brings belongs to everyone.

THE BABY SEALS THE MARRIAGE
The new baby in a stepfamily bonds and extends the entire clan. There is a continuity and future which the baby offers, a shared joy. The stepchildren become half-siblings and are truly a part of the new family.

Of the second wives interviewed who have children in the new marriage, almost half reported that the baby cemented the marriage and put it in first position in their husband's lives. A few women had to deal with a first wife becoming extremely jealous over the birth of their babies. About one-third of the second wives were delighted to be one big, unconventional 'California trend' family where the husband, his ex-wife, her present husband, the second wife, and assorted children all maintain friendly, ongoing contact, including socializing with each other and get-togethers for special occasions and holidays.

No matter how cohesive the blended family seems before a baby is born, preventive family therapy is recommended. By doing this, the problems in the future can be avoided. Blended families are fraught with complex situations, not the least of which is the birth of a new baby. Second wives/stepmothers who devote themselves to the cause and are willing to face the hurdles, reap the rewards of a harmonious family.

HAPPY ENDINGS

Many of us wake up at some time in our lives and realize we are married to the wrong person. Some of us are fortunate enough to end the marriage that doesn't work and remarry our soul mate. Yet a second wife must realize she marries not only a man but his entire past. When the road is getting rough, she needs to take a step back and remind herself that whatever unfolds, this is what she has signed on for and it is a deal she should willingly accept.

When a second wife starts a new life with her husband, the impediments could appear insurmountable. She yearns for something that is all her own with her husband: a fresh start, a history that is exclusively theirs. She may imagine moving far from where he has lived with his first wife and choosing a home together. She might want above all else to have a baby in order to take the marriage beyond couplehood and into a family. Or she might just want her husband all to herself.

The second wife who has self-confidence can acknowledge her husband's past without feeling insecure. After having conducted hundreds of interviews with second wives of all ages, from all parts of the country and social strata, it becomes apparent that though this is the goal, it is not easily achieved. In many cases, a triangle exists between the husband, the first wife, and the second wife. The triangle is loaded with stepchildren, in-laws, and ghosts of one's husband's past. The successful second wife is one who has faith and knowledge which yield the best results in the new marriage. This marriage is also successful if based on intimacy and trust. The sexual component should be strong yet balanced with friendship. There must also be a deep emotional connection and shared goals. The couple has to communicate and support one another. If these salient parts of the marriage are in place, then it will flourish and cannot be threatened.

NECESSARY INGREDIENTS FOR SUCCESSFUL SECOND MARRIAGES
- Intimacy/Passion
- Trust
- Respect
- Sex
- Mutual Support/Equality
- Shared Values/Goals
- Friendship
- Emotional Connection
- Communication

Dr. Donald Cohen reminds us that unresolved issues with a first wife may haunt the second. "If the husband felt unloved and in pain in his first marriage and has not worked through this, he will bring this pain to the second marriage. It is dangerous for the husband to play out such unresolved issues in his new marriage. For example, it may create competition between the first and second wife. On the other hand, if there is total acceptance and tolerance in the marriage and the past is left in the past, the new marriage will flourish."

Some second wives who have been married before feel that neither they nor their husbands would appreciate each other as much if they had not each been through poor first marriages. The emotional dissatisfaction of the first marriage is not repeated because these women and their husbands have higher senses of self; they know what makes them happy and what they want in their next marriage. After an unhappy marriage that lacked energy or commitment, women better understand and appreciate what they get and what they give in their roles as second wives. Second wives of endurance—thirty years or more—view their marriages as worth every effort. The struggle is about putting all the pieces—the children, stepchildren, work, and the ex-wife—in place and balancing things through the life that is forged together. When that balance is achieved, both partners are nurtured and the marriage is an entity unto itself.

A LIFE OF ITS OWN
- His needs are satisfied
- Her needs are satisfied
- The marriage supercedes all others
- They are partners for life

"A second wife cannot forget when she embarks upon a second marriage to a man that it is not as pristine and sparkling a situation as a first marriage would be," comments Dr. Ronnie Burak. "The second wife who is realistic that things might not go her way, especially if she has not been married before and her husband has, will fare better than the second wife who becomes upset when her plans fall apart. Counseling, beforehand if possible, is an excellent method of intervention."

MAKING HAPPINESS HAPPEN
- Seek counseling before making a final commitment
- Do not feel threatened by children's loyalty to their father
- Do not overstep bounds with his children
- Do not engage in denigrating the first wife
- Do not compete with the first wife
- Do not negate the first wife
- Strive to build your own relationship through shared communion and experiences

The expectations of both partners before entering a first marriage may be unreasonable and unrealistic. If the needs of both partners are stated up front in a second marriage, pitfalls can be avoided. Hopefully, there is a maturity, selflessness, and self-awareness that evolves with time and life experience. Preconceived notions are discarded and replaced with a map of reality drawn by both partners. The second wife needs to take stock and determine not to become entangled in a drama with the first wife or the children. At all times, boundaries must be honored. The husband must be as determined as his new wife that his second marriage will succeed. A second wife who sees in her husband the culmination of his prior experience and life lessons can apply these insights to their second marriage.

RISK VERSUS REWARD

It is only if one puts the past to rest that it is possible to go forward. Taking every risk in one's role as second wife brings the ultimate reward of a happy, connected marriage.

Against the odds, we are still a generation that believes in love and marriage. If a man or a woman leaves a first marriage because the partners grew apart, they are dismantling a life in order to find future happiness. It is in our second marriage that we bring these lessons to fruition. We have much to learn about ourselves to hopefully become better people. Thus the past seeds the future. In order to seek the right partner in the second marriage, a person must recognize what was lacking in the first marriage. When a woman who has married before leaves the confines of a poor relationship, she needs to heal enough to invest in a new marriage. When a woman who has never married before marries a man with emotional baggage she is taking a chance that the new marriage will prevail. They both are committing to the future. If the second wife discovers a true soul mate in the second marriage, the second marriage exists as the only marriage.

As a two-time second wife, and after extensively researching the role and its many categories, I know the personal and public persona. Each of us is filled with anticipation and best intentions in a world where the implication of being a second wife is slightly pejorative and ubiquitous. Individually, whatever type of second wife a woman is, we must strive for the richness and benevolence of the experience and shun the problem-laden, narrow path.

I am living testimony to the triumph of the second wife. In order to embark upon my second marriage, so precious in love and spirit, I have battled the shadow of my past and taken responsibility for the enormous adjustment required of my children. I did this because it enabled me to have my life, as it should be. Hopefully, you will achieve the life you wish for as well.

BIBLIOGRAPHY

American Demographics, Vol. 8, No. 5. (May 1996): p. 11.

Du Maurier, Daphne. *Rebecca*. New York: St. Martin's Press, 1993.

"Housework the Second Time." *American Demographics*, June 1996.

Janus, Samuel S. *The Janus Report on Sexual Behavior*. New York: John Wiley & Sons, 1994.

Levinson, Daniel J. *The Seasons of a Woman's Life*. New York: Random House, 1996.

Lofas, Jeanette. *Stepparenting*. New York: NAL-Dutton, 1990.

"Marriage: The Art of Compromise." *American Demographics*, February 1998.

Masters & Johnson. *Heterosexuality*. New York: Random House, 1998.

Moore, Thomas. *Soul Mates*. New York: HarperCollins, 1994.

National Center for Health Statistics. "Monthly Vital Statistics Report." Vol. 43, No. 9, Supplement (April 18, 1995).

National Domestic Violence Hotline. New York, NY. 1-800-799-SAFE.

"Report of Violence Against Women Research Strategic Planning Workshop." Washington, D.C.: National Institute of Justice and United States Department of Health and Human Services, 1995.

Selected Findings of Bureau of Justice Statistics, "Violence Between Intimates" (NCJ 149 259). Washington, D.C.: United States Department of Justice, November, 1994.

"Statistical Abstract of the United States (118th Edition)." Washington, D.C.: United States Census Bureau, 1998.

Zill, Nicholas. "Child Custody, Child Support and Parental Visitation in a National Sample of Children." Washington, D.C.: ChildTrends.